WITHDRAWN

BURTON COLLEGE LIBRARY

84965

A Guide to Authentic e-Learning

D0755965

Part of the groundbreaking Connecti[illegible] e-Learning series, *A Guide to Authentic e-Learning* provides effe[illegible]actical examples to engage learners with authentic tasks in onl[illegible] As technology continues to open up possibilities for innov[illegible]aching and learning opportunities, students and teachers ar[illegible]ntent to accept lecture and text dominated class[illegible]y on information delivery and little else. Situat[illegible]vist theories advocate that learning is best achieved in circumstances resembling the real-life application of knowledge. While there are multiple learning design models that share similar foundations, authentic e-learning tasks go beyond process to become complex, sustained activities that draw on realistic situations to produce important higher-order outcomes.

A Guide to Authentic e-Learning:

Written for Further and Higher Education professionals who teach online, *A Guide to Authentic e-Learning* offers concrete guidelines and examples for developing and implementing authentic e-learning tasks in ways that challenge students to maximize their learning. This essential book provides effective strategies for engaging learners with authentic tasks in online learning settings that can be implemented across many disciplines.

Jan Herrington is Professor of Education in the School of Education at Murdoch University in Perth, Western Australia.

Thomas C. Reeves is a Professor of Learning, Design, and Technology at The University of Georgia, USA.

Ron Oliver is Pro-Vice-Chancellor (Teaching and Learning) at Edith Cowan University in Perth, Western Australia.

Connecting with e-Learning Series
Edited by Allison Littlejohn and Chris Pegler

e-Learning is rapidly becoming a key component of campus-based education as well as a cornerstone of distance learning. However, it remains challenging for many teachers in higher and further education. There are four major reasons for this:

- Learners increasingly expect effective application of technologies; this can be intimidating to teachers/lecturers who are novices at using these technologies themselves.
- Already under pressure for time, teachers need to understand how to design an appropriate blend of online and offline activities, otherwise their learners may end up working unproductively and unhappily.
- Courses need to be sustainable, so that learning materials can be easily generated, stored, retrieved and repurposed.
- Teachers/lecturers are understandably uncertain about how to invest their time and effort in a fast-moving field.

This exciting new series provides relevant guides for both newcomers to teaching in higher and further education and experienced teachers/lecturers developing their practice online. With practical, accessible advice that draws on recent research and the experiences of expert practitioners, each book is relevant to teachers and lecturers worldwide.

Books in the series include:

Preparing for Blended e-Learning
Allison Littlejohn and Chris Pegler

The Educational Potential of e-Portfolios: Supporting personal development and reflective learning
Lorraine Stefani, Robin Mason and Chris Pegler

The website for this series is **connecting-with-elearning.com**

A Guide to Authentic e-Learning

Jan Herrington
Thomas C. Reeves
Ron Oliver

NEW YORK AND LONDON

First published 2010
by Routledge
270 Madison Avenue, New York, NY 10016

Simultaneously published in the UK
by Routledge
2 Park Square, Milton Park, Abingdon, Oxon OX14 4RN

Routledge is an imprint of the Taylor & Francis Group, an informa business

© 2010 Taylor & Francis

Typeset in Minion by
RefineCatch Limited, Bungay, Suffolk
Printed and bound in the United States of America on acid-free paper by
Walsworth Publishing Company, Marceline, MO

All rights reserved. No part of this book may be reprinted or reproduced or utilized in any form or by any electronic, mechanical, or other means, now known or hereafter invented, including photocopying and recording, or in any information storage or retrieval system, without permission in writing from the publishers.

Trademark Notice: Product or corporate names may be trademarks or registered trademarks, and are used only for identification and explanation without intent to infringe.

Library of Congress Cataloging in Publication Data
Herrington, Jan.
A guide to authentic E-learning / Jan Herrington, Thomas C. Reeves, Ron Oliver.
p. cm.—(Connecting with e-learning series)
Includes bibliographical references and index.
1. Internet in education. 2. Continuing education—Computer-assisted instruction.
I. Reeves, Thomas C., 1936– II. Oliver, Ron, 1955– III. Title.
LB1044.87.H47 2009
371.33′44678—dc22 2009034780

ISBN10: 0–415–99799–2 (hbk)
ISBN10: 0–415–99800–X (pbk)
ISBN10: 0–203–86426–3 (ebk)

ISBN13: 978–0–415–99799–7 (hbk)
ISBN13: 978–0–415–99800–0 (pbk)
ISBN13: 978–0–203–86426–5 (ebk)

Contents

Figures

Tables

Series Editors' Foreword

Authenticity in learning design is central to creating learning opportunities for students from which they can benefit and upon which they can draw once they leave formal learning behind. So what makes learning authentic? Why is authenticity important? This book offers an overview of authentic learning supported, enabled and productively partnered with e-learning. *A Guide to Authentic e-Learning* offers a comprehensive and authoritative, yet accessible, introduction to this field.

Current global, societal and technological changes are affecting the way we live and work. There has been a transformation in conventional working patterns to address the greater uncertainty in our lives and the need to adjust to new challenges. Learning is a complex process, dependent on the ability of the learner to re-contextualise the knowledge and skills that they have acquired. Today's learners are expected to be familiar with a wider range of concepts, and, having acquired these, are expected to apply them in a wider range of contexts than ever before. Enabling this level of flexible learning requires a re-examination of formal education, in particular its reliance on decontextualised and abstract forms of learning.

A Guide to Authentic e-Learning offers a comprehensive view of the strengths and limitations of authentic learning within the context of blended e-learning. The authors present contemporary learning approaches that move the reader from "information broadcast" towards transformative approaches in which learners actively and authentically participate. They examine a range of learning activities and contexts, tasks and environments, from simple websites to simulations, within which authentic e-learning offers significant advantages. In particular the book illustrates the potential for authentic e-learning to support learners in adapting to a changing world, clearly identifying current barriers to the translation of classroom learning into learning for life.

In supporting the provision of realistic learning activities, this book embraces the complexity of the real world and engages with the principles that support authentic approaches to teaching and learning in which learning is through realistic, often complex, sometimes challenging, collaborative activity.

The authors, Jan Herrington, Thomas C. Reeves and Ron Oliver, are renowned international experts in the field. Collectively they have drawn on years of experience working with a range of staff in tertiary education who are implementing authentic e-learning. They provide exemplars and experiences from around the world, illustrating ways in which widespread and emerging technologies can be used as cognitive tools, rather than delivery platforms, to support authentic learning and provide exciting opportunities for learning innovation. In particular the text draws from their extensive research activity in abstracting key characteristics of authentic learning and assessment.

As part of the Routledge *Connecting with e-Learning* series, the book is aimed at teachers, academics, librarians, managers and educational support staff around the world who are involved in learning innovation. We hope this book will help you reflect on ways in which Authentic e-Learning might transform your own practice.

Connecting with e-Learning series editors

Allison Littlejohn

Director of the Caledonian Academy and Professor of Learning Technology, Glasgow Caledonian University, UK

Chris Pegler

Senior Lecturer, Open University, UK

Acknowledgments

The authors would like to thank the many dedicated and resourceful teachers and educational designers who have contributed to our understanding of authentic learning, and to their students, who have willingly shared their ideas with us in our research.

We also wish to thank Allison Littlejohn and Chris Pegler, the series editors, for inviting us to write this book, and for their excellent feedback on a draft of this manuscript. We also appreciate the assistance provided by Sarah Burrows, Alexandra Sharp, Donna White and Sue Dickinson at Routledge.

We thank the Australian Research Council and the Australian-American Fulbright Commission for partially funding the research on which this book is based.

Finally, we thank our families, especially our spouses Tony, Trisha and Helen, who have supported us personally throughout the writing of this book.

Introduction

Before we consider *authentic e-learning*, it is necessary to clarify what we mean by *authentic learning* per se. For authentic learning to occur, learners must be engaged in an inventive and realistic task that provides opportunities for complex collaborative activities. Many of the best teachers provide exactly this type of learning experience for their students without necessarily thinking of it as authentic. When asked to recall their most memorable learning experiences from their undergraduate studies, adults often mention the authentic tasks their teachers challenged them to complete, such as conducting a real-world survey or researching local history.

Designing and implementing an authentic learning experience require teachers to take risks that many have been neither prepared nor rewarded for taking. In addition, this approach to enabling student learning may require more effort than standard academic instructional methods such as lectures and discussions. For example, teachers must endeavour to make certain that the authentic task is well supported with guidance and resources.

There are many misconceptions about authentic learning, in particular, as it relates to e-learning. For example, these are some of the arguments and beliefs that have been reported in the literature or anecdotally to argue against the use of authentic approaches in e-learning:

- Students are left to their own devices without support to abstract meaning from the environment
- The problems must be real, so they are not readily accommodated in the classroom
- Students need to complete work for real clients who must be located and contracted every year the course runs

- Students do not get their money's worth because there is no teaching
- Authentic e-learning environments are expensive and time consuming to develop because they require realistic simulations with multiple possible outcomes
- Teachers cannot give lectures (or podcasts of lectures) or set specific readings, because they are too didactic
- Authentic learning promoting diversity of outcome does not allow for the fact that sometimes there is a single correct answer that students must learn
- Authentic tasks are suitable for vocational courses but not for higher education or personal growth areas like literature and the arts
- For some courses there is no real-world application for the knowledge, so there can be no authentic task
- Students cannot perform complex and authentic tasks until they are taught the sub-skills required to complete them
- Authentic tasks are too unwieldy to allow teachers to demonstrate a similar problem through worked examples
- Authentic e-learning environments involve giving lots of examples of real-world practice
- Assessment of authentic e-learning tasks cannot be done at a distance
- Authentic tasks reflect only the teachers' view of authenticity and may not be authentic at all.

None of these objections are impediments to the effective use of authentic learning in higher education. They represent some misconceptions about both the intent and the processes involved in authentic learning, and give the impression that it must be conducted in real work settings, and that it is relatively unsupported. On the contrary, authentic learning can be readily created in university and classroom settings and is ideally suited to computer and web-based delivery. As universities embrace the internet and web-supported learning, the potential exists for authentic learning to be used widely to improve student learning. However, unfortunately the higher education climate today is arguably not conducive to the courageous and imaginative thinking that is required to promote authentic learning.

Impediments to Authentic Learning in Higher Education

Despite the considerable affordances provided by new technologies, the curriculum, delivery and pedagogies in higher education have arguably been placed in a straitjacket, as teachers struggle to create innovative and radical solutions to the problems that abound in the sector—problems such as: increases in student–staff ratios, difficulties in recruiting staff, a decline in the number of academic staff in key areas such as mathematics, poor library holdings, increasing casualisation of the workforce and declining student satisfaction ratings (Commonwealth of Australia, 2001). In the USA, its once vaunted higher education system is increasingly being questioned by scholars as well as the public at large (Newfield, 2008; Bok, 2007). Hersh and Merrow (2005) highlight some of the problems as "athletic scandals, increasing abuse of alcohol and other drugs, grade inflation, escalating costs, and dissatisfaction with the competence of college graduates" (p. 2).

Rapid advances in e-learning technologies have brought into sharp relief the failure of higher education to adapt to changing expectations of society, the workplace and an increasingly discriminating and technologically-capable student body (Ministerial Council for Education, 2005). New online technologies serve two primary goals in higher education. The first is increasing access to higher education opportunities for people who would not otherwise have them, and the second is enhancing the quality and outcomes of higher education. Progress is being made with respect to the first goal (Iiyoshi & Kumar, 2008), but evidence for attainment of the second goal is lacking.

This book offers practitioners in further and higher education the means to question and review the reliance of the sector on pedagogy that promotes decontextualised, abstract forms of learning—learning that frequently remains *inert*. It provides the principles of a more authentic approach to teaching and learning in universities, and offers a range of exemplars that have been implemented and tested in institutions throughout the world. We argue that emerging and established technologies provide exciting opportunities for changing current forms of pedagogy to a more relevant conception of e-learning than universities have so far managed to reflect through the widespread use of learning management systems.

We argue that technologies need to be used as cognitive tools for learning rather than as simply alternative delivery platforms. And we acknowledge that while there is much evidence to support the form of authentic learning that we present, more research is needed to find out more about how and why this approach works, and how to replicate its features consistently in a wider range of subjects and disciplines.

Inert Knowledge

One of the principal claims we make for authentic learning is that knowledge that results from it is more likely to be accessible in problem-solving situations. Learning in schools and universities has traditionally separated *knowing* and *doing* (Resnick, 1987). Historically, the emphasis has been on extracting essential principles, concepts and facts, and teaching them in an abstract and decontextualised form. The idea is that once students have learned something in an abstract form—devoid of contextualised details that can interfere with the key facts and principles—they will be able better to apply this learning in a range of different situations.

However, often this learning remains locked up and inaccessible when it is most needed. There are numerous examples and anecdotes of situations where learned information, facts or principles are needed to solve a particular problem but they fail to be retrieved at the critical moment. For example, a driver with a degree in physics becomes stuck driving in sand and attempts to dig the car out of the sand instead of partially deflating the tyres. Or a home carpenter with a degree in mathematics builds a shelf unit with uneven shelves because of a failure to measure the diagonals of the frame to ensure it is square.

In simple cases such as the aforementioned, there is a failure to access knowledge that is clearly relevant to solving the problem in hand. Information has been stored as facts rather than as tools (Bransford, Sherwood, Hasselbring, Kinzer, & Williams, 1990), and is "welded" to its original occasion of use in the classroom (Brown, 1997), or as Whitehead (1932) so aptly put it, the knowledge has remained "inert."

Failure to Access Relevant Knowledge

Bereiter (1984) recounted an investigation into reading strategies employed by university students, which found that when asked to learn as much of a difficult article on educational psychology as they could in 10 minutes, almost all students started at the beginning and read through the article. When questioned about the techniques employed, they all acknowledged that they knew better strategies and that they had been taught to skim read, check main headings, and read summaries and conclusions. But few had thought to employ these strategies.

In a study by Gick and Holyoak (1980) students were presented with the following extract and asked to memorise the information in the passage:

> A general wishes to capture a fortress in the center of a country. There are many roads radiating outwards from the fortress. All have been mined so that while small groups of men can pass over the roads safely, a large force will detonate the mines. A full scale direct attack is therefore impossible. The general's solution is to divide his army into small groups, send each group to the head of a different road, and have the groups converge simultaneously on the fortress.

Students were then given the following passage of text:

> You are a doctor faced with a patient who has a malignant tumor in his stomach. It is impossible to operate on the patient, but unless the tumor is destroyed the patient will die. There is a kind of ray that may be used to destroy the tumor. If the rays reach the tumor all at once and with sufficiently high intensity, the tumor will be destroyed. At lower intensities, the rays are harmless to healthy tissue, but they will not affect the tumor either. What type of procedure might be used to destroy the tumor with the rays, and at the same time avoid destroying the healthy tissue?

Unless students were specifically told to use the first passage to solve the problem, only 20% used the army analogy to conclude that it was possible to aim the rays from a number of directions to converge on the cancerous tumor. The knowledge from the first story, although memorised, was inert. Commenting on this study, the Cognition and Technology Group at Vanderbilt (1993b) concluded that: "People may be able to retrieve and use knowledge when explicitly asked to do so, and yet fail to spontaneously access it or use it. Under these conditions, the knowledge does them little good" (p. 37).

Research has shown that a similar pattern of response can be found in highly technical areas. For example, Morris and Rouse (1985) found that electronic troubleshooting was not performed well in the field despite intensive formal training in electronics and troubleshooting theories. Another study investigated university students' conceptions of logarithms and why they are used (Bransford, Sherwood et al., 1990). The majority of students had little idea that when logarithms were first invented, they enabled astronomers and mathematicians in the 1600s to easily solve complex calculations with simple addition. Students were asked to nominate what they would take into a test situation which offered prizes for completing large-number multiplication within an hour. Computers, calculators and slide rules were not allowed. Most students did not think to take a book of logarithms. They saw logarithms as relevant to logarithm problems, and as "difficult ends to be tolerated rather than exciting inventions that allowed a variety of problems to be solved" (Bransford, Sherwood et al., 1990, p. 117).

The failure to access and use critical knowledge can have much more serious consequences in contexts where split second decisions must be made as in flying an aircraft. In a book titled *How We Decide*, Lehrer (2009) describes scenarios where pilots, military commanders, physicians, and others involved in life-or-death decisions may fail to access critical knowledge that was "learned" outside a context of application.

Knowledge as a Product

Much of the abstract knowledge taught in universities is not retrievable in real-life problem-solving contexts, because the direct instruction model commonly used in higher education ignores the interdependence of situation and cognition. When learning and context are separated, knowledge itself is seen by learners as the final product of education rather than a tool to be used dynamically to solve problems. Cole (1990) contended that traditional education overemphasises the acquisition of facts and procedures, a situation that Entwhistle, Entwhistle and Tait (1993) argued is bolstered by the nightly quiz shows on television which "publicize and reward . . . incremental, decontextualized knowledge" (p. 335).

Research by Miller and Gildea (1987) explored the discrepancy between the vocabulary that school children learn, and the vocabulary they are taught. They contend that teachers in schools attempt to teach no more than about 200 words per year, yet school children learn about 5000 words per year. Children learn vocabulary efficiently and effectively at this rate (over 13 words per day for up to 16 years) generally without the help of standard vocabulary teaching strategies, such as dictionary exercises. Miller and Gildea's study gave examples of students' attempts to use vocabulary when they were taught in a typical school manner using decontextualised dictionary definitions and exemplary sentences.

For example, one student wrote: "My family erodes a lot," using the excerpted dictionary meaning of *erodes* as "eat out, eats away." Another wrote: "I was meticulous about falling off the cliff" using the definition of *meticulous* as "very careful." This teaching method assumes that each word definition is a discrete, self-contained piece of knowledge, and it ignores the fact that language is developed through "continued, situated use" (Brown, Collins, & Duguid, 1989b, p. 33). Miller and Gildea also maintained that it is ineffective to give an example of the word in a model sentence. For example, given the sentence: "The king's brother tried to usurp the throne," the children concluded "usurp" was equal to "take" and wrote sentences such as "The thief tried to usurp the money from the safe" (Miller & Gildea, 1987, p. 90).

Learners in formal educational settings are typically taught to use symbols in problem solving, a process which often results in the connections between the symbols and the events and objects they represent being lost (Resnick, 1987). In contrast, learners in authentic, everyday situations use the physical elements of the situation directly to help solve the problem, and rarely lose sight of the quest.

We are not suggesting that formal instruction should be abandoned in favour of context-dependent strategies that are learned "on the job." Rather, we believe that there is much of pedagogical significance in the way people learn and apply their understanding in real-life problem-solving situations that can be applied to higher education pedagogical techniques and practices to foster meaningful learning.

Emerging Technologies and Cognitive Tools

When information and communication technologies (ICTs) are used in universities, too often they are seen merely as disseminators of knowledge, that is, where students learn *from* the technologies rather than *with* them as cognitive tools (Jonassen & Reeves, 1996; Kim & Reeves, 2007). The former conception is more common than the latter.

The foundation for the "learning from" approach is "educational communications," that is, the deliberate and intentional act of communicating content to students with the assumption that they will learn something from these communications. The instructional processes inherent in the "from" approach to using media and technology in higher education can be reduced to a series of simple steps:

- Exposing students to messages encoded in media and delivered by technology

- Assuming that students perceive and encode these messages
- Requiring a response to indicate that messages have been received, and
- Providing feedback as to the adequacy of the response.

In contrast, the theoretical foundation for the "learning with" approach is "cognitive tools" that have been intentionally adapted or developed to function as intellectual partners to enable and facilitate critical thinking and higher-order learning (Lajoie, 2000). Jonassen and Reeves (1996) explored the theoretical parameters of cognitive tools, describing them as: "reflection tools that amplify, extend, and even reorganise human mental powers to help learners construct their own realities and solve challenging tasks" (p. 699). Examples of cognitive tools include: databases, spreadsheets, wikis, blogs, expert systems, communications software such as teleconferencing programs, online collaborative knowledge construction environments, media construction software, and modelling tools. The "learning from" approach to using media and technology dominates higher education in both traditional and online classrooms. The "learning with" approach appears ideal for authentic e-learning but it is not in evidence in most university courses at this time, especially in e-learning contexts where teacher-centered models are predominant.

In the cognitive tools approach, media and technology are given directly to learners to use for representing and expressing what they know. Learners themselves function as designers using media and technology as tools for analysing the world, accessing and interpreting information, organising their personal knowledge, and representing what they know to others. Mobile technologies and emerging technologies of "participatory culture" on the Web comprise powerful cognitive tools for authentic learning environments.

Technologies of Participatory Culture

While the Web has undoubtedly made an impact in higher education (Marginson & van der Wende, 2007), most universities have chosen commercial learning management software such as WebCT and Blackboard—now merged as one company and cornering over 75% of the US market (Siemens, 2006). Through these ready-made tools that model information-based modes of delivery, courses typically revert to more transmissive modes (Beetham & Sharpe, 2007). Lectures are podcast, weekly readings are set, and discussion topics are led by the teacher, and all the while plagiarism is increasing, and students use the Web to *search* rather than *research* (Brabazon, 2007).

It is clear from numerous sources (e.g., New Media Consortium) that universities must adapt their methods to fully capitalise on the powerful technologies which are becoming more and more central to the lives of both students and teachers. Mobile technologies such as mobile phones and mp3 players (and increasingly hybrid devices) are technologies that most students have in their pockets. These devices have much potential and can be used as cognitive tools in a range of educational contexts (Herrington, Mantei, Herrington, Olney, & Ferry, 2008; Jacob & Issac, 2008; Sharples, Taylor, & Vavoula, 2005; Traxler, 2007), and yet universities struggle to accommodate them with policies that are unable to account for student-owned technologies (New Media Consortium, 2008).

Web 2.0 functions allow the creation of collaborative, shared knowledge (examples include Wikipedia, YouTube) and the development of *participatory cultures* (Jenkins, 2007). However, even though esteemed publications such as the *Encyclopedia Britannica* now have online versions where users can contribute and edit content, universities are generally reluctant to incorporate such public knowledge sharing into tasks and assessment processes (Conole & Fill, 2005; Kolbitsch & Maurer, 2006). Surowiecki (2004) argued that the shared "wisdom of the crowd" can be more accurate and insightful (because of the range of experience and reflections) than any *single* expert opinion in some problem-solving situations. Others have challenged this view, calling the rise of shared knowledge on the internet "the tyranny of the ignorant" or the "cult of the amateur" (Keen, 2007). Although the debate about the wisdom of crowds versus digital mob rule will continue, higher education cannot afford to ignore the fact of "wikinomics" (Tapscott & Williams, 2006) whereby people around the world are sharing information and acting upon it in transformative ways.

A recent cartoon in the popular *Doonesbury* series by Garry Trudeau highlights the mismatch between traditional pedagogy and new technology in the typical college classroom. In a large lecture hall, a character Zipper is answering his email rather than paying attention to Professor Atkin's lecture. A friend in the class instant messages Zipper to alert him to the fact that the professor has just asked him to name four major greenhouse gases. Zipper asks his friend to stall the professor while he Googles the answer. The friend tells the professor that they can't hear in the back of the hall, and asks her to repeat the question. Professor Atkins says, "I just asked Zipper to name four greenhouse gases." Zipper quickly responds: "Water vapour, CO_2, ozone, and methane," and the clearly surprised teacher replies, "Uh . . . right."

Google and instant messaging are just two of many tools that the Net Generation use on campuses today (Oblinger & Oblinger, 2005). Cloud Computing and Virtual Worlds are two technologies noted by the New Media Consortium as "imminent" (New Media Consortium, 2008). However, most universities have barely conceived the educational potential of these technologies much less anticipated and prepared policies to enable their use in e-learning (NSF Task Force on Cyber-learning, 2008).

Participatory e-Learning

The Vision

The vision of participatory e-learning is compelling. Learners, enrolled in a common unit of study for training, continuing professional development, or the pursuit of an academic degree, will work together online to solve complex problems and complete authentic tasks, using web-based functions and tools to research, create and publish original products. Although they may never meet face-to-face, these highly motivated learners will form strong bonds that encompass productive teamwork, in-depth collaboration, and even lasting friendships. Through intensive engagement in the collaborative solution of authentic problems, the learning outcomes accomplished by these learners will be of the highest order, including improved problem-solving abilities, enhanced communications skills, continuing intellectual curiosity, and robust mental models of complex processes inherent in the performance contexts in which their new learning will be applied.

The Reality

Unfortunately, the reality of online learning is disappointing, at least in higher education so far. There is little evidence that the developers of most e-learning courses in postsecondary contexts have tried to reach, much less attained, the vision described above. While proponents of new technologies argue that we need "to break what has been called the credit-for-contact model" (Twigg, 2003, p. 125) of higher education long dominant in the USA and increasingly being adopted in other countries, most online courses still seek to ensure that students will spend the 45–50 hours of academic contact time required in traditional three credit-hour semester-long courses. Although more than 80% of institutions of higher education in North America now offer some totally online or blended courses (Allen & Seaman, 2003), the majority of these courses appear to remain constrained by traditional assumptions about the processes of "instruction" rather than the development of constructivist learning environments as defined by Wilson (1996) and others.

For example, an Adult Education graduate program at a leading US institution recently graduated its first cohort of students enrolled in its completely online Masters program. The developers of this program promote the equivalence of its online courses and its traditional face-to-face courses. According to the program's published description, the online curriculum does not differ in any substantive way from the on-campus version. Rather than perceiving the development of an online degree program as an opportunity for innovative pedagogy, the faculty members involved in this program intentionally aimed at replicating their pre-existing instructional methods as nearly as possible.

Learning Management Systems in e-Learning

What explains the general failure to design and implement truly innovative interactive collaborative e-learning courses in postsecondary education? At least part of the problem can be attributed to how learning management systems are currently being used to put courses online. Most online courses, including those in the online Adult Education Masters program noted above, are delivered using commercial learning management systems such as Blackboard and WebCT. The "affordances" (Norman, 1988) of these systems tend to promote thinking of online course design as a process of replicating traditional classroom instructional practices such as lecture notes, readings, quizzes, term papers, exams, and the like.

When Britto (2002) investigated faculty intentions and student perceptions of the pedagogical dimensions of WebCT, he found that faculty perceived the benefits of teaching a course using a learning management system as pertaining primarily to the convenience and efficiency of course administration and management, whereas students expressed frustration that the online tools were not employed to support their learning more directly. Other studies have reported similar student frustration with online learning courses for reasons such as confusion about online instructions, failures to get prompt feedback from teachers or tutors, and persistent technical problems (Vonderwell, 2003).

Lombardi (2007) has written of the needs of the new "participatory learners," and how important it is to match learning activities to their experiences of hands-on involvement with Web 2.0 applications. Siemens (2006) has also noted that when students are adept at using participatory technologies and tools on the Web, using learning management systems in their courses is like a step back into the past for them.

We are not suggesting that commercial learning management systems inevitably promote mediocre collaborative online learning, and indeed, there is evidence that they can offer powerful communication tools for instructors and students who have reason and purpose for using them (Herrington, Oliver, & Reeves, 2003). However, generally instructors are unlikely to perceive the opportunities for pedagogical innovation without substantial development support.

Moving from One Medium to Another

Developing innovative collaborative online learning courses is not only hindered by the misapplication of course management tools. We agree with Naidu (2003) that the challenge is more a conceptual one than a technological one. We perceive the primary problem as an inability of teachers and instructional designers to think "out of the box" when it comes to developing e-learning courses. Rather than attempting to make online courses even better than traditional classes, many faculty members and other specialists involved in online course development seem to be content with converting traditional courses into an online format without pedagogical change.

Moving a course from one medium to another, for example from the physical classroom to online, can take different instructional design paths, ranging from attempts to replicate the previous version in the new medium as faithfully as possible to radical changes in the design that take advantage of contemporary learning theories. But the more common approach used in higher education today is replicating the instructional design of traditional face-to-face courses in the online medium. For example, lectures delivered in a traditional classroom are delivered online via PowerPoint with audio or streaming video, the identical textbook is used in both classroom and online versions of a course, and the same multiple-choice or short essay exams are used as the primary means of assessment.

Towards an Authentic Approach to e-Learning

A more radical approach would involve moving away from traditional university course activities (such as lectures, demonstrations, discussions, textbook readings, and examinations) to a course where a single authentic task or project becomes the entire focus of the e-learning course. The next chapter describes the characteristics of such an approach.

Chapter 1

What is Authentic e-Learning?

Any discussion of *authentic e-learning* must begin with an explanation of what we mean by *authentic learning*. It could be argued that learning can be authentic, as we define it, without utilising any *e*-element. Littlejohn and Pegler (2007) noted that "e-learning is commonly taken to mean the use of computers and the internet for learning" (p. 16). With this in mind, however, it is almost impossible to conceive of any authentic learning endeavour in higher education today that does not take advantage of the affordances of computers and the internet. In our view, authentic learning is best executed with powerful computer-based, participatory tools—this is e-learning at its best.

Authentic learning has its foundations in the theory of *situated cognition* or *situated learning*, together with other pedagogical approaches developed over the last two decades, such as *anchored instruction*. The technologies associated with e-learning provide ideal affordances for the approach both in blended and fully online courses.

The Foundations of Authentic Learning: Situated Learning

It was Brown, Collins, and Duguid (1989b) who first synthesised contemporary thinking and research into the theory of *situated learning* and proposed a model of instruction that had implications for educational design and practice. Collins (1988) defined situated learning most simply as: "the notion of learning knowledge and skills in contexts that reflect the way the knowledge will be useful in real life" (p. 2). The model arose out of investigation of highly successful learning situations. They set out to find examples of learning in any context or culture that were effective, and to then analyse the key features of such models. One such model was snow skiing, where learning time had diminished from two years to two weeks as a result of instruction (Burton, Brown, & Fischer, 1984). An analysis of common features found in all the successful models were factors such as: apprenticeship, collaboration, reflection, coaching, multiple practice and articulation (McLellan, 1991).

In proposing their model of situated cognition, Brown et al. (1989b) argued that, contrary to many existing teaching practices which abstract knowledge from context, meaningful learning will take place only if it is embedded in the social and physical context within which it will be used. Typical work in schools and universities is often quite distinct from authentic activity or "the ordinary practices of the culture" (p. 34). Many of the activities undertaken by students are unrelated to the kind performed by practitioners in their everyday work. They proposed the use of *cognitive apprenticeships*, a method designed to "enculturate students into authentic practices through activity and social interaction," and based on the successful traditional apprenticeship model (Brown et al., 1989b, p. 37).

Cognitive Apprenticeship

In an elaboration of the cognitive apprenticeship model, Collins, Brown and Newman (1989) contended that traditional apprenticeships have three characteristics that are cognitively important in a model of situated learning:

1. Learners have continual access to models of expertise-in-use against which to refine their understanding of complex skills.
2. Apprentices often have several masters and have access to a variety of models of expertise leading to an understanding that there may be different ways to carry out a task, and that no one individual embodies all knowledge and expertise.
3. Learners have the opportunity to observe other learners with varying degrees of skill (p. 456).

A critical aspect of the situated learning model is the notion of the "apprentice" observing the "community of practice." This idea was developed by Lave and Wenger (1991), who proposed that participation in a culture of practice can, in the first instance, be observation from the boundary or *legitimate peripheral participation.* As learning and involvement in the culture increase, the participant moves from the role of observer to fully functioning agent. For example, apprentice hairdressers begin to learn the craft of hairdressing by first performing basic and unskilled tasks such as sweeping up hair cuttings and making tea and coffee for customers. Gradually, they are drawn more and more into key professional activities until they are fully qualified hairdressers. All the time spent in the workplace setting exposes them to the professional practices and mores of the role, and they learn the stories and behaviours related to what it means to be a hairdresser. Such peripheral but important knowledge is difficult if not impossible to teach in a decontextualised and abstract manner.

Legitimate peripheral participation enables the learner to progressively piece together the culture of the group and what it means to be a member. "To be able to participate in a legitimately peripheral way entails that newcomers have broad access to arenas of mature practice" (p. 110). Lave and Wenger (1991) proposed that the main functions of legitimate peripheral participation are to enable the learning of the language and stories of a community of practice, and to learn how to speak both within and about the practice, and yet this opportunity is denied students in many learning settings in higher education.

The Debate about Situated Learning

While the publication of the idea of situated learning met with much interest and acclaim in the early 1990s, it was also widely challenged and debated. Many of the criticisms of attempts to use situated learning as a model of instruction were based on how closely the learning environment resembled, not a cognitive apprenticeship, but a traditional apprenticeship. For example, Tripp (1993) presented a narrow set of criteria to define situated learning, which equated very much with a standard apprenticeship. In a response to the original Brown, Collins, and Duguid article (1989a), Wineburg (1989) argued that the abstract representation of knowledge was at least as effective as the situated learning approach and yet much more readily implemented in the classroom.

However, the principal theorists of situated learning consistently argued that their model, when further researched and developed, would be a model for teaching with practical classroom applications (Brown et al., 1989b; Brown, Collins, & Duguid, 1989a; Brown & Duguid, 1994; Collins, 1988; Collins et al., 1989). For those who questioned the appropriateness of the situated learning framework in conventional classrooms, the application of the model to e-learning was a further step removed from the traditional apprenticeship role. For example, Hummel (1993) described a distance education course on Soil and

Environment which was based on ideas from situated learning theory. Hummel rejected the idea that the program was "true" situated learning by virtue of the fact that it was computer-based: "Instructional designers who apply situated learning theory by implementation in electronic media should realize that they take an important step away from this theory . . . courseware becomes the learning environment and not the authentic situation" (p. 15). Similarly, Tripp (1993) contended that computer-based simulations were not sufficient, and reiterated that "true expertise is learned by being exposed to experts" (p. 75).

As the discussions and debates progressed however, there was increasing agreement that computer- and web-based representations and "microworlds" did provide a powerful and acceptable vehicle for the critical characteristics of the traditional apprenticeship to be located in the classroom environment. Reeves (1993a), for example, considered that one of the major benefits of a well-designed computer-based environment is its ability to include "opportunities for simulated apprenticeships as well as a wealth of learning support activities" (p. 107).

Many of the researchers and teachers who explored the model of situated learning at this time accepted that the computer could provide an alternative to the real-life setting, and that such technology could be used without sacrificing the authentic context that is such a critical element of the model. McLellan (1994) summarised these approaches by pointing out that while knowledge must be learned in context according to the situated learning model, that context can be: the actual work setting, a highly realistic or "virtual" surrogate of the actual work environment, or an anchoring context such as a video or multimedia program (p. 8).

Critical Characteristics of Situated Learning for a Model of Authentic Learning

Brown, Collins, and Duguid (1989b), in their original article, presented a *nascent* theory of situated learning. From the start they suggested that their model was an attempt to begin the process of developing a theoretical perspective for successful learning that cognitive science had, to date, not been able to explain.

Lave and Wenger (1991) cautioned that the conception of situated learning was substantially "more encompassing in intent than conventional notions of 'learning in situ' or 'learning by doing' for which it was used as a rough equivalent" (p. 31). The challenge put to researchers was to identify the critical aspects of situated learning to enable it to translate into teaching methods that could be applied in the classroom.

Although McLellan (1994) summarised the key components of the situated learning model as: apprenticeship, collaboration, reflection, coaching, multiple practice, and articulation of learning skills (p. 7), the contributions of various theorists and researchers, including the original authors of the model, had expanded and refined the notion to a much more comprehensive and far-reaching framework for classroom application.

Our own work has built on that body of work and has used a design research approach (van den Akker, Gravemeijer, McKenney, & Nieveen, 2006b; Reeves, Herrington, & Oliver, 2005) to propose and test draft design principles for authentic learning based on situated learning and other related research and literature. The characteristics of authentic learning that emerged from that research are described in detail below.

Elements of Authentic Learning

The framework of authentic learning is based on the proposal that usable knowledge is best gained in learning settings that feature the following characteristics (Herrington & Oliver, 2000). Authentic learning designs:

1 Provide authentic contexts that reflect the way the knowledge will be used in real life
2 Provide authentic tasks
3 Provide access to expert performances and the modelling of processes
4 Provide multiple roles and perspectives
5 Support collaborative construction of knowledge
6 Promote reflection to enable abstractions to be formed
7 Promote articulation to enable tacit knowledge to be made explicit
8 Provide coaching and scaffolding by the teacher at critical times
9 Provide for authentic assessment of learning within the tasks.

Each of these elements is now explained in more detail.

An Authentic Context that Reflects the Way the Knowledge will be Used in Real Life

In designing e-learning courses with authentic contexts, it is not enough to simply provide suitable examples from real-world situations to illustrate the concept or issue being taught. The context needs to be all-embracing, to provide the purpose and motivation for learning, and to provide a sustained and complex learning environment that can be explored at length (e.g., Brown et al., 1989b; Honebein, Duffy, & Fishman, 1993; Reeves & Reeves, 1997).

In a practical sense, this means that before beginning an e-learning design, a teacher needs to ask questions about the course or unit that is being designed, and where and how the knowledge will be used. Specifically, before beginning to plan for an authentic context, the following questions need to be considered:

- What knowledge, skills and attitudes will students ideally have after completing the course?
- Where and how would students apply this knowledge in real life?
- What context might be possible and appropriate in an e-learning course to enable students to learn the knowledge, skills and attitudes of the course?

An authentic context provides important contextual information for learners. Jonassen (1991a) contended that context provides "episodic memory cues that make the acquired knowledge more memorable" (p. 37). Norman (1988) illustrated this idea by pointing out that if someone arranges a meeting with you at 5.30 pm, you do not have to consciously memorise the time, place and person. The details are easily remembered because they fit readily into your cognitive structure. Within learning environments, Rogoff (1984) defined context as "the problem's physical and conceptual structure as well as the purpose of the activity and the social milieu in which it is embedded" (p. 2).

Avoiding Oversimplification of Context

Teachers and designers of e-learning courses are often tempted to design learning sites that simplify learning by breaking up complex processes and ideas into step-by-step sequences. Indeed, these approaches align with the systems model of instructional design, which specifies that the instructional sequence should progress from simple to complex (Gagné,

Briggs, & Wager, 1992). However, the tendency to simplify complex cases and situations, particularly in initial instruction, can only serve to impede the later acquisition of more complex understandings (Spiro, Feltovich, Jacobson, & Coulson, 1991b). Spiro, Vispoel, Schmitz, Samarapungavan, and Boeger (1987) argued that examples and cases must be studied as they naturally occur, "not as stripped down 'textbook examples' that conveniently illustrate some principle" (p. 181). Errors of oversimplification can also compound each other. For example, Feltovich, Spiro and Coulson (1989, cited in Spiro et al., 1991b) identified more than 12 serious misconceptions held by the majority of medical students they tested, the origins of which they were able to trace to oversimplification of the initial presentation of the concepts.

It is not necessary to simplify learning contexts to enhance learning. Indeed, designing realistic levels of complexity in a learning environment can help to make learning easier. Honebein, Duffy and Fishman (1993) gave the example of a study with students who disliked fractions and who found them difficult to learn. These students were asked to design computer software that would teach fractions to students one year younger than themselves. This meant that the students had to learn what was important about fractions before they could teach it to others. Honebein, et al. noted that:

> When the project was complete, the students had learned not only about fractions but also about software design and instructional design . . . and were so absorbed by the challenges . . . they practically "forgot" that they were also learning about fractions. (p. 95)

Spiro et al. (1987) strongly criticised the tendency to oversimplify in learning environments. They accused such practice as motivated by convenience rather than effectiveness of the learning design:

> Simplification of complex subject matter makes it easier for teachers to teach, for students to take notes and prepare for their tests, for test-givers to construct and grade tests, and for authors to write texts. The result is a massive "conspiracy of convenience." (p. 180)

Is it ever appropriate to simplify contexts in education? Spiro et al. (1991a) conceded that simplification may be appropriate when two essential conditions are met: the learning is at an introductory level and it is conducted in a well-structured domain. However, Honebein et al. (1993) argued against oversimplification at any level. They recommended that the complexity of the learning environment should reflect the complexity of the environment expected in the final performance.

The aim should therefore be to assist the learner in functioning in the environment rather than to simplify it. Oren (1990) pointed out that excessive demands on learners can be reduced by modifying the design of the e-learning context while retaining complexity, for example by limiting the number of options immediately available for novice users but making them accessible to more advanced users. An example of how this might be achieved in an authentic manner is given by Maor and Phillips (1996), who describe the development of a software package on *Birds of Antarctica.* In order to maintain complex learning, but to avoid an overwhelming inundation of data, students using the program assume a role on board a ship as "junior researchers." As their ability in dealing with the instruments and interpretation grows, they move to become "senior researchers" with access to increasingly more sophisticated variables and data.

Recommended e-Learning Design Features

Several implications for e-learning design can be drawn from the research into authentic context. In designing e-learning courses with authentic contexts, it is not enough to simply provide suitable examples from real-world situations to illustrate the concept or issue being taught. The context must be all-embracing and provide a sustained and complex learning setting that can be explored at length. More specifically, an e-learning course which purports to use an authentic context needs to provide:

- a physical environment which reflects the way the knowledge will ultimately be used (Brown et al., 1989b; Collins, 1988; Young & McNeese, 1993);
- a design to preserve the complexity of the real-life setting with "rich situational affordances" (Brown et al., 1989b; Collins, 1988; Young & McNeese, 1993).

Authentic Tasks

The e-learning course needs to provide ill-defined activities which have real-world relevance, and which present a single complex task to be completed over a sustained period of time, rather than a series of shorter disconnected examples (Bransford, Vye, Kinzer, & Risko, 1990; Brown et al., 1989b; Reeves & Reeves, 1997; Lebow & Wager, 1994).

When designing authentic tasks for their courses, teachers need to ask questions such as:

- What kind of activities are conducted in the real world that use the knowledge, skills and attitudes that are the focus of the course?
- How is this knowledge applied to answer real-world questions and solve real-world problems?

Activities in Learning

Tasks, activities, investigations and problems are at the heart of student involvement in formal learning contexts. Teachers provide such tasks to enable students to interact with the learning environment and to practice newly acquired skills. However, often the kind of tasks and activities used in educational settings do not have the intended effect, and simply lead to an acculturation to the practices of classrooms rather than the real-world transfer teachers expect. For example, Clayden, Desforges, Mills, and Rawson (1994) pointed out that elementary school students' efforts to make sense of classroom experiences generally lead them to focus on working practices rather than abstract ideas. "What they learn from the classroom experience is how to do work, how to be neat, how to finish on time . . . and how to tidy away" (p. 164).

While these comments are most appropriate for classrooms in schools, the same conclusions may be drawn for the design of e-learning courses. Students learn how to invoke "sub-optimal" schemes to enable them to proceed, rather than deal with the content in a way that promotes true understanding. The approach of many e-learning tasks is to employ a design that provides steps, procedures, hints, suggestions, and facts which neatly add up to the "correct" solution. Many of these tasks are so "well designed" that they fail to account for the nature of real-world problem solving, where the solution is rarely neat and the salient facts are rarely the only ones at students' disposal.

Recommended Design Features

Many of these characteristics of authentic tasks overlap with other elements of the situated learning model, but they nevertheless provide a useful frame of reference for the elements required in a course featuring authentic activities. Consequently, the e-learning course needs to provide:

- tasks that have real-world relevance (Jonassen, 1991b; Brown et al., 1989b; Young, 1993; Winn, 1993; Resnick, 1987; Cognition and Technology Group at Vanderbilt, 1990a);
- ill-defined tasks that allow students to define the tasks and sub-tasks required to complete the activity (Bransford, Vye et al., 1990; Young, 1993; Cognition and Technology Group at Vanderbilt, 1990b; Collins et al., 1989);
- a sustained period of time for investigation (Bransford, Vye et al., 1990; Cognition and Technology Group at Vanderbilt, 1990b);
- the opportunity for the detection of relevant versus irrelevant information (Young, 1993; Cognition and Technology Group at Vanderbilt, 1990a);
- tasks that can be integrated across subject areas (Jonassen, 1991b; Bransford, Vye et al., 1990; Bransford, Sherwood et al., 1990).

Access to Expert Performances and the Modelling of Processes

In order to provide expert performances, the online learning course needs to provide access to expert thinking and the modelling of processes, access to learners in various levels of expertise, and access to the social periphery or the observation of real-life episodes as they occur (Collins et al., 1989; Brown et al., 1989b; Lave & Wenger, 1991). The facility of the Web to create global communities of learners who can interact readily via participatory technologies, also enables opportunities for the sharing of narratives and stories. Teachers and designers for this element need to focus on how the course environment might provide access to expert or professional knowledge, skills and attitudes in real-world problem solving.

Apprenticeships and the Role of the "Master"

Expert performances and the modelling of processes have their origins in the apprenticeship system of learning, where students and crafts-people learned new skills under the guidance of an expert (Collins et al., 1989). Important elements of expert performances are found in modern applications of the apprenticeship model, such as internship (Jonassen, Mayes, & McAleese, 1993), and case-based learning (Riesbeck, 1996), and increasingly through internet-based guidance in e-learning contexts, such as in medical procedures conducted at a distance under the guidance of an expert.

Access to expert performances allows students to observe a task before it is attempted. Such access enables narratives and stories to be accumulated, and invites the learner to absorb strategies that employ the social periphery (legitimate peripheral participation) (Lave & Wenger, 1991; Brown & Duguid, 1993). The capabilities and strengths of e-learning technologies are more than adequate to provide a "window onto practice" (Brown & Duguid, 1993, p. 14). For example, uploaded movies of experts performing skills—such as a teacher asking open-ended questions, a nurse using reflective listening with a patient, a building adviser assessing foundations, or a farmer judging the quality of produce—allow students the opportunity to observe the experienced practitioner at work.

Gott, Lesgold and Kane (1996) described computer-based learning programs entitled *Sherlock 1* and *Sherlock 2*, that were designed to teach specialised electronics troubleshooting in avionics. After the student has solved a troubleshooting problem, he or she can review the activity with a "walk through" the actions taken. The student can also compare these actions with what an expert might have done, with options such as a side-by-side listing of an expert's decisions with the most recent decisions produced by the student. Collins and colleagues (1989) pointed out that students often fail to use all the resources at their disposal when solving a problem because they have never observed and reflected upon the processes required. Collins gave the example of students being unable to use good models of writing acquired through their own reading as they have no understanding of the strategies used to produce that text.

Levels of Expertise

An important aspect of expert performances in an e-learning course is that it enables the learner to compare his or her performance or understanding to that of an expert in the field (Collins, Brown, & Holum, 1991; Collins, 1988; Candy, Harri-Augstein, & Thomas, 1985). Collins, Brown, and Newman (1989) have also pointed out that it is important for students to be able to compare their performance with others at various levels of expertise. Often, it is the person who has only recently acquired the knowledge or skill who is in the best position to share the key elements of the constructs, or correct misconceptions that might be hindering understanding.

Learning from the Lecture

Some have a mistaken belief that there is no role for any didactic sharing of knowledge in authentic learning, and that it is similar to pure discovery learning where students must themselves discover knowledge without direct assistance. In this sense, there is a belief that there is no role for the lecture in authentic environments.

However, the lecture has a role if one considers that the lecturer or instructor is an expert who can share and model expert performance. There is a strong theoretical and pedagogical foundation for this form of direct knowledge sharing, as those who attend conferences will be well aware. Professionals clearly gain much from direct exposition of peer research and findings, and the lecture presentation is an efficient means to transfer this information if the participants have an appropriate context within which to understand and process the new information.

However, we caution that while the lecture can play an important role in higher order learning, in itself it is insufficient to provide the elements of authentic learning.

Recommended Design Features

In order for the e-learning course to provide expert performances, the learning course needs to offer:

- access to expert thinking and modelling processes (Collins et al., 1989; Collins, 1988; Candy et al., 1985);
- access to learners in various levels of expertise (Collins et al., 1989);
- opportunity for the sharing of narratives and stories and access to the social periphery (Brown et al., 1989b; Brown & Duguid, 1993; Lave & Wenger, 1991).

Multiple Roles and Perspectives

In order for students to be able to investigate a problem or task from more than a single perspective, it is important to enable and encourage students to explore different perspectives on the topics from various points of view, and to "criss cross" the learning environment repeatedly (e.g., Collins et al., 1989; Honebein et al., 1993; Spiro et al., 1991a).

From a pedagogical point of view, teachers and designers need to think about the key perspectives that exist in the subject area, and to also research controversies, debates and discussion that have characterised the area in its recent history.

Single Perspectives are Inadequate

The examination of issues and problems from multiple perspectives has been defined as an important cognitive activity (Honebein et al., 1993). In discussing instruction which puts forward a single, "correct" interpretation, Spiro, Feltovich, Jacobson, and Coulson (1991b) contend that "single perspectives are not *false*, they are *inadequate*" (p. 22). For example, Klein and Hoffman (1993) point out that experience per se does not equal expertise. They cite their own earlier research on firefighters where rural volunteer firefighters with 10 years' experience were not as expert as those who had spent one year in a "decaying inner city" (p. 205). Simple accumulation of practice from a single perspective is not sufficient to ensure expertise. Complexity can help to enhance a student's understanding of the subject area. Instead of being exposed to a single expert view, students can become aware of the differences of opinion that characterise all fields (Sandberg & Wielinga, 1992), and to assess these complex and competing perspectives.

Multiple Examination of Situations and Problems

Spiro, Feltovich, Jacobson, and Coulson (1991a) included multiple perspectives as a critical component of their Cognitive Flexibility Theory. They contended that "visiting the same material at different times, in rearranged contexts, for different purposes, and from different conceptual perspectives is essential for attaining the goals of advanced knowledge acquisition (mastery of complexity and preparation for transfer)" (p. 28). They argued that any single examination of material will fail to notice salient factors which may be apparent from only a different perspective, and possibly then only on the second or third exploration. The "psychological demands" in the examination of a complex case are too great for students to be able to acknowledge all the relevant connections, particularly for non-adjacent material, without an examination of the material from multiple perspectives.

Spiro, Feltovich, Jacobson, and Coulson (1991a) described a project entitled "Exploring Thematic Structure in *Citizen Kane.*" Students are able to explore the film *Citizen Kane* from a number of different suggested perspectives. For example, instead of accepting that the meaning of the film can be encapsulated in a single agreed-upon theme, students can select different themes such as "wealth corrupts" or "the hollow, soulless man." The student can then examine in close proximity five scenes from the film that illustrate this theme. (It is assumed that the student has already seen the film in its entirety.) The student can also access expert commentary once they have viewed the scenes.

In another program (Cognition and Technology Group at Vanderbilt, 1990a; Bransford, Vye et al., 1990) students used the feature-length film *Young Sherlock Holmes* as an anchor for investigating story writing, and the history of the Victorian era. They investigated historical aspects such as authenticity and inventions (Should Watson be riding in a carriage? Was the car invented then?); scientific concepts such as the climate, weather and geography (Does it snow in December?); and literary elements such as grammar, plot and character development. Students used the video for a full semester to examine the film in detail from multiple perspectives. Young (1993) described repeated viewing of the film *Young Sherlock Holmes*, suggesting that the use of the same resource for a whole semester invokes images of "students bored to tears when viewing the film for the tenth or thirteenth time. But . . . it was the changes in understanding that proved motivating, not the original presentation of the situation" (pp. 49–50).

In contrast, many e-learning courses and resources are designed in a linear instructional format, which assumes that the learner begins at the beginning and works through to the conclusion. Such courses provide inadequate experiences for students in dealing with complex issues.

Recommended Design Features

In order for students to be able to investigate the task from more than a single perspective, it is important for the e-learning course to provide or enable:

- different perspectives on the topics from various points of view (Brown et al., 1989b; Collins et al., 1989; Cognition and Technology Group at Vanderbilt, 1990a, 1993a; Lave & Wenger, 1991; Bransford, Sherwood et al., 1990);
- the opportunity to criss cross the learning environment or resource (Spiro et al., 1991a; Young, 1993; Spiro et al., 1991b).

Collaborative Construction of Knowledge

The opportunity for users to collaborate is an important design element, particularly for students who may be learning at a distance. Tasks need to be addressed to a group rather than an individual, and appropriate means of communication need to be established. Collaboration can be encouraged through appropriate tasks and communication technology (such as discussion forums, social networking, wikis, etc.) (e.g., Brown et al., 1989b; Collins et al., 1989; Hooper, 1992; Reeves & Reeves, 1997).

Cooperation versus Collaboration

Collaboration and the opportunity to collaboratively construct knowledge are seen as important elements of an authentic e-learning model. However, simply placing students in groups will not necessarily result in collaboration. Students must also work on a common task with an appropriate "incentive structure," that is, rewards based on the performance of the group (Hooper, 1992).

Katz and Lesgold (1993) pointed out that collaboration is more than cooperation: "Cooperation . . . involves a division of labour in achieving a task. Collaboration happens synchronously; cooperation is either synchronous or asynchronous" (p. 289). Jonassen's (1995) discussion of collaboration also emphasised learners' social roles in "exploiting each other's skills while providing social support and modeling and observing the contributions of each member" (p. 60). Forman and Cazden took this definition even further by suggesting that true collaboration is not simply working together but also "solving a problem or creating a product which could not have been completed independently" (cited in Repman, Weller, & Lan, 1993, p. 286).

Computers, e-Learning and Collaboration

Research has shown that the use of computers per se has a tendency to promote cooperation and collaboration among students and their teachers. Dwyer (1995) reported that in the *Apple Classroom of Tomorrow (ACOT)* study there was a dramatic decrease in teacher-led activities and a corresponding increase in cooperative activities. Collins (1991) listed increased cooperation as one of eight major trends observed in schools that have adopted computers.

While there is some support for the notion that computers can provide a useful means to enhance individual "personalised" knowledge (Ambrose, 1991), an evaluation of 60 cooperative learning research studies found that 72% of the studies reported positive outcomes for cooperative activities, while only 8% reported positive outcomes for non-cooperative activities (Repman et al., 1993). Qin, Johnson, and Johnson's (1995) meta-analysis of 63 studies of higher-order learning and problem solving found that cooperative efforts resulted in better problem solving than competitive efforts (in 55, cooperation outperformed competition; in 8, competition outperformed cooperation). Dunlap and Grabinger (1996) also argued that because complex problems often require unorthodox or unconventional approaches, collaboration allows students to "share the risk" (p. 79). Many other studies (Slavin, 1996; Del Marie Rysavy & Sales, 1991; Hooper, 1992) have shown that there are clear educational advantages to be derived from collaboration among students.

Recommended Design Features

Collaboration has much support in the literature as an important design element, not only in its own right, but also as an enabling device for several other characteristics of the authentic learning model described in this chapter, such as coaching and articulation. In order to support collaboration, the e-learning course needs to provide:

- tasks that are completed in pairs or groups rather than individually (Brown et al., 1989b; Collins et al., 1989; Young, 1993; Resnick, 1987; Alessi, 1996; Hooper, 1992)
- appropriate incentive structure for whole group achievement (Hooper, 1992).

Reflection

In order to provide opportunities for students to reflect on their learning, the e-learning course needs to provide an authentic context and task, as described earlier, to enable meaningful reflection. It also needs to provide non-linear organisation to enable students to readily return to any element of the site if desired, and the opportunity for learners to compare themselves with experts and other learners in varying stages of accomplishment (e.g., Boud, Keogh, & Walker, 1985; Kemmis, 1985; Collins & Brown, 1988).

Conscious Reflection and Learning

Reflection is one aspect of a complex number of interrelated functions that contribute to task performance (Ridley, 1992), an aspect which is gaining increased attention in recent years after almost disappearing from consideration for many years under the influence of learning models that were based on behaviorism (von Wright, 1992). The role of reflection has long been recognised in the military, and in simulations and gaming, as *debriefing* (Thatcher, 1990; Pearson & Smith, 1985).

Boud, Keogh, and Walker (1985) defined reflection as: "those intellectual and affective activities in which individuals engage to explore their experiences in order to lead to new understandings and appreciations" (p. 19). These authors stressed that such reflection must not occur solely at the unconscious level: "it is only when we bring our ideas to our consciousness that we can evaluate them and begin to make choices about what we will or will not do" (p. 19). Boud, Keogh, and Walker (1985) defined the process of reflection as consisting of three related stages:

1 *Returning to the experience*: recollecting the salient features of the experience, recounting them to others.
2 *Attending to feelings*: accommodating positive and negative feelings about the experience.
3 *Re-evaluating the experience*: associating new knowledge, integrating new knowledge into the learner's conceptual framework.

Norman (1993) described two types of thinking that can be used by students in learning: experiential and reflective. Collen (1996) has drawn a distinction between the two, by likening experiential thinking to the rapidly changing images of a music video clip, compared to the concerted mental effort required by reflective thinking. Norman contended that many e-learning tasks promote experiential thinking at the expense of reflective thinking. The predominance of computer programs that require a single user to produce rapid responses to predetermined low-level tasks is an example of the movement towards the acceptance of "experience as a substitute for thought" (Norman, 1993, p. 15).

Prompts to Reflect are Usually Insufficient

Designers of computer-based programs have attempted to provide design elements which explicitly aim to give opportunities for students to reflect on learning as they proceed. In a description of REALs (Rich Environments for Active Learning), Dunlap and Grabinger (1996) advised that students should be encouraged to reflect by asking themselves, or by being prompted by the teacher to ask, questions such as: "Which strategies did you use? Which ones worked? Which ones didn't work? What would you do differently next time? . . . What was your single most important difficulty in solving the problem?" (p. 72). This type of reflection corresponds closely with Boud et al.'s (1985) second stage of *Attending to feelings*, and this approach can support effective metacognitive reflection on performance.

Chee (1995) described a computer-based multimedia project designed using elements of situated learning. The program aimed to teach students an object-oriented programming language entitled Smalltalk. In order to promote reflection, a *Reflect* button could be selected by students. Questions appear which "either possess deeper conceptual significance, or involve subtleties related to programming practice" (p. 152). For example, when the question "What are the key differences between a class and an instance of that class?" appears, and students have spent time reflecting, they can play a movie of an expert expressing his or her view of the issue. Chee notes: "In this way, students can gauge to what extent they have come to appreciate the subject domain in the way that an expert does" (p. 154). However, externally stimulated reflection such as described in these projects may not be integral to the cognitive processes of the students and, if not, is likely to be ignored. Candy, Harri-Augstein, and Thomas (1985) believed that reflection is not facilitated simply by allowing time for it, or providing questions or prompts. Kemmis (1985) pointed out that we do not reflect in a vacuum: "We pause to reflect . . . because the situation we are in requires consideration: how we act in it is a matter of some significance" (p. 141). Such reflection, one might argue, is only possible in an e-learning course that provides an authentic task within an authentic context, not at the prompting of an external agent.

Reflection as a Process and a Product

Some theorists see reflection as both a *process* and a *product* (Collen, 1996; Kemmis, 1985), and that it is action-oriented (Kemmis, 1985). Knights (1985) contended that reflection is not the kind of activity which its name suggests—a solitary, internal activity—but a two-way process with the aware attention of another person: "Without an appropriate reflector, it cannot occur at all" (p. 85). This view is strongly supported in the literature by others who have pointed out that reflection is a social process (Kemmis, 1985), and that collaboration on tasks enables the reflective process to become apparent (von Wright, 1992).

Recommended Design Features

This review of the research and literature on reflection suggests that, in order to facilitate reflection, the learning course needs to provide:

- authentic context and task requiring decision making (Brown et al., 1989b; Norman, 1993);
- non-linear organisation of materials and resources to enable students to return to any element if desired (Boud et al., 1985; Kemmis, 1985; Collins & Brown, 1988);
- the opportunity for learners to compare themselves with experts (Collins et al., 1991; Collins, 1988; Candy et al., 1985);
- the opportunity for learners to compare themselves with other learners in varying stages of accomplishment (Collins et al., 1989);
- collaborative groupings of students to enable reflection with aware attention (Knights, 1985; von Wright, 1992; Kemmis, 1985).

Articulation

In order to produce an e-learning course capable of providing opportunities for articulation, the tasks need to incorporate inherent—as opposed to constructed—opportunities to articulate, collaborative groups to enable articulation, and the public presentation of argument to enable defence of a position (e.g., Edelson, Pea, & Gomez, 1996; Collins et al., 1989; Lave & Wenger, 1991).

Speech and Learning

Counsellors and psychologists have long been aware of the importance of verbalisation in beginning to effect change in problematic behaviours. A frequently quoted psychological law of counselling is: "I learn what I believe as I hear myself speak." Similarly, Baktin (1986) contended that "any true understanding is dialogic in nature" (cited in Brown & Campione, 1994, p. 267). The implication is that the very process of articulating in speech enables formation, awareness, development, and refinement of thought.

In education, the work of Vygotsky (cf. Davydov, 1995) has profoundly influenced the way educators see the role of articulation in learning. Vygotsky believed that speech is not merely the vehicle for the expression of the learner's beliefs, but that the act of creating the speech profoundly influences the learning process. Vygotsky wrote: "Thought undergoes many changes as it turns into speech. It does not merely find expression in speech; it finds reality and form" (cited in Lee, 1985, p. 79).

Vygotsky believed that intellectual development occurs first between people in a social context before it is internalised within the individual:

> Any function in the child's cultural development appears twice, or on two planes. First it appears on the social plane, and then on the psychological plane. First it appears between people as an interpsychological category, and then within the child as an intrapsychological category. (Cited in Wertsch, 1985b, pp. 60–61.)

Accordingly, the process is not a passive one, but a dynamic construction of personal ownership of learning through articulation and reflection (McMahon & O'Neill, 1993). This active process is reflected in Mercer's (1996) comment that: "Talk is now recognised as more than a means for sharing thoughts: it is a social mode of thinking" (p. 374).

The Role of Articulation

The role of articulation has also been recognised in the value of peer tutoring. Research on peer tutoring (Forman & Cazden, 1985) has suggested that reasoning and problem solving is facilitated by "cognitive reorganization induced by cognitive conflict" (p. 330). Cognitive conflict occurs when students with disparate viewpoints challenge each other's understanding, and is most likely to occur when students are required to achieve consensus. Pea (1991) argued for the importance of publicly defending a position in presentations to critics, who may be other students or specialists and experts on the topic. Pea described a project where students composed computer-based multimedia presentations and where one of the key elements was the argumentation and persuasion of the product. The importance of developing arguments both for and against the proposal was highlighted, and these arguments were presented in formal presentation open to critiquing. Pea suggested that such activity "might fundamentally change the nature of learning by creating rich conversational artefacts for discussion and presentation" (p. 65).

Chee (1995) described a multimedia project designed using elements of situated learning. In order to accommodate articulation as an element as students use the package, the designers of the program included an *Articulate* button. When students click the button, they are given questions that require them to articulate answers "either to themselves, or to a friend" (p. 151). Questions include: "How do you determine the superclass of a new class that you are going to define? What are the differences between the pseudo-variables *super* and *self*? What situation can cause an infinite loop when the method of *new* is invoked?" (p. 151). Questions such as these, requiring only low-level factual responses, appear to be more like a revision strategy, totally unlike the rich opportunities articulation affords such as described by Edelson, Pea, and Gomez (1996):

> The act of speaking requires an individual to place a structure and a coherency on his or her understanding that may lead the individual to recognize gaps in that understanding or forge new connections between formerly disconnected knowledge . . . The social act of attempting to share and reconcile the knowledge of different individuals motivates learning in a way that is much rarer . . . among solitary learners (p. 152).

In spite of this strong argument from the research for the value of articulation in learning, many e-learning courses are used quietly where a solitary student interacts with the computer in silence. Lave and Wenger (1991) pointed out that being able to speak the vocabulary and tell the stories of a culture of practice is fundamental to learning, yet some e-learning courses ensure almost by default that the learning remains tacit.

Recommended Design Features

In order to enable opportunities for articulation, the e-learning course needs to provide:

- a complex task incorporating inherent, as opposed to constructed, prompted opportunities to articulate (Edelson et al., 1996; Collins et al., 1989; Collins, 1988; Bransford, Sherwood et al., 1990);
- collaborative groups to enable social then individual understanding (Edelson et al., 1996; Mercer, 1996);
- public presentation of argument to enable articulation and defence of learning (Pea, 1991; Lave & Wenger, 1991).

Coaching and Scaffolding

In order to accommodate a coaching and scaffolding role principally by the teacher (but also by other students), the e-learning course needs to provide the opportunity for more able partners to assist with scaffolding and coaching, as well as the means for the teacher to support learning via appropriate communication technologies (e.g., Collins et al., 1989; Greenfield, 1984).

The Zone of Proximal Development

A systems approach to the design of learning (Gagné et al., 1992) proposes that the best way to deal with complexity is to simplify the topic by breaking it down into its component parts. However, Perkins (1991) suggested that the temptation to oversimplify learning environments should be resisted, and instead designers and teachers should search for new ways to provide appropriate scaffolding and support. An authentic e-learning course provides for coaching at critical times, and scaffolding of support, where the teacher provides the skills, strategies, and links that the students are unable to provide to complete the task. Gradually, the level of support (the scaffolding) is reduced until the student is able to stand alone.

The foundation for the notion of scaffolding lies in Vygotsky's (1978) "zone of proximal development," described as "the distance between the actual developmental level as determined by independent problem solving and the level of potential development as determined through problem solving under adult guidance, or in collaboration with more capable peers" (p. 86).

Scaffolding in Learning

Vygotsky's ideas prompted Bruner and others to develop the notion of scaffolding (Wertsch, 1985a), described by Greenfield (1984) as comprising five salient characteristics. According to Greenfield, in both the building and the educational sense, scaffolding:

1 Provides a support.
2 Functions as a tool.
3 Extends the range of the worker.
4 Allows the worker to accomplish a task not otherwise possible.
5 Is used selectively to aid the worker where needed (p. 118).

Many e-learning designers believe their courses should be self-contained resources that include everything the student needs to learn a particular topic. However, teachers who require students to work individually on computer-based tasks are denying them the benefits of not only collaboration, but also expert assistance—providing hints, suggestions, critical questions, and the "scaffolding" to enable them to solve more complex problems.

Some argue that computer-based resources can fulfil the coaching role, and some programs are designed to "eliminate pedagogical roles for teachers," to effectively make them "teacher-proof" (cf. Reeves, 1993b). Collins et al. (1989) pointed out that coaching is highly situation-specific and is related to problems that arise as students attempt to integrate skills and knowledge, a role that is still best performed by the teacher. Dreyfus and Dreyfus (1989) insisted that: "Computers will not be first-rate teachers unless researchers can solve four basic problems: how to get machines to talk, to listen, to know and to coach" (p. 139).

New Roles for the Teacher

Coaching in an authentic e-learning course requires "powerful, but different roles for teachers" (Choi & Hannafin, 1995, p. 67), roles that require interactions with students to occur mainly at the metacognitive level (Savery & Duffy, 1996). On this point, Jonassen (1993) maintained that unless the teacher initiates the required change in approach, students may continue to use e-learning resources in the same low-level manner they use books, browsing for factual information: "Knowledge construction usually accedes to knowledge reproduction. Typically, there is only one perspective worth memorising—the teacher's—because that is what will be tested. Teachers find it difficult to give up control" (p. 37).

The teacher as coach is a fundamental and integral part of an e-learning course that provides a substantial scaffolding and coaching support for students.

Recommended Design Features

In order to accommodate a coaching and scaffolding role principally by the teacher, the learning course needs to provide:

- collaborative learning, where teachers and more able partners can assist with scaffolding and coaching (Collins et al., 1989; Collins, 1988; Young, 1993);
- coaching and scaffolding assistance is available for a significant portion of the activity (Harley, 1993; Collins, 1988; Griffin, 1995; Young, 1993).

Authentic Assessment

In order to provide integrated and authentic assessment of student learning, the e-learning course needs to provide: the opportunity for students to be effective performers with acquired knowledge, and to craft polished performances or products in collaboration with others. It also requires the assessment to be seamlessly integrated with the activity, and to provide appropriate criteria for scoring varied products (e.g., Wiggins, 1993; Reeves & Okey, 1996; Linn, Baker, & Dunbar, 1991; Duchastel, 1997; Bain, 2003).

Standardised Assessment

Assessment of student learning is an integral and necessary component of any pedagogical model. Conventional assessment procedures, such as standardised tests, have been criticised in much of the literature on assessment. For example, Leone Burton (1992) commented on the disservice the widespread use of such tests have done to the learning of mathematics:

> If the Oxford Dictionary is to be believed, assessment is the estimation of value for the purpose of fixing and imposing a fine! Norm-referenced, summative assessment has imposed a fine on millions of learners of mathematics by failing them, and has done a disservice to the discipline by reifying those who succeed and the mathematics on which their success is based (p. 1).

Many such writers argue that it is futile to apply standardised, norm-referenced tests to the assessment of learning in more constructivist courses. For example, Entwhistle, Entwhistle, and Tait (1993) contended that assessment procedures profoundly affect the way students learn, and that "providing a constructivist teaching environment will have little effect on the quality of learning while conventional assessment procedures remain in place" (p. 353). Young (1993) also noted that "assessment can no longer be viewed as an add-on to an instructional design or simply as separate stages in a linear process of pre-test, instruction, post-test; rather assessment must become an integrated, ongoing, and seamless part of the learning environment" (p. 48).

This view is also held by Gardner (1992), who maintained that norm-referenced, formal tests and assessment materials are not sensitive enough to account for cultural differences, and they are rarely useful in determining students' level of competence. As evidence, he cited the work of some of the researchers into learning in context (Lave & Wenger, 1991; Lave, Murtagh, & de la Rocha, 1984; Rogoff, 1984; Scribner, 1984) and pointed out that these studies have revealed that often those who fail on formal measures of calculating or reasoning are able to exhibit excellent command of the same skills in their everyday context.

In many e-learning courses, students continue to be assessed by the conventional methods of norm-referenced tests, essays, and examinations which are generally based on the assumption that there is an objective reality which can be judged as right or wrong. Thus, testing items are confined to simple multiple choice or other low-level means to assess students' knowledge.

Authentic Assessment

A common definition of authentic assessment is one such as given by Torrance in the introduction to the edited papers entitled *Evaluating Authentic Assessment*:

> The basic implication of the term [authentic assessment] seems to be that the assessment tasks designed for students should be more practical, realistic and challenging than what one might call "traditional" paper-and-pencil tests (Torrance, 1995, p. 1).

Such a definition would appear to cover the general meaning of a variety of terms used in the literature to describe alternative forms of assessment, such as *authentic assessment*, *performance-based assessment*, *school-based assessment*, and *portfolio assessment*. There has been some discussion in the literature about the distinction that can be drawn between *authentic* and *performance-based* assessment. Many authors use the terms interchangeably (Torrance, 1995) but Reeves and Okey (1996) pointed out the critical difference is one of the degree of authenticity required in the assessment—the "fidelity" of the task to the conditions under which the performance would normally occur. Meyer (1992) drew a useful distinction between the two by pointing out that while performance assessment focuses on the student response that is to be examined, authentic assessment, while referring to the performance, focuses on the context in which the response is performed. Meyer noted that in using this framework, "it is difficult to imagine an authentic assessment which would not also be a performance assessment" (p. 40).

Two frequently cited criticisms of authentic assessment (Reeves & Okey, 1996) are that authentic assessment does not allow easy comparisons among students, and it does not provide information about generalisability to other contexts. Reeves and Okey conceded that the first criticism is a valid one, and one which must be resolved by a more general consensus about the purpose of assessment. The second concern regarding generalisability, Reeves and Okey contended, is one which proponents of authentic assessment would dismiss on the grounds that they *deliberately* seek to situate learning within the context of the real world, "a world in which the much vaunted generalizability of standardized tests may have little relevance" (p. 193). This theme was also taken up by Young (1995), who argued that assessment needs to be viewed in a more functional manner and validated, not solely by its stability as a psychometric instrument, but more critically by its real-world usefulness.

For example, Wiggins (1990) focused on the *process* of assessing, and has refined characteristics which assist in the design and use of authentic assessment. He drew comparisons with "traditional" types of assessment to help clarify the distinction. Table 1.1 summarises Wiggins' differentiation of authentic and traditional assessment.

Recommended Design Features

In order to provide authentic assessment of student learning, the e-learning course needs to offer:

- the opportunity for students to be effective performers with acquired knowledge, and to craft polished performances or products (Wiggins, 1990, 1993, 1989);
- significant student time and effort in collaboration with others (Linn et al., 1991; Kroll, Masingila, & Mau, 1992);
- the assessment to be seamlessly integrated with the activity (Reeves & Okey, 1996; Young, 1995);
- multiple indicators of learning (Lajoie, 1991; Linn et al., 1991).

A Framework for Implementation

This chapter has described nine key elements of an authentic e-learning approach based on literature and research into situated learning, anchored instruction, collaborative learning, scaffolding, authentic assessment, and other relevant research. The combined guidelines

Table 1.1 A Comparison of Authentic and Traditional Assessment (Wiggins, 1990)

Authentic assessment	*Traditional assessment*
Direct examination of student performance on worthy intellectual tasks	Relies on indirect or proxy items
Requires students to be effective performers with acquired knowledge	Reveals only whether students can recognise, recall or "plug in" what was learned out of context
Present the student with a full array of tasks	Conventional tests are usually limited to pencil-and-paper, one-answer questions
Attend to whether the student can craft polished, thorough and justifiable answers, performances or products	Conventional tests typically only ask the student to select or write correct responses–irrespective of reasons
Achieves validity and reliability by emphasising and standardising the appropriate criteria for scoring varied products	Traditional testing standardises objective "items" and the one "right" answer for each
"Test validity" should depend in part upon whether the test simulates real-world "tests" of ability	Test validity is determined by matching items to curriculum content
Involves ill-structured challenges that help students rehearse for the complex ambiguities of professional life	Traditional tests are more like drills, assessing static and too-often arbitrary elements of those activities

provide a useful, integrated model for the instructional design of an e-learning course that would enable the authentic elements to be operationalised.

In Chapter 2, the task—the key element in any authentic learning design—is described in more detail.

Chapter 2

Authentic e-Learning Tasks

Of all the design elements of an authentic e-learning course—indeed, of any learning design—it is the task that matters most.

A well-crafted task, and the activities students engage in to complete it, can enable and facilitate complex learning, and motivate and engage students in its execution. There has been a great deal written about authentic tasks and activities in recent times as the influences of constructivist philosophy and advances in technology impact on educational theory, research and development. As a result, the role of activities in courses of study has grown to the point where they are no longer relegated to the role of a vehicle for *practice* of a skill or process. A well-designed task can be so much more than an opportunity for students to practice and apply their learning.

In this chapter, we propose that the task students perform as they complete a course of study is the single most important element in the design of the learning course. A complex and sustained task can motivate students to learn. It can provide meaning and relevance to complex content, enable collaborative problem solving, justify the creation of polished products, and provide integrated assessment of achievement. Indeed, it can be the central organising element of an entire course of study.

Activity as Practice

In the past, the view of activities as practice (such as exercises set by the teacher) was the norm. Brophy and Alleman (1991) defined activities as: "Anything students are expected to do, beyond getting input through reading or listening, in order to learn, practice, apply, evaluate, or in any other way respond to curricular content" (p. 9). Similarly, Lockwood (1992) stated that activities "encourage and affirm learning . . . [they]

may take many forms, but essentially, they encourage the learner to respond to the text rather than remain passive" (flyleaf).

Definitions such as these, which spring from an earlier, more teacher-centered paradigm of teaching and learning, now appear inadequate. The influence of a constructivist philosophy, of problem-based and case-based learning, and the use of immersive scenarios and participatory technologies have placed the activity that students complete, as they study, firmly at the heart of the curriculum.

Under the influence of more "instructivist" or teacher-centered approaches, activities were seen as a vehicle for practice. For example, in a systems approach to learning (Gagné et al., 1992) the activity or task that students complete is described in a list of nine events of instruction as: "Eliciting the performance," and is an opportunity for the student to show that he or she has mastered the skill and is able to demonstrate it to the teacher's satisfaction. The systems model is based on a behaviourist approach and on the assumption that if skills and sub-skills are taught in the right order, in a systematic and comprehensive manner, then effective learning will occur. Dick and Carey (1990) described the use of practice and feedback in the classroom:

> Not only should [learners] be able to practice, but they should be provided feedback or information about their performance . . . that is, students are told whether their answer is right or wrong . . . Feedback may also be provided in the form of reinforcement. Reinforcement for adult learners is typically in terms of statements such as "Great, you are correct" (p. 138).

Compare this fairly simplistic approach to some of the learning courses designed from a more constructivist philosophy. For example, in an undergraduate engineering course described by Reeves and Laffey (1999) the students' task is to plan a mission to Mars, and to design a research station including a renewable power source to sustain life once a station is established. The task gives a purpose and meaning to the learning that will occur without predetermining and limiting the scope and sequence of the enquiry.

Academic Problems vs Practical Problems

There has been a great deal written about the differences between the kinds of tasks and problems we face in real-world situations and those typically designed into courses of study. For example, Sternberg, Wagner, and Okagaki (1993) differentiated between the kinds of problems learners face in academic situations and practical, real-world applications. They stated that academic problems tend to be: formulated by others, well defined, complete in the information they provide, characterised by having only one correct answer, characterised by having only one method of obtaining the correct answer, disembedded from ordinary experience, and of little or no intrinsic interest. For example, it is unlikely that the following typical mathematics textbook exercise would ever be encountered in this form in any realistic context, or that students would necessarily know when to apply it in appropriate circumstances:

> $2x + 1 = 7$. Solve for x

Similarly word problems, while attempting to provide a real-world context, often fail to replicate the essential elements of a meaningful and realistic problem. For example:

> Jenny and her friend were on holiday and they visited a winery. They bought 2 one-litre bottles of wine, 3 bottles each containing 750 millilitres, and two half-litre bottles of wine. What was the total quantity of wine bought?

Why does the student need to know how much wine Jenny and her friend bought? If the total was needed to write on a customs declaration, or the weight was likely to make their suitcases too heavy, or Jenny needed to calculate her likely blood alcohol level after consuming this wine, this is important contextual information that is missing from the problem description. As it stands, the problem remains a simple and almost pointless algorithm with little descriptive detail to make it realistic. Bottge and Hasselbring (1993) have pointed out that such word problems are inadequate because:

> They describe situations in a textual rather than a contextual form; they typically include key words such as "in all" or "how many more" that can trigger a specific number operation—unlike real problems that offer no such clues; and there is usually only a single correct answer, which takes only a few minutes to solve (p. 36).

In direct contrast to the academic approach, practical problems tend to be characterised by: the key roles of problem recognition and definition, the ill-defined nature of the problem, substantial information seeking, multiple correct solutions, multiple methods of obtaining solutions, the availability of relevant prior experience, and often highly motivating and emotionally involving contingencies (Sternberg et al., 1993, p. 206).

Key differences between the school-based approach and real-life approach have also been developed and summarised by Lebow and Wager (1994) (see Table 2.1). While the differentiation between the two approaches is largely within the context of classroom instruction, the same distinctions may be drawn for the design of e-learning courses, particularly when the resources on the site are limited to important or key facts rather than a range of information. In completing tasks and solving problems online, students frequently learn to invoke "sub-optimal" schemes to enable them to proceed, rather than deal with the content in a way that promotes true understanding. Many of these online programs are so tightly designed to process student input that they fail to account for the nature of real-world problem solving, where the solution is rarely neat and the salient facts are rarely the only ones at students' disposal.

In contrast, a number of authors suggest that authentic tasks should be ill-defined so that students must find as well as solve the problems. Learners need to have opportunities to: explore a situation with all the complexity and uncertainty of the real world, have a role in determining

Table 2.1 Real-life versus In-school Problem Solving (Lebow & Wager, 1994)

Real-life	*In-school*
Involves ill formulated problems and ill-structured conditions.	Involves "textbook" examples and well-structured conditions.
Problems are embedded in a specific and meaningful context.	Problems are largely abstract and decontextualised.
Problems have depth, complexity and duration.	Problems lack depth, complexity, and duration.
Involves cooperative relations and shared consequences.	Involves competitive relations and individual assessment.
Problems are perceived as real and worth solving.	Problems typically seem artificial with low relevance for students.

the task and how it might be broken up into smaller tasks, select relevant information, and find solutions that suit their needs. Because authentic activities mirror real-world activities, they require students to use teamwork, interpersonal skills, technology, decision making, and other skills to complete the task successfully (Perreault, 1999).

Defining Authentic Tasks

A number of authors have contributed to the definition of characteristics of authentic tasks. For example, Young (1993) listed the attributes of real-life problems which need, where possible, to be replicated in authentic tasks. The problem must provide:

- Ill-structured complex goals;
- Opportunity for the detection of relevant versus irrelevant information;
- Active/generative engagement in defining problems as well as solving them;
- Involvement of the student's beliefs and values;
- An opportunity to engage in collaborative interpersonal activities (p. 45).

Others have also discussed the importance of providing an authentic context to the task. Jonassen (1991b) noted that authentic activities have real-world relevance and utility, and recommended that authentic tasks be integrated across the curriculum. Similarly, Bransford, Vye, Kinzer, and Risko (1990) described the following criteria for authentic activities to maximise the effectiveness of the approach:

- A single complex problem should be investigated by students;
- Students identify and define their own questions;
- Students must have the opportunity to experience the problem from a number of different perspectives;
- Students work on the problem over a "reasonably long period of time" (p. 394), that is weeks rather than days;
- Activities are logically related to the problem.

Many other theorists and researchers (e.g., Gordon, 1998; Lebow & Wager, 1994) have also emphasised the importance of designing collaborative, rather than independent, learning activities, and others such as Duchastel (1997) have pointed out the importance of diversity, rather than uniformity, of outcome. The Cognition and Technology Group at Vanderbilt (1990b) have stressed the importance of complexity and the necessity of providing an environment capable of sustained examination.

Elements of Authentic Tasks

As described above, many writers and theorists have suggested quite specific design criteria for tasks which, if implemented well, can enhance students' learning as they engage in activities that reflect the critical characteristics of genuine roles and activities of professionals in real-world settings. Authentic tasks are an integral component of situated learning environments, and it is useful to describe their design more fully in order to explore their effective use in e-learning courses. In reflecting on the characteristics of authentic activities described by researchers, we have derived design characteristics of authentic tasks for e-learning (Herrington, Oliver, & Reeves, 2003; Herrington, Reeves, Oliver, & Woo, 2004):

Authentic Tasks have Real-World Relevance

Activities match as nearly as possible the real-world tasks of professionals in practice rather than decontextualised or classroom-based tasks (e.g., Brown et al., 1989b; Jonassen, 1991b; Lebow, 1993; Oliver & Omari, 1999; Cronin, 1993; Young, 1993; Winn, 1993; Resnick, 1987; Cognition and Technology Group at Vanderbilt, 1990a).

Authentic Tasks are Ill-Defined, Requiring Students to Define the Tasks and Sub-Tasks needed to Complete the Activity

Problems inherent in the activities are ill-defined and open to multiple interpretations rather than easily solved by the application of existing algorithms. Learners must identify their own unique tasks and sub-tasks in order to complete the major task (e.g., Lebow & Wager, 1994; Bransford, Vye et al., 1990; Cognition and Technology Group at Vanderbilt, 1990a).

Authentic Tasks Comprise Complex Tasks to be Investigated by Students over a Sustained Period of Time

Activities are completed in days, weeks and months rather than minutes or hours, requiring significant investment of time and intellectual resources (e.g., Bransford, Vye et al., 1990; Lebow & Wager, 1994;

Cognition and Technology Group at Vanderbilt, 1990b; Jonassen, 1991b).

Authentic Tasks Provide the Opportunity for Students to Examine the Task from Different Perspectives, Using a Variety of Resources

The task affords learners the opportunity to examine the problem from a variety of theoretical and practical perspectives, rather than a single perspective that learners must imitate to be successful. The use of a variety of resources rather than a limited number of preselected references requires students to detect relevant from irrelevant information (e.g., Young, 1993; Spiro et al., 1987; Bransford, Vye et al., 1990; Cognition and Technology Group at Vanderbilt, 1990b).

Authentic Tasks Provide the Opportunity to Collaborate

Collaboration is integral to the task, both within the course and the real world, rather than achievable by an individual learner (e.g., Lebow & Wager, 1994; Young, 1993; Gordon, 1998).

Authentic Tasks Provide the Opportunity to Reflect

Tasks need to enable learners to make choices and reflect on their learning both individually and socially (e.g., Young, 1993; Myers, 1993; Gordon, 1998).

Authentic Tasks can be Integrated and Applied Across Different Subject Areas and Lead Beyond Domain-Specific Outcomes

Tasks encourage interdisciplinary perspectives and enable diverse roles and expertise rather than a single well-defined field or domain (e.g., Jonassen, 1991b; Bransford, Sherwood et al., 1990).

Authentic Tasks are Seamlessly Integrated with Assessment

Assessment of tasks is seamlessly integrated with the major task in a manner that reflects real-world assessment, rather than separate artificial assessment removed from the nature of the task (e.g., Reeves & Okey, 1996; Young, 1995; Herrington, & Herrington, 1998).

Authentic Tasks Create Polished Products Valuable in their Own Right rather than as Preparation for Something Else

Activities culminate in the creation of a whole product rather than an exercise or sub-step in preparation for something else (e.g., Barab, Squire, & Dueber, 2000; Gordon, 1998; Duchastel, 1997).

Authentic Tasks Allow Competing Solutions and Diversity of outcome

Tasks allow a range and diversity of outcomes open to multiple solutions of an original nature, rather than a single correct response obtained by the application of rules and procedures (e.g., Duchastel, 1997; Bottge & Hasselbring, 1993; Young & McNeese, 1993; Bransford, Vye et al., 1990; Bransford, Sherwood et al., 1990).

Authentic e-Learning Tasks

Well-designed authentic tasks are able to guide learning in entire courses of study. They are not provided simply to enable students to practice skills taught in more didactic, content-focused ways. They are integral to the way students approach and study the course, and provide meaning to complex curricula (Woo, Herrington, Agostinho, & Reeves, 2007).

The affordances of a web-based delivery serve only to strengthen the impact of an authentic task on student learning, if other elements of authentic learning designs are also in place, such as strong support provided by the teacher and collaborators.

But how might such complex tasks look in an e-learning course? Some examples of courses that use substantial authentic tasks follow. They range from simple websites that capitalise on a well-described task to well-resourced multimedia simulations.

Research Methods

In a post-graduate unit titled *Research Preparation: Research Methods* (Angus & Gray, 2002), students do not learn research methods by studying texts describing research methodologies and appropriate applications. Instead they work virtually in a graduate research center (Figure 2.1) where they are given the task of investigating the impact of the closure of a rural school on the community.

Figure 2.1 The graduate research center in *Research Methods*.
Source: Max Angus & Jan Gray, Edith Cowan University

They do this using both qualitative and quantitative methods, and they are assisted by two virtual researchers who have collected data from the community and assembled them in raw form. The students examine school records, population data, newspaper reports, interviews with teachers, parents and community members, and other documents (e.g., Figure 2.2). Students produce a report that analyses the impact of the closure of the school on the rural community.

Introductory Biology

In an introductory biology course for online delivery (described in Koenders, 2002) students investigate a simulation of the discovery of new life forms, and are introduced to the interpretation of microscopic images of cellular structures. In the scenario, students are given a role as a biologist who has joined an expedition to a remote lake in Siberia, where several microorganisms are found that cannot be classified. They "collect" the specimens and return to the university to analyse them. On the website, they are provided with images of unicellular organisms apparently unknown to science. Students are assigned to groups of four where they analyse the specimens and prepare a report. The scenario is not drawn in an elaborate, resource-intensive manner, but built up through the creation of an interesting and engaging idea.

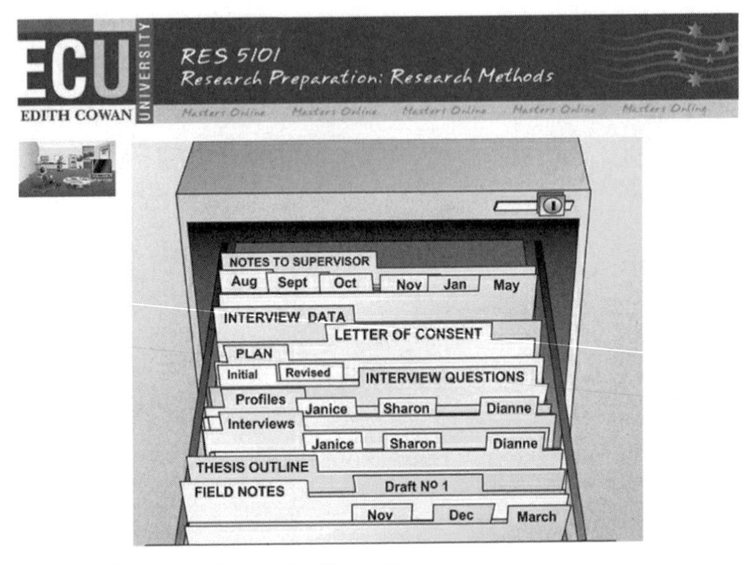

Figure 2.2 Qualitative data in the filing cabinet.
Source: Max Angus & Jan Gray, Edith Cowan University

"Writing in Organizations"

In a very early example of complex activity, Pennell, Durham, Orzog, and Spark (1997) described a web-based environment, "Writing in Organizations," part of the third-year curriculum for Bachelor of Arts (Communication Studies) where students learn business communication skills by accepting temporary employment in a virtual recording company. They are given the task of preparing a report on whether the company would benefit from the introduction of an internal newsletter. In order to complete this activity, students make appointments, keep a physical diary, "interview" the director and other employees, and write letters, memos and reports. Figure 2.3 shows the text of the interview with Mario, the External Communication Manager of the company, including a list of possible questions on the left that the interviewer can ask.

Swedish Language

In a language course conducted in Finland (cf. Saukko in Leppisaari, Vainio, & Herrington, 2009), students learn the Swedish language by

Figure 2.3 Interviewing one of the employees in *Virtual Records*.
Source: Marsha Durham & Russ Pennell

immersing themselves in the realistic context of job seeking, including a variety of situations requiring language proficiency. By the end of the course, students are able to talk about themselves and their education in Swedish, are able to navigate job applications in their field, conduct key work tasks, and handle customer contact situations. Contact teaching covers oral content, and students build work-related vocabulary and written skills in the online component.

Teacher Education in ICTs

In a core ICT subject for Early Childhood pre-service teachers, students create a digital story book in order to learn mobile technologies and information and communication technologies (ICT) applications appropriate for early childhood settings (Olney, Herrington, & Verenikina, 2009). The course is designed to provide pre-service early childhood educators with the knowledge and skills of implementing ICT in a variety of early childhood settings.

Over six weeks of the semester, students are required to research and write a story suitable for young children, and to then use iPods and a range of other technologies and software (such as PowerPoint,

Inspiration, iMovie, iPhoto, GarageBand) as necessary to create a digital version of their story.

North American Fiction and Film

In a semester-long course titled *North American Fiction and Film* (Fitzsimmons, 2006) (Figure 2.4) students study novels written by North American writers such as Melville, Hemingway, DeLillo, Vonnegut, Atwood, and Esquival, and they view film versions of the same works. In the course, they are given the role of Editorial Board Members of an online scholarly journal (Figure 2.5), to which they submit book reviews and articles based on their study of the literature. The students collaboratively design a guide for novice reviewers on how to write a book review. The teacher of the course is the journal editor, and an edition of the journal is published online at the end of the semester. A range of literary resources, articles and reviews are accessible from the website.

Business Management

In a course on business management negotiation skills (Jones, 2006) targeted at managers, human resource managers and employee relations

Figure 2.4 Main interface of *North American Fiction and Film.*
Source: John Fitzsimmons, Central Queensland University

North American Fiction & Film

Getting Started | Tasks | Library | Online Resources | Discussion List | Support
Memorandum 1 | Task Schedule | Suggested Reading schedule

Memorandum 1

To:	New Board Member
From:	Editor, John Fitzsimmons
Date:	16 July
Topic:	Special Issue of Naff_Online

Dear Colleague

Congratulations on being appointed to a position on the editorial board of our online journal, NAFF_Online. We are currently working to produce our first issue, which has been dubbed a "Special Issue". Our audience will be both academic and general (ie academics, students, and interested members of the public).

In this Special Issue, which we do not expect to have ready until the end of the Winter term, it has been decided to have both essays and book review articles. I have set up a draft Splash_Page for the issue, but I am happy to take suggestions on alternatives. The final decision about the Splash_Page and the structure of the issue will come from the full Board.

I would like you to produce one book review article, and one essay for the journal. I would also like you to produce a 20 minute conference paper for our NAFF_Online conference on Friday 12 October (see task schedule below for details). I want to include a conference summary, and possibly some selected papers in this Special Issue.

Figure 2.5 Memo inviting students to join Editorial Board.
Source: John Fitzsimmons, Central Queensland University

practitioners, students engage with realistic problems in a virtual restaurant. A number of issues arise within the restaurant that require a negotiated solution, centering on wages and working conditions, health and safety, and equity in the workplace. Students take roles as manager, Maitre d', waiters, bar staff, chef or kitchen staff to negotiate acceptable solutions.

History of World War I

In a web-based learning activity titled *Not Just A Name On A Wall* (Morrissey, 2006) high school students learn the history of World War 1 by researching a real soldier whose name is taken from a local memorial tower or plaque. The task was designed for students in a small rural high school, and the first thing they are required to do is select a name from the war memorial in the center of their town (Figure 2.6). Many of the soldiers came from families in the district, so it is possible that students

Figure 2.6 The War Memorial with names in *Not Just a Name on a Wall.*
Source: Peter Morrissey, www.notjustanameonawall.com

could choose someone who was related, such as a great-great-uncle. Once the student has chosen a name, the story of that soldier is researched using a range of resources freely available on the Web for this purpose (such as research websites created and maintained for the Australian War Memorial Website and the National Archive of Australia) (Figure 2.7). The student researches the soldier and his battalion, and creates a story of his service and experiences during the war. Some of the students' stories have been published in the local newspaper around the times of significant commemorative days (such as Anzac Day and Memorial Day in Australia), and others have been uploaded and published on the Web.

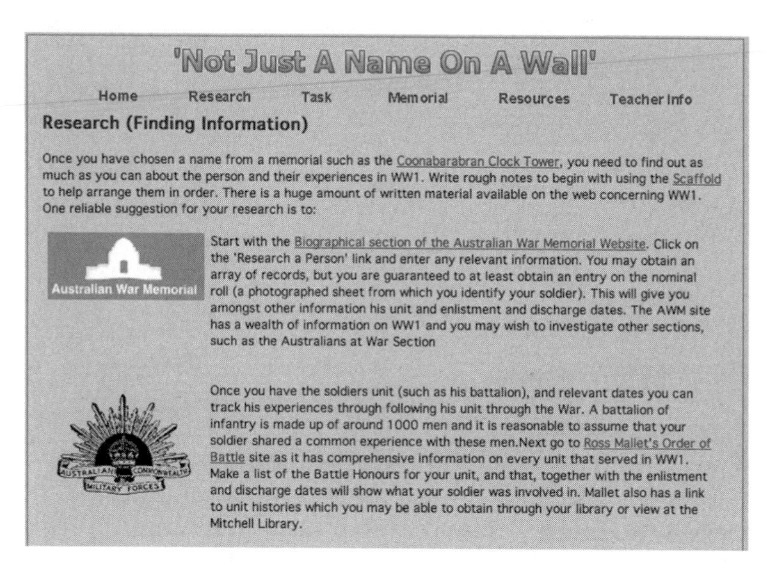

Figure 2.7 Resources and web links for researching a soldier's history.
Source: Peter Morrissey, www.notjustanameonawall.com

Shakespeare's Plays

In an English-language course in a high school in the Philippines (Ambat, 2008), students use technology to understand and appreciate a Shakespearean play through an authentic task of filming the play in a modern language, or their own vernacular, and setting. First, students modernise the language of a selected Shakespearean play in teams by researching it on the Internet and finding resources that help them understand the original script. They then localise the setting to reflect either the modern local community or ancient community customs and traditions. For example, the balcony scene from *Romeo and Juliet* shows Juliet is standing on a hill near a hut, with Romeo in the bushes below. The students design, perform and film the play, and edit it using MovieMaker. Lastly, students reflect on the process by writing their personal insights and analysis of the play.

e-Learning Evaluation

Students in a post-graduate level e-learning course titled *E-Learning Evaluation* work in small groups to plan, conduct, and report an evaluation of an actual e-learning program for real-world clients (Liu, Oh, & Reeves, 2009, April) (see Figure 2.8). The major task in this course

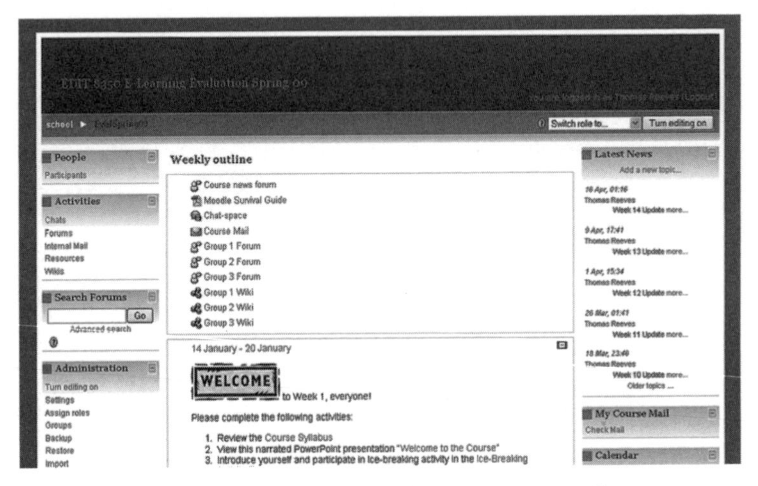

Figure 2.8 Screen capture of e-learning evaluation course moodle menu.
Source: Thomas C. Reeves, University of Georgia

approximates the real-world work of professional evaluators. The task requires significant investments of time and intellectual resources—approximately 10–15 hours per week of sustained effort over the length of a 16-week semester. Effective group work is essential to most evaluation projects, and thus collaborative work is required in the course. Self-regulated learning skills are also demanded as students must balance individual and group activities in the course.

The complexities of the realistic and often unpredictable activities inherent in e-learning evaluation require learners to make choices and reflect upon and self-regulate their own learning. The activities enable students to play diverse roles such as project manager, data collector, statistician, and report writer. Playing these different roles allows students to develop robust expertise rather than inert knowledge. The final evaluation report is submitted to the real-world client after several rounds of expert and peer assessment. The final evaluation report becomes a key part of each learner's professional portfolio.

Putting the e-learning evaluation course online has opened the course up to learners from around the world, and the course has attracted learners from Australia, Canada, Europe, and South Africa as well as the USA. Widely dispersed, the students work in virtual teams to accomplish the authentic tasks of planning, conducting, and reporting an e-learning evaluation. The evaluation clients are also widely distributed, and none of them is co-located with the learners in the course. This dispersion of clients and co-workers replicates the daily experience of many 21st century knowledge workers (Friedman, 2005).

Local Government

In a vocational course on local government (the *Local Government Toolbox*), each of the units is presented in the form of a problem, typical of those that confront people in local government. Once again, the authentic setting casts the learner in the role of a government administrative assistant confronted by a series of authentic tasks.

In one task, learners explore issues surrounding a contaminated landfill and then formulate recommendations and give a presentation. The environment provides access to the resources needed for the learner to create a reasonable solution to the problem. Resources and supports within the web environment provide information on the local setting to enable the students to undertake the problem. The tasks, resources and supports are provided to the students in the various objects they find in their virtual office, including an in-tray with the tasks, a filing cabinet with office information, and newspapers and letters for the contextual information. The telephone and computer in the office are the learners' communication tools.

Legal Studies

In the units of study in a legal studies course (the *Legal Administration Toolbox*), students learn skills associated with working in a legal office (Figure 2.9). Students assume the role of a legal assistant in a law firm and undertake a series of tasks as the context for their learning. In each unit, students are given an authentic task to complete. In the unit on creating legal letters, for example, their task is to successfully create a legal letter from a dictated message. Their task comes to them in the form of an email in their office setting. The resources and supports they need to learn the appropriate skills and knowledge to create the legal document, with the given information, are provided in the online learning environment within the virtual office.

Online Teaching and Learning

In a *Graduate Certificate in Online Teaching and Learning* (Herrington & Oliver, 2006) authentic tasks assist new online teachers to have the confidence to design and plan effective online learning courses themselves.

Figure 2.9 The interface of the legal office.
Source: Australian Flexible Learning Framework, © Commonwealth of Australia

The course is strongly student-centered, with authentic assessment of tasks. The first unit of four in the course, entitled "Online Teaching and Learning," was designed to explore issues associated with the creation of effective learning courses, and draws heavily on recent theory and research. The student takes on a role in a scenario set in a fictitious university. Figure 2.10 shows the main interface of the course where students are able to access resources by clicking the appropriate item. The student is required to evaluate a website that has been set up as an exemplar for a consortium of universities planning to develop a joint online course. The students then, in collaboration with other students (posed as representatives from the other universities), recommend a set of guidelines for website development, and then redesign the original website (or one of their own choosing) according to those guidelines. While comprising a single sustained task, the activity can be evaluated at three points.

Coastal and Marine Systems

Coastal and Marine Systems (Lavery, 2001, in Herrington et al., 2004) is a post-graduate, web-based course where tasks are specifically designed to mirror typical problems that a coastal manager or an environmental consultant might encounter. For example, in one major task it is postulated that a marina has been constructed, and as part of the

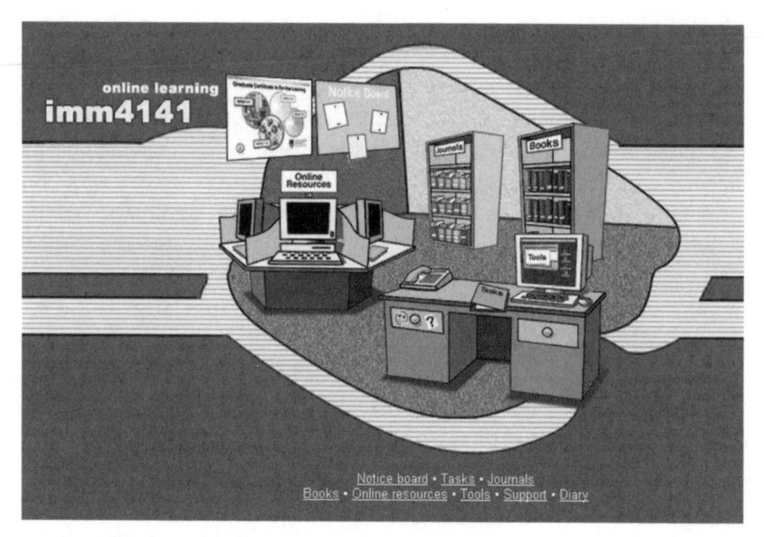

Figure 2.10 The interface for *Online Teaching and Learning*.
Source: Jan Herrington & Ron Oliver, Edith Cowan University

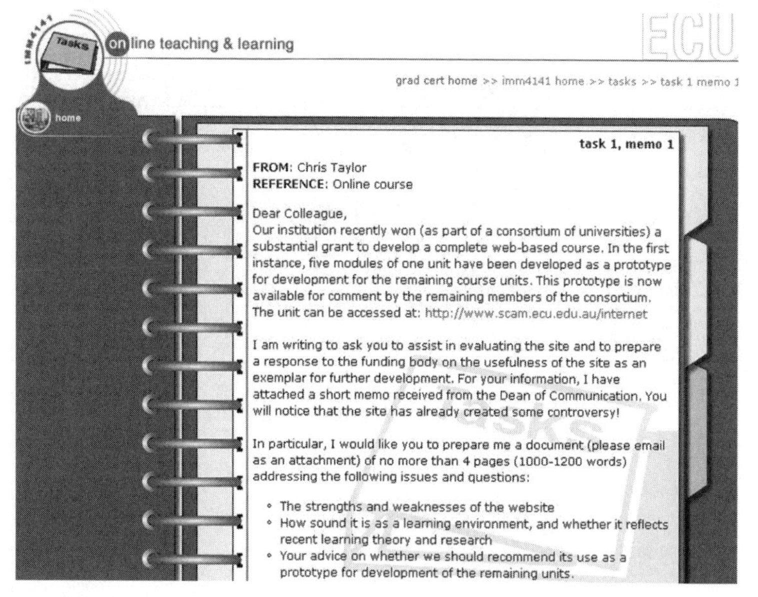

task 1, memo 1

FROM: Chris Taylor
REFERENCE: Online course

Dear Colleague,
Our institution recently won (as part of a consortium of universities) a substantial grant to develop a complete web-based course. In the first instance, five modules of one unit have been developed as a prototype for development for the remaining course units. This prototype is now available for comment by the remaining members of the consortium. The unit can be accessed at: http://www.scam.ecu.edu.au/internet

I am writing to ask you to assist in evaluating the site and to prepare a response to the funding body on the usefulness of the site as an exemplar for further development. For your information, I have attached a short memo received from the Dean of Communication. You will notice that the site has already created some controversy!

In particular, I would like you to prepare me a document (please email as an attachment) of no more than 4 pages (1000-1200 words) addressing the following issues and questions:

- The strengths and weaknesses of the website
- How sound it is as a learning environment, and whether it reflects recent learning theory and research
- Your advice on whether we should recommend its use as a prototype for development of the remaining units.

Figure 2.11 The task presented in a memo in *Online Teaching and Learning*.
Source: Jan Herrington & Ron Oliver, Edith Cowan University

ongoing approval process, annual monitoring of water quality is required (Figure 2.12). The monitoring encompasses water inside the marina as well as a site several hundred meters outside the marina, in well-flushed ocean conditions. The students are provided with a set of real data collected by the course teachers from inside and outside the marina, and they are required to analyse and interpret the data, and draw conclusions as to whether the water quality within the marina is different to that outside, and if so explain the possible causes. The evaluation is presented as a report within the context of the renewal of the marina license. The course is constrained, to a degree, by the requirements of the learning management system (originally the plan included a more realistic interface with clickable visual links and metaphors) but nevertheless, the task incorporates critical characteristics of authentic learning.

Youthwork

In a vocational course for youth workers (*Youthwork Toolbox*), learners develop skills and knowledge through a series of authentic tasks set in a youthwork village (Figure 2.13). Each of the units in the module is presented in the context of a different authentic task, and learners

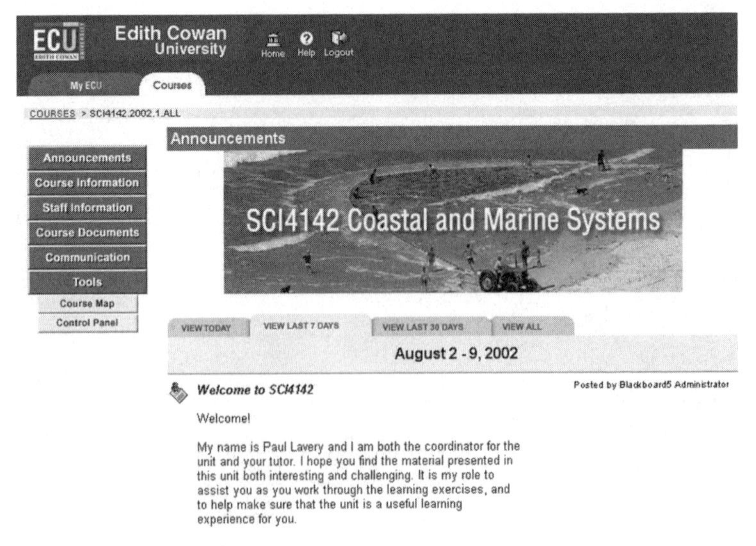

Figure 2.12 Main interface of *Coastal and Marine Systems*.
Source: Paul Lavery, Edith Cowan University

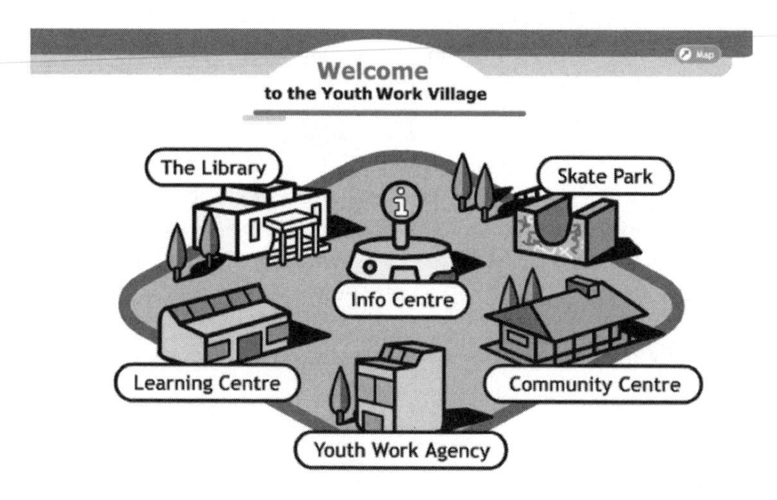

Figure 2.13 Main interface of the youthwork village.
Source: Australian Flexible Learning Framework, © Commonwealth of Australia

assume the role of a youthworker to undertake tasks to develop their capabilities. Learning outcomes are judged by the quality of the products developed. In a unit on visual communication, for example, learners are required to create a poster advertising an upcoming event. In order to create the poster, they need to learn and apply a range of skills and competencies. Within the youthwork village, the learners are provided with plentiful resources and supports for learning the particular skills that they need in the development of the poster.

Film and Television

In a Bachelor of Creative Industries course specialising in Television, McKee (2008) described an authentic project involving the creation of a series of short "blipcoms" of a comedy program for a telecommunications company. The movies were designed for distribution on mobile phones. Students worked on the movies over two semesters, overseen by a staff member who took the role of producer. The students worked together with the staff in teams to write the scripts for a dark comedy "sitcom" series of one-minute episodes, which were edited by the producer. In the production phase, the students worked as crew in the university's television studio. Directors from the industry were also brought in, effectively modelling professional behaviour for students.

Resources for Realising e-Learning Courses

While many of the e-learning examples given above have involved the creation of simulated workplaces and as such, incorporate extensive resources such as graphics, video, and sound files, other examples are less resource-intensive while still retaining fidelity to the authentic characteristics described. The learning courses described have varying degrees of fidelity to the characteristics of authentic tasks defined earlier, and all have strong linkage to real-world professional practice. In particular, they illustrate how a whole course of study (or a major part of it) can be encapsulated within complex, realistic tasks.

The foundations of this approach can be explained using logic mapping.

The Underlying Logic of Online Authentic Tasks in Higher Education

The concept of using logic maps or systems models to represent the theory or logic of teaching and learning practices has a long history. For example, in 1963, John B. Carroll introduced a model of school learning that has influenced educational researchers and curriculum specialists for more than four decades. In a 25-year retrospective look at his model, Carroll (1989) expressed surprise that his model had attracted as much attention as it had over the years, but also went on to state that "the model could still be used to solve current problems in education" (p. 26).

We believe Carroll's confidence in his model is still warranted today, and thus we have used it as an inspiration for the logic map described below to represent the model of authentic tasks as a foundation for teaching and learning online.

Logic Mapping

Carroll's original model was a formal, quasi-mathematical one in which three of the five classes of variables that can explain variance in school achievement are expressed in terms of time. The structure of the Carroll Model is represented in Figure 2.14. Each of the factors in the model is explained below.

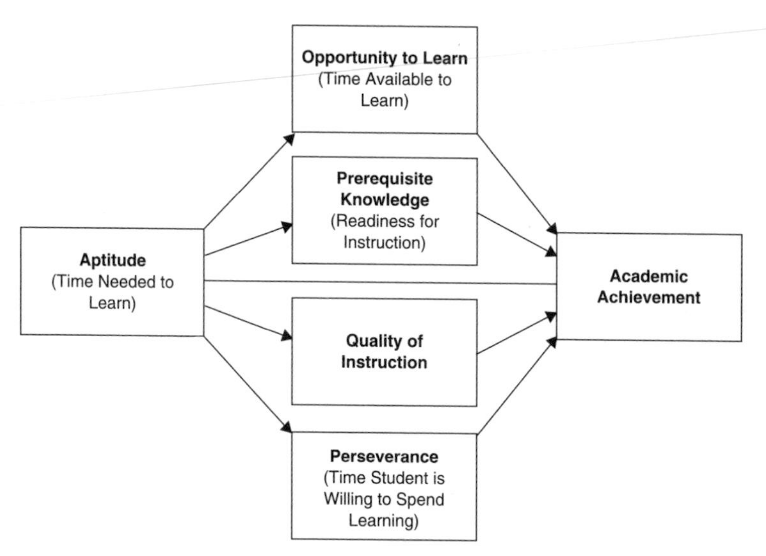

Figure 2.14 Carroll's model of school learning (Carroll, 1989).

Aptitude

An influential factor in Carroll's model is his interpretation of aptitude as "the amount of time a student needs to learn a given task, unit of instruction, or curriculum to an acceptable criterion of mastery under optimal conditions of instruction and student motivation" (Carroll, 1989, p. 26). Rather than viewing aptitude as a score on a standardised test, Carroll viewed most learners as capable of desirable levels of academic achievement, provided enough time. This temporal interpretation of aptitude has influenced many, for example, Benjamin S. Bloom (1971, 1977), credited as the founder of the Mastery Learning instructional model.

Opportunity to Learn

The amount of time available for learning within a curriculum defines the "opportunity to learn" factor. Carroll pointed out that a weakness of many school schedules (e.g., 180 days a year divided into 60-minute classes devoted to different subjects) is that they provide less time than lower-aptitude students need to achieve a given set of objectives. Academic semesters may impose similar restraints on learning time, although the most recent evidence shows that most higher education students fail to use their learning time wisely (Kuh, 2001). Content "covered" in a curriculum is another variable included in the "opportunity to learn" factor.

Ability to Understand Instruction

This factor includes language comprehension and learning skills, variables Carroll regarded as individual differences subject to development or enhancement. In Carroll's view, learners who develop better learning skills will be able to decrease the amount of time they require for learning, and in effect, increase their aptitude for learning. This factor also relates to the readiness or preparedness of the student for learning as well as any prerequisite knowledge the learner is expected to have.

Quality of Instruction

An often-misinterpreted factor in Carroll's model of school learning is quality of instruction. Carroll emphasises structural aspects of instruction such as knowledge of objectives, access to content, and carefully planned and clearly specified instructional events. Carroll (1989) clarified that this does not mean that learning tasks must be broken down into small steps and subjected to drill and practice, defending his model as encompassing a wide range of instructional events, from direct tutorials to field trips.

Perseverance

The perseverance factor, often viewed as an operational definition of student motivation, also has a temporal interpretation. Perseverance is the amount of time a student is willing to spend on learning a given task or set of objectives. According to Carroll, if students have similar aptitudes (i.e., they need approximately the same amount of time to accomplish a certain learning task), then any of them who put forth more effort (i.e., spend more time) will attain higher achievement. Of course, if more time is not available for extra effort to be performed, then the perseverance factor will have little impact.

Academic Achievement

Carroll's model is focused on academic achievement of the kind usually measured by standardised achievement tests or by the grades achieved in academic courses. Typical achievement indicators predicted by the classes of variables in Carroll's model include course grades, grade-point-average (GPA), achievement test scores, and graduation rates.

A Logic Map of an Authentic Tasks-based Higher Education Course

Using Carroll's model as an inspiration, Figure 2.15 is intended to represent the underlying logic of the authentic tasks-based model described above and exemplified by the courses we have illustrated. Each of the factors in the model is explained below. There are five classes of factors in our logic map of an authentic tasks-based learning environment: *Input*, *Design*, *Engagement*, *Instructor*, and *Outcome* factors.

Input Factors

Three factors are included in our specification of the *Input* class of factors: aptitude and individual differences, cultural habits of mind, and origins and strengths of intrinsic motivation.

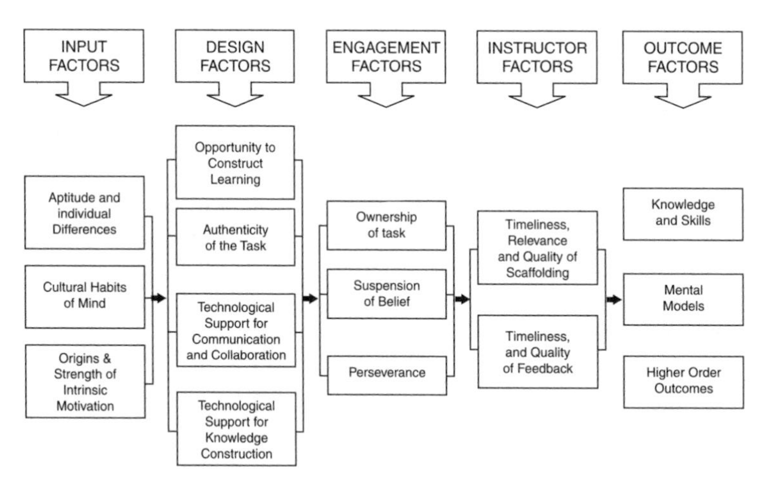

Figure 2.15 Logic map of authentic tasks-based learning environment.

Aptitude and Individual Differences

Whereas Carroll (1963, 1989) defined aptitude in terms of the time a student needs to learn a task, our model includes a richer analysis of the characteristics a learner brings to contemporary e-learning. The diversity reflected in most higher education populations today demands a more complex portrayal. Certainly, aptitude in Carroll's sense is still relevant, but there are numerous other individual differences that should be considered when designing interactive learning environments (Jonassen & Grabowski, 1983). Locus of control, learning styles, anxiety, tolerance for ambiguity, prior experience, interests, attitudes, and disabilities are just a few of the individual difference variables that can vary among the participants in online learning courses.

Cultural Habits of Mind

Some cultures emphasise rational problem solving and critique, whereas others place more value on normative communication and shared understanding. The importance of cultural influences on learning has been given increasing attention in higher education recently, although relatively few interactive learning courses have been designed to take advantage of cultural differences. We view sensitivity to cultural diversity and pluralism as a "meta-value" that should influence virtually every aspect of human activity, including the design and implementation of online learning courses. The role of cultural habits of mind in learning is an area in great need of research.

Origin of Motivation

Two primary forms of motivation are extrinsic (outside the learning environment, e.g., rewards such as degree diploma) and intrinsic (integral to the learning environment, e.g., intellectual curiosity aroused by an authentic task). Intrinsically motivating learning is elusive regardless of the context, but our research suggests that learners vary in their capacity for intrinsic motivation. The type of motivation affecting the learner is inevitably an important variable in explaining the effects of web-based learning.

Design Factors

Four factors are included in our specification of the *Design* class of factors: opportunity to construct knowledge, authenticity of the task, technological support for communication and collaboration, and technological support for knowledge construction.

Opportunity to Construct Learning

Most existing online courses used for distance education appear to employ reductionist direct instruction addressing a series of easily measurable objectives in sequence. As described in this chapter, online learning courses can enable learning opportunities through authentic tasks to be done or real-world problems to be solved that have relevance for learners. This factor includes the time available for learning as well as the extensiveness of the content encompassed in the design of the task.

Authenticity of the Task

Higher education instructors often try to design assignments and tasks that have relevance to their students, but usually fall short. They might add contextual elements to an assignment, but most students are savvy enough to know when such "authenticity" is just window dressing. Adopting large-scale, authentic tasks involves taking risks that learners may initially fail to appreciate because it takes the students out of their normal comfort zone. Given the evidence that decontextualised academic tasks lead to short-lived and inert knowledge (Cognition and Technology Group at Vanderbilt, 1990a), the risk is well worth taking.

Technological Support for Communications and Collaboration

Few complex authentic tasks can be accomplished by individual learners, and hence it is important to provide a technological infrastructure that enables high fidelity communication and collaboration among learners in distance education. The standard discussion tools and chat rooms provided in common learning management systems may suffice in many cases as they have in some of our examples, but more research is needed to advance the degree to which ICTs support the levels of substantive communication and collaboration desired in e-learning.

Technological Support for Knowledge Construction

In the process of accomplishing authentic e-learning tasks, collaborating learners will need to develop prototype knowledge representations that can be easily shared, critiqued, edited, and refined over time. This will require the provision of "cognitive tools" for learning (Jonassen & Reeves, 1996), including both off-the-shelf software and web-based participatory tools such as wikis and blogs.

Engagement Factors

Three factors are included in our specification of the *Engagement* class of factors: ownership of task, suspension of disbelief, and perseverance.

Task Ownership

Brown, Collins, and Duguid (1989b) emphasised the importance of task ownership in situated cognition, that is, learning that is tied to the retrieval cues in the environments in which the learning will be used. Learning tasks may be primarily academic (writing an essay about the role of women in colonial Australia) or primarily authentic (conducting research on the effects of pollutants in local streams on marsupial populations). Academic tasks dominate the lives of most learners, regardless of whether they are at a distance or not. Cognitive learning theory (Winn & Snyder, 1996) indicates that the ways in which knowledge and skills are initially learned affect the degree to which these abilities can be used in other contexts. By emphasising authentic tasks that students "own" for themselves, authentic online learning courses may enhance the transfer of knowledge and skills.

Suspension of Disbelief

Because authentic tasks require students to immerse themselves in cognitive activities that mirror real-world professional practice, often the conditions of their involvement need to be described within a scenario or well-formulated problem description. Sometimes, depending on the design of the task and its setting, this requires some suspension of disbelief if, for instance, students are asked to imagine that they are the professionals and they can learn enough to solve a major problem or accomplish a significant feat (such as planning a mission to Mars). With time and appropriate support, students can readily engage with these tasks when they suspend disbelief and allow themselves to become immersed in the problem.

Perseverance

Whereas Carroll (1963) defined perseverance as the amount of time a student is willing to spend on learning a given task, we think this factor must also include factors such as *metacognition* and *reflection*. Metacognition refers to a learner's awareness of objectives, ability to plan and evaluate learning strategies, and capacity to reflect on one's progress and adjust learning behaviours to accommodate needs (Flavell, 1979). In short, metacognitive skills are the skills one has in learning to learn. Learners in any kind of higher education context vary widely in their capacity for hard work, their metacognitive skills, and their powers of reflective thinking.

Instructor Factors

Two particular factors are included in our specification for the *Instructor*: timeliness, relevance and quality of scaffolding; and timeliness, relevance and quality of feedback.

Timeliness, Relevance and Quality of Scaffolding

Scaffolding refers to the role of the instructor in providing sufficient directions to get learners started on the right path when confronted with a complex authentic task, reining learners in when they stray too far from a feasible path to task completion, pointing students to useful resources, nurturing clear communication and fruitful collaboration, and in general providing learners with just enough support so that they accomplish the tasks primarily through their own efforts. Scaffolding requires a difficult balancing act between providing too much support, whereby an authentic task may become just a matter of following directions, and too little support that can lead to task failure and learner frustration.

Timeliness, Relevance and Quality of Feedback

Evaluations of distance education again and again identify poor feedback as the most significant flaw in most online courses. Even in the most authentic online learning course, an instructor has a responsibility to provide learners with relevant and accurate feedback in a timely manner. Ideally, the feedback should approximate the kinds of review and encouragement that people in the real world would receive when tackling the same kind of task.

Outcome Factors

Three factors are included in our specification for the *Outcome*: knowledge and skills, mental models, and higher order outcomes. Instead of the traditional achievement indicators in Carroll's (1963) model, a richer analysis of the types of outcomes of contemporary higher education is needed.

Knowledge and Skills

The first outcome is knowledge and skills. Cognitive psychology has enriched our understanding of the mental states that result from learning to include constructs such as concepts, schema, rules, and skills (Winn & Snyder, 1996). Authentic task-based online learning courses do not rely upon traditional academic tests to assess knowledge and skills, but seek evidence of growth in these areas through performance analysis and assessment of artifacts created during the accomplishment of the task.

Mental Models

It may seem strange to separate "mental models" from other types of knowledge and skills, but developing robust mental models is such an important outcome in higher education that it deserves special attention. In the USA, a large-scale investigation of student engagement in traditional higher education (Kuh, 2001) illustrated the alarming degree to which students are failing to develop deep learning. University graduates must be able to activate appropriate mental models, use them to interpret new information, assimilate new information back into those models, reorganise the models in light of the newly interpreted information, and use the newly aggrandised mental models to explain, interpret, or infer new knowledge (Norman, 1983). Mental models are the mental structures we use to "understand systems and solve problems arising from the way systems work" (Winn & Snyder, 1996, p. 123).

Higher-Order Outcomes

Although many in academe remain primarily concerned with the transmission of existing knowledge and skills in their fields, others also intend students to develop higher-order outcomes such as problem-solving abilities, creativity, curiosity, and the desire for lifelong learning.

Higher-order outcomes such as framing and resolving ill-defined problems, or exhibiting intellectual curiosity, are rarely directly observable. Although measures of variables such as curiosity have been developed, these types of outcomes must usually be inferred from students' performance on a range of alternative assessments. An inherent advantage of authentic tasks is that the assessment of higher-order outcomes is embedded in the final product that provides evidence of task accomplishment.

Applying Authentic Tasks

The logic map illustrated in Figure 2.15 and described above represents a first step in illuminating the logic underlying authentic task-based online learning courses.

Authentic tasks form the basis of a learning design that appears to hold considerable promise for the delivery of e-learning units and courses. In this chapter we have discussed and described a framework for designing authentic learning based on the prescription of an authentic task that is holistic and complex. In the next chapter, we describe learning tasks and activities that appear to have a semblance of authenticity, but, we argue, are lacking in essential elements of the design model.

Chapter 3

What is *Not* Authentic e-Learning?

While authentic approaches to e-learning may be intuitively appealing, the approach is often misinterpreted. Many educators begin with the belief that to be authentic, such learning opportunities must be *real*. While real settings and problems are appropriate, it is sometimes very difficult for teachers to arrange a real setting for the task for many students, year after year as the course runs. For example, courses that involve work to be done for real clients can be time consuming and problematic to arrange, and there may be other legal considerations such as occupational health and safety and intellectual property issues.

Our research has provided principles to guide the development of realistic and complex e-learning tasks that are not *real* but *cognitively real*, that is, they provide opportunities to think and act as an expert would, and are much more readily implemented in higher education classes.

Nevertheless, it is sometimes difficult to create realistic and complex tasks that can prompt and frame the learning of a range of skills and concepts without simplification. Sometimes tasks have a semblance or veneer of authenticity but they are not capable of supporting deep learning and sustained activity.

Non-authentic Tasks

In many higher education courses, the tasks given often have little resemblance to the kinds of activities and problems people face in real-world situations.

In some disciplines it may be accepted that a task is quite abstract and decontextualised. For example, most designers and teachers would recognise that a mathematics problem such as that shown in Figure 3.1,

Let F be the vector field on $\Re^3$
given by $F(x,y,z) = (2xz, -x, y^2)$
Evaluate
$$\iiint_V \underline{F} dV = \left(\iiint_V 2xz\,dV, -\iiint_V x\,dV, \iiint_V y^2\,dV\right)$$
where V is the region bounded by the surfaces
$x = 0$, $y = 0$, $y = 6$, $z = x^2$ and $z = 4$

Figure 3.1 Mathematics problem example.

while complex and important, has few of the characteristics of authentic tasks (such as an authentic context).

Myers (1993) developed three criteria for measuring the authenticity of an activity:

1 The activity provides opportunities for the students to achieve something that they perceive as real or genuine
2 The activity challenges, inspires and empowers learners to take risks and exceed personal limitations, and
3 The activity makes some difference in the lives of the learners (p. 72).

These characteristics are also similar to those suggested by Sternberg, Wagner, and Okagaki (1993), who differentiated between the kinds of problems learners face in academic situations and the kind they face in practical, real-world applications. Practical problems can be characterised by the ill-defined nature of the problem, the need for substantial information seeking, multiple (as opposed to a single) correct solutions, and multiple methods of obtaining solutions (Sternberg et al., 1993, p. 206).

However, academic problems tend to be much more structured and formulaic. They are formulated by the teacher, well defined, complete in the information they provide, have only one correct answer and usually only one method of obtaining the correct answer. They are disembedded from ordinary experience, and of little or no intrinsic interest for students. Differences between academic and real-life approaches have also been investigated by Lebow and Wager (1994), who noted that students perceive academic problems as artificial and not very relevant, whereas authentic problems are perceived as realistic and worth solving.

The elements of authentic e-learning courses described in Chapter 1, and the characteristics of tasks described in Chapter 2, can also be used as design guidelines against which to assess the authenticity of e-learning activities.

Misconceptions of Authenticity of Tasks

When designing authentic tasks it is easy to misconstrue the approach, and to conclude that it is enough to include real-world examples. There are many misconceptions regarding the form that authentic tasks should take. The main misconceptions include the following, where teachers mistakenly believe that these types of tasks fulfil the requirements of authenticity:

Word Problems

Word problems, while attempting to provide a real-world context, frequently fail to replicate the essential elements of a meaningful and realistic problem. For example, consider:

> There are 25 people in a room. How many handshakes would there be if everyone shook hands with every other person?

There are key mathematical strategies required to solve this problem, but important contextual elements are missing from the problem description to make it authentic and relevant. Why would anyone need to know the answer to this question?

A well-known example of a false word problem is: If there are 26 sheep and 10 goats on a ship, how old is the captain? This is an example of what Schoenfeld (1991) called *nonreason*, that is, a willingness to engage in activities that don't make sense. Collins (1988) also discussed *suboptimal schemes* for remembering information to pass tests, which explains why many children give the number 36 as the answer to this problem.

A more complex example from physics might be a question such as the following:

> If a person jumps off a moving bus, how would that affect the speed of the bus?

Again, a sophisticated knowledge of Newtonian motion is needed to solve this problem, but initial consideration of the question might bring in contextual factors which have not been considered within the description of the problem. For example, a student considering an actual instance of someone jumping off a bus (as opposed to an academic word problem) might reflect on why the person jumped, where they jumped from, the weight of the person, and what the driver of the bus did immediately before and after the jump—none of which technically influences the solution.

Bottge and Hasselbring (1993) have pointed out that such word problems are inadequate because they simply provide a textual, rather than a contextual form.

Thematic Approaches

Thematic approaches to interdisciplinary studies, while worthwhile and complementary to understanding an issue across diverse subject areas, are usually presented as non-authentic tasks. For example, a thematic task might require students to study the four seasons from the perspectives of science, poetry/writing, mathematics, geography and music.

While such academic endeavour may result in many associations and networks across discipline areas, it is unlikely that such a learning context would result in deep and transferable knowledge for two key reasons. First, thematic approaches are generally constructed solely to suit a curriculum focus rather than as an investigation of a genuine and realistic issue or problem. Secondly, there is rarely a polished product that might be useful in a real-world context—in most cases the product of these tasks resembles an academic assignment.

Most Computer Games

Most computer games, even educational ones, fail as authentic tasks on a number of counts. Games have the capacity to reflect real-world contexts and endeavours, using realistic and almost perfect 3D images that enable users to readily engage within their worlds. This is one of their main strengths and they have the potential to represent powerful authentic learning settings.

However, most immersive and real-world type games are designed purely for recreational purposes and learning becomes incidental to their purpose. Although there are growing numbers of multi-player games, they are usually designed for a single player and, while they can create opportunities for real reflection, the ultimate aim is to finish the game rather than to create a genuine and useful product. The failure to engage players in genuine productivity is the key weakness in computer games when measured against authentic task criteria.

Some PBL problems

Problem-based learning (PBL) tasks that are based on Howard Barrows' model of medical education can be engaging and authentic. Two key features of his PBL approach comprise first, a rich problem that can be freely explored, and secondly, student-centered learning (Hmelo & Evensen, 2000). These characteristics align well with the characteristics of authentic tasks.

However, many PBL problems present a problem situation that requires a known, best-practice solution, and few PBL tasks require a realistic product beyond the solution of the problem. For example, the PBL genetics problem *When Twins Marry Twins* (Allen, 1999) requires students to solve a complex and genuine problem, but the student is advised that the problem 'can be researched by consulting the textbook alone, and has a content focus that easily fits within the framework of a conventional course' (Para 6).

An authentic task, as we have described it, would not be able to be completed by reference to a single source of information.

Complex Problems Simplified

In some cases, course teachers and designers have access to rich and detailed resources, such as simulations or web-based resources, which recreate workplaces and other contexts for exploration, but instead of capitalising on the rich complexity of these environments, teachers sometimes reduce and simplify the task.

Such environments have much potential to be used with authentic tasks. For example, a simulated laboratory workplace, created in Quicktime VR, presenting a panorama of the room, would allow students to explore the entire laboratory by panning around and moving in to inspect aspects of interest (Figure 3.2).

A teacher of Occupational Health and Safety (OHS) could give students an overall authentic task requiring them to inspect the virtual laboratory and write an OHS report pointing out risk factors, as a professional might be required to do (this was how the panorama

Figure 3.2 One segment of the virtual lab panorama in Quicktime VR.
Source: Janis Jansz, Edith Cowan University

environment was used as an authentic task in its original course). However, a weaker approach would be one where the teacher simplified the inspection process, perhaps by breaking the task down into sub-steps, and giving specific questions to answer, such as:

- What biological materials are present in the lab?
- What biological hazards are evident?
- How many instances of contamination exist in the lab?
- What preventive measures should be in place?

Spiro et al. (1987) are very strong in their criticism of such oversimplification: practice, they maintain, is motivated by convenience rather than concern for student learning.

Summary of Tasks against Characteristics

These five task examples are shown in summary form in Table 3.1 below, where each type of task is matched against the characteristics of authentic tasks described in detail in Chapter 2.

Table 3.1 Non-authentic Tasks matched to Characteristics of Authentic Tasks

Authentic tasks:	Word problems	Thematic approaches	Computer games	Some PBL problems	Complex problems simplified
Have real-world relevance		✗	✗		
Are ill defined	✗				✗
Comprise complex tasks investigated over time, using variety of resources	✗			✗	
Provide the opportunity to examine the task from different perspectives	✗		✗		
Provide the opportunity to collaborate			✗		
Provide the opportunity to reflect			✗		
Lead beyond domain-specific outcomes				✗	✗
Are seamlessly integrated with assessment			✗		✗
Create polished products valuable in their own right	✗	✗	✗	✗	✗
Allow competing solutions and diversity of outcome			✗		

While each of these example tasks has shortcomings, all of them could be enriched to create engaging and authentic tasks for students with the application of the critical elements used as design guidelines. It depends on the overall approach and design, its complexity, and whether there is a realistic and genuine artefact that results from the activity.

Continuum of Authentic Characteristics

There is arguably no such thing as a perfect task—one that matches exactly all the characteristics that have been described as contributing to the design of an authentic task. However, it is useful when designing and reviewing tasks and overall learning courses to consider the dimensions on a continuum as shown in Table 3.2 (this technique was used by Reeves & Reeves, 1997, to gauge effective dimensions of interactive learning on the Web). In this way, a designer or teacher can follow the guidelines in Column 2 and reflect upon the guiding questions in Column 4 to assess each characteristic, and then build up a picture of the entire design by connecting a line between points on the continuums.

Table 3.2 could be used at different times to assist with the design and review of an authentic e-learning course. It could be used in the early planning stages to act as a prompt to ensure that different elements have been accounted for in the design. For example, a teacher might be prompted to plan a teleconference to allow students to speak in their own voices and articulate their understanding, or to strengthen collaborative work. At the review stage, the continuum items can be assessed and joined to give a visual representation of the entire course or unit. Any aspects that veer significantly to the left can be assessed and attended to as required.

Figure 3.3 below demonstrates (in part) how two quite different e-learning courses might be illustrated on the task dimension of the table. The task on the right is more authentic as judged on all the elements because it provides a realistic and complex task that requires decision-making by students, and takes a few weeks of a semester course to complete. The task on the left is a more academic decontextualised one, with limited—albeit relevant—resources, taking only minutes or hours to complete.

Figure 3.3 below demonstrates (in part) how two quite different e-learning courses might be illustrated on the task dimension of the table. The task on the right is more authentic as judged on all the

Table 3.2 Continuum of Characteristics to Gauge Authenticity

Element of authentic learning	*Guidelines for implementation*	*Continuum of characteristics* *Non-authentic*	➔	*Authentic*	*Guiding questions*
Provide authentic context that reflects the way the knowledge will be used in real life	A physical/virtual environment that reflects the way the knowledge will ultimately be used	Decontextualised	➔	Realistic	Does the context of the course represent the kind of setting where the skill or knowledge is applied?
	A non-linear design to preserve the complexity of the real-life setting	Fixed	➔	Flexible	Is the pathway students take through the learning environment flexible, where students are able to move around at will?
Provide authentic tasks	Tasks that have real-world relevance	Academic	➔	Real world	Does the task mirror the kind of task performed in real-world applications?
	Ill-defined complex activities that provide an opportunity for students to define the tasks and sub-tasks required to complete the activity	Multiple small tasks	➔	Complex tasks	Is the task presented as a series of small sub-steps or as an overarching complex problem?
	A sustained period of time for investigation	Short time	➔	Long time	Do students work on the task for weeks rather than minutes or hours?
	The opportunity for the detection of relevant versus. irrelevant information	Limited information	➔	Broad information	Are students able to choose information from a variety of inputs, including relevant and irrelevant sources?

	Tasks that can be integrated across subject areas	Single discipline	→	Multi-disciplinary	Are tasks and strategies relevant to other disciplines and broader knowledge?
Provide access to expert performances and the modelling of processes	Access to expert thinking and modelling processes	Direct instruction	→	Expert performance	Does the learning environment provide access to expert skill and opinion?
	Access to learners with various levels of expertise	Expertise	→	Levels of expertise	Does the learning environment allow access to other learners at various stages of expertise?
	Opportunity for the sharing of narratives and stories and access to the social periphery	Didactic, core	→	Narrative, peripheral	Are students able to hear and share stories about professional practice?
Provide multiple roles and perspectives	Different perspectives on the topics from various points of view	Single view	→	Multiple perspectives	Are students able to explore issues from different points of view?
	The opportunity to criss-cross the learning environment or resources	Single pathway	→	Multiple pathways	Are students able to use the learning resources and materials for multiple purposes?
Support collaborative construction of knowledge	Tasks are completed in pairs or groups rather than individually	Cooperation	→	Group collaboration	Are students able to collaborate (rather than simply cooperate) on tasks?
	Appropriate incentive structure for whole group achievement	Individual grade	→	Group grade	Are grades given for group effort, rather than individual effort?

(Continued overleaf)

Table 3.2 Continued

Element of authentic learning	*Guidelines for implementation*	*Continuum of characteristics* *Non-authentic*	→	*Authentic*	*Guiding questions*
Promote reflection	Authentic context and task that require decisions to be made	Pre-determined steps	→	Decision making	Are students required to make decisions about how to complete the task?
	Non-linear organisation of resources to enable students to return to any element if required	Linear	→	Non-linear	Are students able to move freely in the environment and return to any element to act upon reflection?
	The opportunity for learners to compare themselves with other in varying stages of accomplishment	No facility to compare	→	Able to compare	Can students compare their thoughts and ideas to experts, teachers, guides, and to other students?
	Groupings of students to enable reflection with aware attention	Individual	→	Group	Do students work in collaborative groups that enable discussion and social reflection?
Promote articulation	Inherent, as opposed to constructed, opportunities to articulate	Little discussion	→	Much discussion	Does the task require students to discuss and articulate beliefs and growing understanding?
	Groups to enable articulation	Individual	→	Group	Does the environment provide collaborative groups and forums to enable articulation of ideas?

	Public presentation of argument to enable articulation and defence of learning	Little articulation	→	Presentations	Does the task enable presentation and defence of arguments?
Provide coaching and scaffolding	Collaborative learning, where more able partners can assist with scaffolding and coaching	Unsupported	→	Partner coaching	Are more knowledgable students able to assist with coaching?
	Coaching and scaffolding assistance is available for a significant portion of the activity	Unsupported	→	Scaffolded	Is a teacher, guide or helper available to provide contextualised support?
Provide for authentic assessment of learning within the tasks	The opportunity for students to be effective performers with acquired knowledge, and to craft polished performances or products	Raw	→	Polished	Are products or performances polished and refined rather than incomplete or rushed drafts?
	Significant student time and effort in collaboration with others	Brief	→	Extended	Do students participate in the activity for extended periods of time?
	The assessment to be seamlessly integrated with the activity	Separate tests	→	Integrated assessment	Are students assessed on the product of the investigation, rather than by separate testing?
	Multiple indicators of learning	Single measure	→	Multiple measures	Are there multiple assessment measures rather than a single measure?

Element of authentic learning	Guidelines for implementation	Continuum of characteristics Non-authentic ➡ Authentic	Guiding questions
Provide authentic tasks	Tasks that have real-world relevance	Academic ➡ Real world	Does the task mirror the kind of task performed in real world applications?
	Ill-defined complex activities that provide an opportunity for students to define the tasks and sub-tasks required to complete the activity	Multiple small tasks ➡ Complex task	Is the task presented as a series of small sub-steps or as an overarching complex problem?
	A sustained period of time for investigation	Short time ➡ Long time	Do students work on the task for weeks rather than minutes or hours?
	The opportunity for the detection of relevant versus. irrelevant information	Limited information ➡ Broad information	Are students able to choose information from a variety of inputs, including relevant and irrelevant sources?
	Tasks that can be integrated across subject areas	Single discipline ➡ Multi-disciplinary	Are tasks and strategies relevant to other disciplines and broader knowledge?

Figure 3.3 Example use of continuum for authentic and academic task.

elements because it provides a realistic and complex task that requires decision-making by students, and takes a few weeks of a semester course to complete. The task on the left is a more academic decontextualised one, with limited—albeit relevant—resources, taking only minutes or hours to complete.

Enabling Activities

In this chapter, we have provided descriptions of a range of tasks which have some authentic elements but that, in themselves, do not provide the rich opportunities for learning which an authentic e-learning course provides. This is not to say that these types of tasks are not useful enabling activities. Indeed, if any one of the examples given here were included within a more complex overarching authentic task, it would provide useful skills and learning opportunities. However, each on its own is insufficient, or as articulated by Spiro, Feltovich, Jacobson, and Coulson (1991b), not false but inadequate.

In the next chapter we explore in more depth the realism required in an authentic e-learning course, and the suspension of disbelief that is often required by learners to fully engage with authentic tasks.

Chapter 4

How Real does Authentic e-Learning Need to be?

A persistent question that arises in considering and planning for authentic e-learning is: how real does it need to be? Should the courses we design have realistic elements similar to real-world situations (such as in life-like simulations), or indeed, should the problem setting actually be real?

We argue that while real learning contexts and realistic simulations can comprise excellent examples of authentic e-learning designs, neither is essential to prompt the "cognitive realism" necessary for learners to benefit from the approach (Herrington, Reeves, & Oliver, 2007).

Increasing Relevance in Learning

Since the development of factory model schools (Rist, 1973), reality and real-world practice have been insufficiently used to convey meaning or alternative views in traditional classrooms, much to the detriment of learners. Even in higher education contexts, where arguably there are numerous opportunities to providing learning opportunities beyond the walls of the lecture hall, teaching has largely been limited to abstract talk, text, and tests.

Fortunately, in the last decade or more, under the influence of constructivist philosophy (Fosnot, 1996) and more student centred approaches, many teachers in colleges and universities have tried to make learning more relevant to students by creating opportunities for them to apply their learning in realistic, if simulated, situations. Service learning, co-ops, internships, apprenticeships, and other strategies have been used to expand learning options for postsecondary students. At the same time, many teachers have attempted to use technology such as computers and video to recreate the essence of real situations in order to design authentic learning experiences for students. Efforts to recreate reality, sometimes in a more appealing and idealistic form, are not new, and can be traced back to the development of perspective in art.

Simulations and Virtual Reality

Throughout history, people have attempted to escape the real world by surrounding themselves with more appealing representations of reality. The artistic representation of realistic landscapes has existed at least since the Hellenistic Greeks with the development of perspective in art, which allowed the placement of objects in "believable space" (Greenhalgh, 2002, p. 2). Affluent citizens of Greece surrounded themselves with panoramic landscapes on the walls of their rooms, representing idyllic scenes. The artists worked to make these panoramas as realistic as possible to allow the occupants of the rooms to experience an alternative reality. As skills with portraying perspective in art developed during the Renaissance, *trompe l'oeil* ("the art of deception") paintings became increasingly popular, providing viewers with a more appealing visual aspect than reality would permit within available time and space.

In recent years, simulations have become popular in industry and retail areas such as in building construction scheduling, architecture, interior design and landscaping (Green & Sulbaran, 2006) where the facility to create an immersive three-dimensional representation of ideas can have obvious benefits for planning, evaluation, marketing, and training. Some of the advantages of using simulations in educational contexts include:

1. Simulations are useful when fieldwork is physically or financially impractical, dangerous, or involves decisions that are too risky for novices, such as managing an organisation.
2. Simulations require students to make choices and deal with complexity, to choose relevant from irrelevant information.
3. Learning is (almost) experiential, not only in providing the look and feel of the real world but also in allowing students to discover the consequences of actions in ways textbooks and tutorials do not, by experimentation.
4. A computer can present information and choices personalised to the learning level and style of the student, through scaffolding, which can be dis-erected as proficiency increases. Students can have sources of online help that are tailored to the problem and their progress, not a generalised textbook.

5 Simulation learning has an "immersive" quality quite different from classroom or home study experiences. It can create the experience Csikszentmihalyi (1992) described as flow—an intense feeling of engagement more easily observed amongst students playing computer games, board games, watching a movie or reading a novel than in classroom learning.
6 Finally, simulations can have a powerful ability to facilitate metacognitive learning. Goodman (1995) argued that beyond allowing students to put theory into practice, simulations are prime vehicles for facilitating "practice in theory," for example, through formulating generalisations about the studied world (Standen & Herrington, 1996, pp. 834–835).

Simulations vary in their complexity and their resemblance to real-world practice, from simple representations on computer screens to fully immersive virtual reality.

Immersive Learning and Virtual Reality

Rosenberg (2006) promoted the potential of interactive simulations for learning:

> Through the power and creativity of simulations and the ubiquitous nature of the Internet, scenarios can be created that rival the real world, making training more relevant, more effective, more challenging, and, where appropriate, more fun. Indeed, technology-based games and simulations represent one of the fastest growing segments of the e-learning industry, and the US government is now fully engaged in simulations and games, even for highly sensitive areas like the military and homeland security (pp. 47–48).

The United States space program, the airline industry, the military, and medical schools have a long history of using simulations to provide learning situations with high degrees of verisimilitude to real-life environments. The US space program uses highly realistic, computer-generated simulations to train astronauts to cope with highly critical situations. Murray and Cox (1989) described the total realism of the simulations used to train astronauts on the Apollo missions, and how mission controllers were able to relate fully to situations simulated in training, with perhaps the exception proving the rule: for example, a mission controller's amazed response to the presence of dust on a real mission on the moon (something that was not included in the simulations).

Virtual reality technology enables simulations so realistic in aircraft training that people react spontaneously and automatically to the environment as if they were really experiencing it. For example, McLellan (1991) related a trainee pilot's experience in an aircraft simulator:

> Part of the drill is that we lose an engine at a critical period in the take-off. And I made the rotation and I did everything I possibly could and the thing rolled to the right and crashed . . . I yelled and everybody else yelled . . . It is so realistic that it's almost frightening (p. 33).

Macedonia and Rosenbloom (2001) described collaboration among the military, academia and Hollywood to create realistic and immersive simulations for military training. Maximum verisimilitude to genuine combat and other situations is required. The simulation described by Macedonia and Rosenbloom was designed to be used for training soldiers about to engage in combat or peace-keeping missions in foreign countries. This simulation included a full briefing on the mission, weapons, political factions, strategies and immersion in the culture of the city. Describing the experience of a soldier in this simulation, Macedonia and Rosenbloom wrote: "The sights, sounds and smells of the city immediately bombard him . . . the scene is a rich and confusing tapestry of life" (p. 90). The elements of real-life situations are included to ensure that soldiers can account for peripheral events sometimes not accounted for in training situations.

In medicine, patient simulators that allow students to practise procedures under realistic conditions on simulated patients have created many opportunities for early skill development prior to practice on real patients. For example, at Harvard Medical School, a simulator for practising bronchoscopy is used where a flexible fiberoptic bronchoscope is "snaked" down the trachea to inspect the airways leading to the lungs. The director of the program stated that: "The tissues look real, even seem to move when touched. The simulator patient breathes and has a heartbeat; he coughs if the user hits an airway wall" (Rabkin, 2002).

What are the characteristics of such simulations that enable realistic fidelity to the genuine situation and provide valuable training and preparation for the real situation? Macedonia and Rosenbloom (2001) proposed that there are "six thrusts crucial to verisimilitude" that are worthy of further investigation and research:

1 Immersion: providing compellingly realistic experiences.
2 Networking and databases: organising, storing, and distributing content.
3 Story: providing compelling interactive narratives that propel experiences.
4 Characters: replacing human participants with automated ones.
5 Setup: authoring and initialising environments, models, and experiences.
6 Direction: monitoring, directing, and understanding experiences (p. 86).

Simulations based on design criteria such as the six listed above, with full plot development and character representation, may be effective in certain learning situations. They are, however, extremely resource-intensive and costly to develop. They also have certain limitations implicit in their development, such as predetermined outcomes that need to be predicted and created within the parameters of the scenario itself.

Realistic or Real?

How real does a learning setting need to be to ensure quality learning outcomes? Some argue that only a real problem situation should be presented, with no simulation at all. For example, Savery and Duffy (1996) nominated two guiding forces in developing problem-based scenarios: first, that the problems must raise the concepts and principles relevant to the content domain, and secondly that the problems must be real. They stated:

> There are three reasons why the problems must address real issues. First, because the students are open to explore all dimensions of the problem there is real difficulty of creating a rich problem with a consistent set of information. Second, real problems tend to engage learners more—there is a larger context of familiarity with the problem. Finally, students want to know the outcome of the

> problem—what is being done about the flood, did AT&T buy NCR, what was the problem with the patient? These outcomes are not possible with artificial problems (p. 144).

Is it necessary then, when incorporating authentic learning experiences into learning courses, to design totally real or highly realistic simulations? Is the physical or simulated reality of a learning situation a critical component of effectiveness? Research into the realism of learning environments indicates that maximum fidelity does not necessarily lead to maximum effectiveness in learning, particularly for novice learners (Alessi, 1988).. Smith (1987), in his review of research related to simulations in the classroom concluded that the "physical fidelity" of the simulation materials is less important than the extent to which the simulation promotes "realistic problem-solving processes" (p. 409), a process Smith described as the "cognitive realism" of the task (Smith, 1986).

Based on our own research, we propose that the physical reality of the learning situation is of less importance than the characteristics of the task design, and the engagement of students in the learning setting. When the central task or activity is the vehicle for study of the entire course, its design must incorporate a range of complex facets and options to enable and motivate students to learn from its completion. However, the contexts and tasks do not need to be real (at least in the sense proposed by Savery and Duffy, 1996), nor need they comprise complicated plots and well-defined characters, or anticipate selected outcomes (in the way proposed by Macedonia & Rosenbloom, 2001). They do not need to have a verisimilitude approaching virtual reality. Instead they should aim to provide a "cognitive realism" rather than reality itself. For example, the learning courses described in Chapter 2 have varying degrees of fidelity to reality, but all have strong linkage to real-world professional practice, and to the "cognitive realism" described by Smith (1986). The scenarios are not drawn in elaborate, resource intensive ways, but are built up through the creation and development of realistic and engaging ideas.

The Nature of Authenticity

In spite of the growing evidence of the success of these authentic e-learning courses, they are not without their problems. One issue that has emerged strongly from a number of different sources is the nature of authenticity, and how "authentic" environments are often the creation of the teachers', authors' and instructional designers' imaginations, and are thus inevitably someone's *view* of what is authentic. Petraglia (1998b) has been critical of this shortcoming, calling it "the real world on a short leash" (p. 53).

There is nevertheless, much evidence to suggest that these learning environments can provide a great deal of meaning to otherwise decontextualised facts and skills, and can enhance the transfer of deep and lifelong learning (Barab & Landa, 1997).

At what point do students become engaged, if ever, in these scenarios? Is there a pattern to their acceptance of the terms of the authenticity, and how important is the suspension of disbelief? (Herrington, Oliver, & Reeves, 2003.)

Pre-authentication in Learning Experiences

Some maintain that it is impossible to design truly authentic learning experiences. Petraglia (1998b, 1998a) argued that authenticity can be neither "predetermined nor preordained," and such attempts often result in little more than "preauthentication," that is, "the attempt to make learning materials and environments correspond to the real world prior to the learner's interaction with them" (p. 53). He gave the example of a task of balancing a cheque book, a task which may be authentic for a 21-year-old, but hardly for a 5-year-old. Even amongst the older age group, many factors contribute to whether they would find the task authentic—some would find "any given lesson in personal finance irrelevant, inaccurate, or otherwise inappropriate" (p. 59). Barab, Squire and Dueber (2000) argued that authenticity occurs "not in the learner, the task, or the environment, but in the dynamic interactions among these various components . . . authenticity is manifest in the flow itself, and is not an objective feature of any one component in isolation" (p. 38).

Petraglia (1998a) believed that learners need to be *persuaded* that they are participating in an authentic learning experience. This idea is also adopted by Kantor, Waddington and Osgood (2000) who, when referring to the kinds of goal-based scenarios they design for Anderson Consulting, argued that:

> No matter how realistic the case . . . nor how authentic the conditions and tools . . . [it] is not the same as a work environment. It is a simulation of a client engagement in which the participants tacitly agree to go along with an interpretation of job reality which we have crafted (pp. 211–212).

There is increasing evidence that in order to fully engage with an authentic task or problem-based scenario, students need to engage with a process that is familiar to moviegoers throughout the world—the suspension of disbelief. For example, consider the suspension of disbelief that audiences must undergo to enable them to become engaged with movies such as *Star Wars*, *Mad Max*, *The Matrix*, *The Truman Show*, and *Back to the Future*. Audiences need to accept the worlds that have been created, no matter how unlikely. Once the initial suspension of disbelief has occurred, it is only inconsistencies within the parameters of the plot itself that cause dissonance in the viewer. In other words, once the viewer has accepted the fundamental basis for the simulated world in which he or she is immersed, engagement with the story and message of the film is entirely feasible.

In authentic e-learning courses that are scenario-based, where conditions, characters, circumstances and parameters are drawn to simulate a real-life context for learning, a similar suspension of disbelief is required. For some students, there appears to be some misapprehension about the approach, because it is so different from the more academic approaches with which they are familiar. Many students initially perceive authentic environments to be non-academic, non-rigorous, time wasting and unnecessary to efficient learning. It is often only when the suspension of disbelief occurs that these students see the complexity and the value of the learning design.

In this vein, Kantor, Waddington, and Osgood (2000) have a well-defined level of authenticity for their goal-based scenarios, largely designed for business consulting training:

> We make them authentic to the degree that the staging of theatrical productions is authentic. We provide physical props (plans, offices, desks) . . . We locate furniture, phones, computer equipment, flip charts and white boards in the team rooms to promote the right mix of team collaboration and communication, creation of work products and research activities. These levels of authenticity are set to the degree that such models of communication require, but no more (p. 222).

Willing Suspension of Disbelief

The term "willing suspension of disbelief" was first used by the early nineteenth-century poet Samuel Taylor Coleridge. The term has been applied to many instances of human response to the arts, as noted by Milburn (n.d.):

> [Coleridge's] original turn of the phrase was in reference to the reader's response to poetry, but everyone immediately realized he had summarized most of the human experience of art generally . . . Whether you're talking about a Spielberg movie, a Stephen King novel, a twitch-em-up video game, a multi-decibel rave, or a simple TV sitcom, they all require the same thing of spectators/ participants: a willing suspension of disbelief. (Para no. 6.)

However, the idea is also highly relevant to education. Laurel (1993) likened the willing suspension of disbelief to engagement: "Engagement is what happens when we are able to give ourselves over to a representational action, comfortably and unambiguously. It involves a kind of complicity" (p. 115).

In initial contact with authentic learning designs as described here (see Herrington, et al., 2003), many students *willingly* and instantly engage with enthusiasm. Similarly, there is often a ready acceptance of the characters and parameters of the scenarios developed using authentic tasks, described by Laurel (1993) as a willingness "to think and feel in terms of both the content and conventions of a mimetic context" (p. 115). Students can become so immersed in the learning context that has been created for them that they begin to see the characters as real. The veracity of the e-learning design and its physical representation on the website is not a critical factor for those students who were able to engage with the context from the outset. The quality of the graphics and images is also not seen as important to students if they have accepted the basic context of the scenario. Even simple two-dimensional sketches are acceptable to students if they are engaged.

This observation that many, particularly younger, students have little trouble adapting to the conventions and conduct of web-based scenarios may be a legacy of popular computer and strategy games that have successfully incorporated complex and sustained scenarios in their design. Nevertheless, these responses cannot be considered to be restricted only to this age group, as many students across all ages show immediate and sustained acceptance of authentic learning designs.

Delayed Engagement

The capacity of authentic learning settings to promote students' willing suspension of disbelief is a powerful outcome and one that appears to hold strong prospects for enhancing the effectiveness of a range of learning settings which promote knowledge construction. However, many students experience problems with learning courses that focus on learner-centered tasks and activities. For example, Taplin (2000) has noted that students may have difficulty in changing dependent learning habits, that problems can arise if students are not self-motivated and that many are accustomed to teacher-centered modes of instruction and are unhappy when this directed support is withdrawn. Others such as Hoffman and Ritchie (1997) have found that some students experience discomfort at "the increased degree of freedom they experience" when they are accustomed to "comprehension and synthesis of instructor-specified information, based on instructor-formulated learning objectives, and participation in instructor-led learning activities" (p. 100). Some students resist authentic approaches to such a degree that reports of angry emails and accusations of not being taught or not getting their money's worth are not uncommon. For instance, Taplin (2000) reported from one of the teachers participating in her study: "One participant found that there was very strong resistance—almost to the point of mutiny—from one group of students because 'they are too exam oriented. They didn't take it easily when accepting the new teaching mode' " (p. 293).

Few students in our experience, however, have any sustained resistance to authentic approaches although there is sometimes initial inability to accept the learning experience wholeheartedly. Such resistance is not unexpected in environments where many resources must be accessed and novel processes must be undertaken to find the critical knowledge that will assist with the problem.

Similarly, frustration can arise simply because of the similarity of these authentic learning tasks to the kind of uncertain and messy tasks that people are often required to do in their professional lives. Students need to be given the time and space to make these mistakes. In all the environments using authentic tasks examined to date in our own research, even reluctant students were reported to have engaged within a few weeks of the semester.

These findings provide support for the use of authentic environments for e-learning. Our research suggests that the use of authentic settings encourages and supports learners in their development of skills in self-regulation and self-learning, factors which have been seen to inhibit other forms of e-learning. The capacity of the learning design to encourage students' willing suspension of disbelief appears also to encourage self-direction and independent learning—important success factors in e-learning.

Scaffolding and Support

Teacher support and peer scaffolding are often suggested as strategies that may assist students who are reluctant to engage with student-centered and problem-based tasks to persevere beyond the initial weeks of frustration and uncertainty.

As teachers move to adopt learning settings that focus on student-centered rather than teacher-centered learning activities, the need for strategies to support and encourage learners in what are sometimes unfamiliar and discomforting activities becomes an important element in the design process. Support for students in the early weeks of immersion in student-centered online learning is crucial. This is particularly important when isolation can be an additional mitigating factor against successful engagement with the course. Taplin (2000) has noted that acceptance of problem-based learning scenarios, in addition to the usual difficulties in conventional situations, is often exacerbated by distance because of the students' physical isolation.

By facilitating the willing suspension of disbelief, students become immersed in the setting and such immersion can provide the motivation that is needed for the initial perseverance. Once students have persevered with what can initially be quite discomforting and unfamiliar settings, they are able to develop the forms of familiarity and the skill sets required so that the authentic setting no longer provides a distraction from the cognitive engagement that higher-order learning requires.

We do not agree with one of Taplin's respondents who contended that: "As educators, we can't [just worry about pleasing] the students by not doing it at all. Rather we have to gradually brainwash them . . . otherwise they will lose their competitiveness in this society" (p. 495). We believe, like O'Reilly (2000), that there is a need to humanise the online experience with greater compassion, empathy and open-mindedness. Authentic learning settings appear to be able to provide support in the initial stages of learning, enabling students to experience a suspension of disbelief, and through these means to be encouraged to persevere with their learning through initial difficulties when the need for learner engagement is paramount to learning success.

Addressing the Full Range of Educational Outcomes

Another area where authentic e-learning has enormous potential to enhance higher education relates to the importance of addressing the full range of educational outcomes. Government agencies and think-tanks have defined the critical outcomes for 21st century learners (Partnership for 21st Century Skills, 2007; CEO Forum on Education and Technology, 2001), including all four of the learning domains (cognitive, affective, conative, and psychomotor). Traditional pedagogical methods primarily address the cognitive learning domain (Anderson & Krathwohl, 2001), often to the neglect of the other domains.

In the next chapter, the relationship between authentic e-learning and the often neglected conative domain is explained.

Chapter 5

Authentic e-Learning and the Conative Learning Domain

A 2005 Public Broadcasting System (PBS) television documentary in the USA titled *Declining by Degrees: Higher Education at Risk*, presented ample evidence that Americans do not know enough about the outcomes of higher education, but that it is convenient for all involved (faculty, students, parents, alumni, legislators, donors, and the taxpaying public) to pretend that high-quality teaching and learning are occurring. In a book by the same name (Hersh & Merrow, 2005), Schneider (2005) highlights the problem:

> Americans are increasingly cynical about their public institutions and public leaders. But their skepticism does not extend to the content of a higher education. Most students—and the public as a whole—assume without question that whatever students choose to study in college, they will learn what they need to know for today's competitive and complex environment. But in practice, college figures in the public imagination as something of a magical mystery tour. It is important to be admitted; it is also important to graduate with a degree. But what one does in between, what students actually learn in college, is largely unknown and largely unchallenged (p. 62).

It is curious, if not outrageous, that in the absence of reliable and accurate information about the outcomes of higher education, students and their parents have increasingly come to rely upon commercial ratings of colleges and university provided by commercial enterprises such as *US News and World Report* and the *Princeton Review*. The criteria factored into the ratings provided by these for-profit ventures fail to include meaningful data about student learning or academic achievement. Instead, numerous proxy indicators of the quality of a higher education are used, such as the average Scholastic Aptitude Test (SAT) scores of entering freshmen, and selectivity as measured by the ratio of students admitted to students applying. The administrators of most colleges and universities in the USA claim that they pay little attention to such rankings (Ehrenberg, 2005), but in reality they do. An analysis by Zemsky, Wegner, and Massy (2005) indicated that what the *US News and World Report* rankings essentially measure is competitive advantage with respect to attracting the best students. In other words, the rankings are primarily about inputs rather than outputs.

What should Higher Education Students Learn?

Student learning outcomes in higher education are traditionally defined in relationship to three learning domains: cognitive, affective, and psychomotor. The cognitive domain relates to the capacity to think or one's mental skills. As originally defined by Bloom et al. (1956) and revised by Anderson and Krathwohl (2001), the cognitive domain has six levels ranging from *remembering* to *creating* (see Figure 5.1).

The affective domain (Krathwohl, Bloom, & Masia, 1964) is about emotions and feelings, especially in relationship to a set of values. It ranges from *receiving* or becoming aware of stimuli that evoke feelings to manifesting behaviour characterised by a set of consistent and predictable *values* (see Figure 5.2). The psychomotor domain (Harrow, 1972) is concerned with the mastery of physical skills ranging from reflexive movements to exhibiting appropriate body language in *non-discursive communication* (see Figure 5.3).

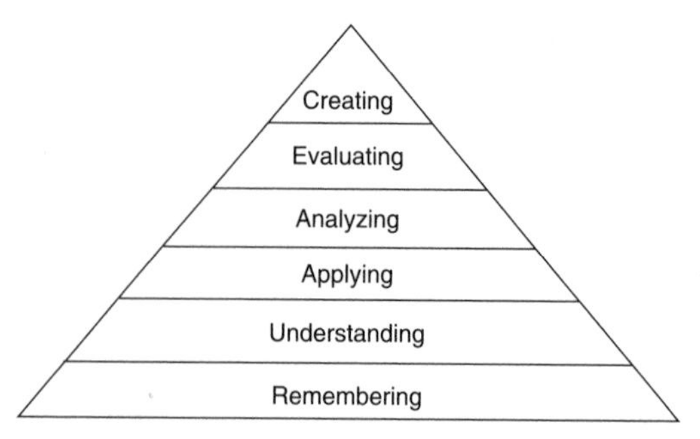

Figure 5.1 Revised taxonomy of the cognitive domain (Anderson & Krathwohl, 2001).

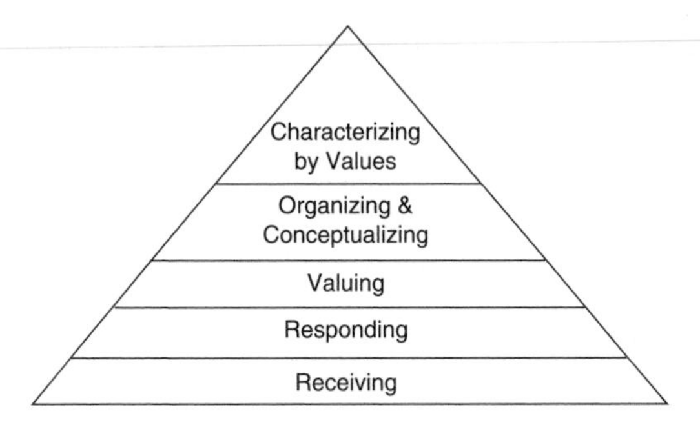

Figure 5.2 Taxonomy of the affective domain (Krathwohl et al., 1964).

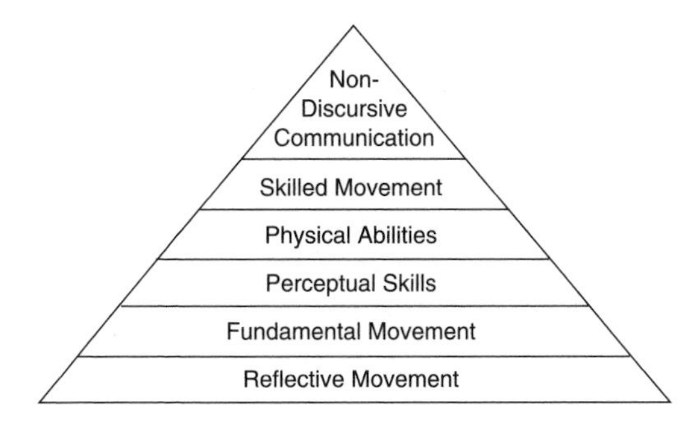

Figure 5.3 Taxonomy of the psychomotor domain (Harrow, 1972).

None of these domains is completely satisfactory. Despite their flaws, these domains are often referred to in faculty development seminars. Sperber (2005) argues that most instruction in higher education is focused on the cognitive domain rather than the affective or psychomotor domains. In addition, even within the cognitive domain much more attention is paid to the lower half of the domain (remembering, understanding, and applying) than it is to the arguably more important upper half (analysing, evaluating, and creating). This problem stems largely from the relative ease with which the skills encompassed in the lower half can be taught and tested within most disciplines. Teaching and assessing the cognitive skills required for analysis, evaluation, and creation takes more time and effort than many, if not most, academic staff believe they have.

Most alarmingly, an entire domain is largely ignored in higher education today. Whereas the cognitive domain is concerned with thinking, the affective with valuing, and the psychomotor with skilled behaviour, the neglected conative domain (Snow, Corno, & Jackson, 1996) is associated with action. Someone may possess the cognitive capacity, affective values, and physical skills to perform a given task (e.g., washing hands thoroughly before interacting with patients in a clinic), but whether that person possesses the will, desire, drive, level of effort, mental energy, intention, striving, and self-determination to actually perform the task at the highest standards possible remains an unanswered question (Gawande, 2007).

The conative domain focuses on conation or the act of striving to perform at the highest levels. Despite the obvious importance of this type of learning outcome, the literature on higher education teaching, learning, and assessment is practically uninformed by consideration of the conative domain. The roots of conation can be traced all the way back to Aristotle who used the Greek word *orexis* to signify striving, desire, or the conative state of mind. Kolbe (1990) contrasted the cognitive, affective, and conative domains as illustrated in Figure 5.4.

Given the increasingly global nature of competition (Friedman, 2005), the higher education graduate of the 21st century can ill afford to enter the world of work without the opportunity to develop expertise across all four domains of learning. Figure 5.5 illustrates a comprehensive array of the learning domains that every college or university graduate should possess.

Unfortunately, very few institutions of higher education collect evidence that their graduates leave their institutions with comprehensive achievement across the four domains. The US National Center for Public Policy and Higher Education, an independent, non-profit, non-partisan organisation, compiled a report titled *Measuring Up 2000: The State-by-State Report Card for Higher Education*, which found that

Cognitive	**Affective**	**Conative**
• To know	• To feel	• To act
• Thinking	• Feeling	• Willing
• Thought	• Emotion	• Volition
• Epistemology	• Esthetics	• Ethics
• Knowing	• Caring	• Doing

Figure 5.4 Comparison of cognitive, affective, and conative domains (Kolbe, 1990).

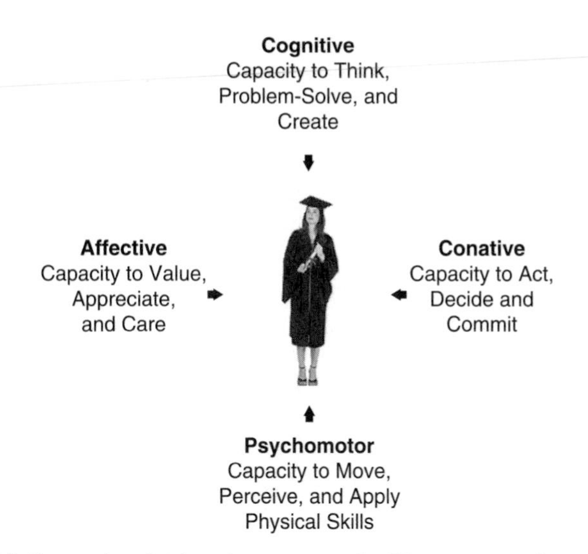

Figure 5.5 Comprehensive learning outcomes for 21st century college graduates.

data relevant to state-by-state comparisons of higher education institutions was widely accessible with respect to preparation, participation, affordability, completion rates, and benefits, but data related to learning was simply unavailable.

The Role of Learning Assessment

Regardless of the field or discipline, there is a set of meta-outcomes that cut across the four domains. The following list, while not exhaustive, suggests the scope of these outcomes:

- accessing and using information,
- communication skills using multiple media,
- demonstrating understanding accompanied by deep reflection,
- applying rules and procedures to structured and unstructured problems,
- being creative,
- thinking critically,
- making sound judgments,
- problem solving,
- being committed to life-long learning,

- exhibiting intellectual curiosity,
- proactively seeking to extend knowledge in one's discipline,
- exhibiting ethical behaviour.

Meta-outcomes of this kind will not be achieved in higher education unless they are assessed. This conclusion is supported by strong evidence that if something is not assessed in higher education, then it is not learned (Bain, 2004). The bottom line is that assessment drives learning (Oosterhof, Conrad, & Ely, 2008). Perhaps it is just human nature, but university students choose to focus their study efforts on the things about which they know they will be tested and graded. Most students quickly come to recognise that they can get good grades by cramming for tests and then quickly forgetting what they have memorised to allow themselves to focus on other pursuits. Most teachers are familiar with the typical questions asked by undergraduate students in higher education courses such as: "Are we responsible for knowing that material?" or "Is this content going to be on the test?"

Teachers recognise the desire of students to focus their study efforts, minimal as they are, on accumulating the "knowledge" that will be tested, and in far too many cases, instructors give in to these wishes rather than pushing their students to achieve at higher levels.

When John Merrow, the producer of *Declining by Degrees*, was asked what was the most shocking discovery he found when he was visiting various institutions of higher education across the USA for his television documentary, he responded:

> NOT that students are binge drinking, NOT that athletics is a business, and NOT that most students don't seem to have to work very hard to get good grades, because we knew those things. What came as a surprise was what one of our experts calls "the non-aggression pact" between professors and students. It amounts to an unspoken compact: don't ask too much of me, and I won't expect much from you. This allows the faculty members to concentrate on what their institution values: publications, research and getting grants. And it means that students get good grades and can float though college with plenty of time for socializing, networking and other activities. Few complain, even though to an outsider it's pretty clear that the emperor has no clothes. That came as a shock.

Ideally, university instructors should design their learning assessments as if "testing and grading are not incidental acts that come at the end of teaching but powerful aspects of education that have an enormous influence on the entire enterprise of helping and encouraging students to learn" (Bain, 2004, p. 150). But the reality is sadly otherwise. If we want our university graduates to possess the 21st century skills outlined above, assessment must focus on these higher-order types of outcomes (as described in Chapter 7).

Accordingly, university and college instructors must devote much more effort to the task of assessment because it is the lifeblood of good teaching. This is no easy task. In the USA, a large percentage of entering college students must enrol in remedial courses in mathematics, reading, or composition (Atwell, Lavin, Domina, & Levey, 2006). There is ample evidence that numerous students are graduating from high school without the academic preparation required to engage in higher-order learning and assessment. When this fact is combined with the growing pressure on faculty members in research universities to fund and conduct research and on instructors in teaching universities and colleges to teach more students with fewer resources, higher education certainly does seem to be "declining by degrees" (Hersh & Merrow, 2005).

Are Today's Postsecondary Students "Millennials" or "Generation Me"?

Although some people both within and outside academe are questioning the assumed high quality of American higher education (Hersh & Merrow, 2005), others are predicting that a new kind of student is entering our institutions of higher learning that is extraordinary in the technological sophistication and drive to achieve. Raschke (2002) proclaimed that "Colleges and universities are about to be beset by a new generation of learners whose skills and expectations derive from growing up on the net" (p.68). In recent years, much has been written in both popular and scholarly literature about the generation of students entering higher education today called by various monikers such as *Generation Y*, *Millennials*, and the *Net Generation* (Howe & Strauss, 2000; Coomes & DeBard, 2004; Oblinger & Oblinger, 2005; Tapscott, 1998). Howe and Strauss (2000, p. 4) who wrote ". . . today's teens are recasting the image of youth from downbeat and alienated to upbeat and engaged" have predicted that the Americans born between 1982 and 2000 constitute the next "greatest generation" that will out-achieve previous generations such as the *Baby Boomers* (born 1943–1960) and *Generation X* (born 1961–1981). However, the evidence for such optimism appears to be largely drawn from surveys and focus groups conducted with young people living in affluent suburbs, sometimes in the presence of their parents.

The results of the National Survey of Student Engagement (NSSE) conducted by Indiana University paint a much less upbeat picture of the current generation of college undergraduates than that of Howe and Strauss (Kuh, 2001). Conducted every year since 2000 and involving more than 600 colleges and universities in the USA, NSSE indicates that undergraduate students are much less engaged in learning activities known to foster academic achievement than expected by their professors (Kuh, Kinzie, Schuh, & Whitt, 2005). The average university instructor expects undergraduate students to be engaged in classes or labs 10–15 hours per week and out-of-class studying for another 25–30 hours per week. This is not an unreasonable expectation, but the NSSE data showed that 20% of students spend less than five hours per week studying, 25% spend 6–10 hours per week, 48% spend 11–30 hours per week, and only 7% exceed the 30 hours per week expected by their teachers. Kuh, Laird, and Umbach (2004) highlight five essential strategies for increasing student engagement:

1 increasing student–faculty interaction;
2 engaging students in active, collaborative learning activities;
3 encouraging more achievement-oriented "time-on-task" among students;
4 setting high academic challenge;
5 providing continuous timely feedback (p. 26).

All of these strategies have implications for assessment, but the last two especially so. Unless teachers raise the level of the objectives they are trying to achieve so that they encompass all four learning domains in their assessments, students will not be compelled to become more academically engaged. In addition, unless teachers are willing to become more engaged in high-quality teaching themselves, especially with respect to providing continuous timely feedback through better assessment strategies, any increased student interest in academic engagement will diminish quickly.

The imperative to focus assessment on the full range of learning domains takes on even more significance when taking into account a more realistic portrayal of today's university students than the overly optimistic one presented by Howe and Strauss (2000), Schooley (2005), and others. Twenge (2006) used empirical data collected over the past

50 years to dismiss most of the optimistic claims about Millennial students, stating that:

> My perspective on today's young generations differs from that of Neil Howe and William Strauss, who argue in their 2000 book, *Millennials Rising*, that those born since 1982 will usher in a return to duty, civic responsibility, and teamwork. Their book is subtitled *The Next Great Generation* and contends that today's young people will resemble the generation who won World War II. I agree that in an all-encompassing crisis today's young people would likely rise to the occasion—people usually do what needs to be done. But I see no evidence that today's young people feel much attachment to duty or to group cohesion. Instead, as you'll see in the following pages, young people have been consistently taught to put their own needs first and to focus on feeling good about themselves. This is not an attitude conducive to following social rules or favoring the group's needs over the individual's . . . Our childhood of constant praise, self-esteem boosting, and unrealistic expectations did not prepare us for an increasingly competitive workplace and the economic squeeze created by sky-high housing costs and rapidly accelerating health care costs. After a childhood of buoyancy, GenMe is working harder to get less.

Whereas most other generational researchers have taken a cross-sectional approach to their research wherein they distributed surveys to, or conducted interviews with, members of different generations at the same point in time, Twenge (2006) painstakingly analysed the results of studies that involved school children, adolescents, and college students completing well-designed, validated questionnaires in the 1950s, 60s, 70s, 80s, 90s, and the early 2000s. This enabled her to compare, for example, the attitudes of the Baby Boomer generation expressed when they were adolescents with the attitudes of GenMe expressed during their adolescence. A sample of her findings derived from data collected from 1.3 million young Americans since the 1950s include:

- In 2002, 74% of high school students admitted to cheating whereas in 1969 only 34% admitted such a failing.
- In 1967, 86% of incoming college students said that "developing a meaningful philosophy of life" was an essential life goal whereas in 2004 only 42% of GenMe freshmen agreed.
- In 2004, 48% of American college freshmen reported earning an

A average in high school whereas in 1968 only 18% of freshmen reported being an A student in high school.
- In the 1950s, only 12% of young teens agreed with the statement "I am an important person" whereas by the late 1980s, 80% claimed they were important.
- In the 1960s, 42% of high school students expected to work in professional jobs whereas in the late 1990s, 70% of high schools expected to work as a professional.
- In a recent poll, 53% of GenMe mothers agreed with the statement that a person's main responsibility is to themselves and their children rather than making the world a better place whereas only 28% of Boomer mothers agreed.

We argue that regardless of whether you believe that the students entering higher education are the next "best and brightest" generation or a generation of layabouts who expect the world to be handed to them, authentic e-learning provides important benefits for 21st Century students. Authentic e-learning is especially powerful with respect to the role of assessment in relationship to conative as well as cognitive, affective, and psychomotor outcomes.

Assessment Advances

Bain (2004) described how the best teachers in higher education focus their teaching assessment activities on "critical thinking, problem solving, creativity, curiosity, concern for ethical issues" as well as "breadth and depth of specific knowledge" and the "methodologies and standards of evidence used to create that knowledge" (pp. 8–9). In addition, they use assessment "to help students learn, not just rate and rank their efforts" (p. 151).

Pellegrino, Chudowsky, and Glaser (2001) describe an assessment triangle (see Figure 5.6) wherein: "the corners of the triangle represent the three key elements underlying any assessment . . . a model of student cognition and learning in the domain, a set of beliefs about the kinds of observations that will provide evidence of students' competencies, and an interpretation process for making sense of the evidence" (p. 44).

The *cognition* corner is based upon a theory of learning underpinning the set of knowledge, skills, attitudes, and habits of mind to be measured. For example, if a teacher subscribes to a constructivist theory of learning (Fosnot, 1996), his or her assessments should focus on cognition related to the production of original representations of

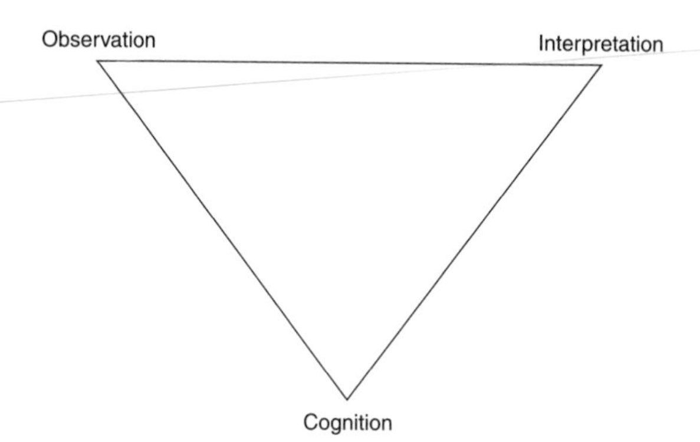

Figure 5.6 The assessment triangle (Pellegrino et al., 2001).

knowledge as opposed to the regurgitation of textbook knowledge. The *observation* corner refers to the tasks or performances that educators design to provide evidence that students have learned. The nature of this evidence should be linked to the cognitive learning theory in such a way as to support the decisions derived from the assessment results. Employing the principles of constructivist learning theory, a teacher is likely to observe the learner's learning through the analysis of tangible phenomena such as portfolios, products, or performances. The *interpretation* corner "expresses how the observations derived from a set of assessment tasks constitute evidence about the knowledge and skills being assessed" (Pellegrino et al., 2001, p. 48).

With a constructivist learning theory in mind, a teacher might design a rubric that expresses levels of quality for the portfolio, product, or performance being assessed (Miller, 2005). Online learning supports other unique forms of alternative assessments such as electronic portfolios, discussion boards, and blogs (Oosterhof et al., 2008). In authentic e-learning, the assessment is embedded within the learning design in such a way that the traditional distinctions between learning and testing fade away.

Obviously, no assessments are perfect, and all fail to some degree to provide completely reliable and valid evidence of student learning. Some inference is always required because assessments inevitably oversimplify the full capacity students possess to perform across all four domains of learning. As Pellegrino et al. (2001) clarify: "A crucial point is that each of the three elements of the assessment triangle not only must make sense on its own, but also must connect to each of the other two elements in a meaningful way to lead to an effective assessment and sound inferences" (p. 49). This implies the need for alignment, not just within an assessment but between assessment and the other critical factors that define e-learning.

Alignment is the Key

The success of any learning design, including authentic e-learning, is determined by the degree to which there is adequate alignment among eight critical factors: (1) goals, (2) content, (3) instructional design, (4) learner tasks, (5) instructor roles, (6) student roles, (7) technological affordances, and (8) assessment. Evaluations of traditional, online, and blended approaches to tertiary teaching indicate that the most commonly misaligned factor is assessment (Reeves & Hedberg, 2003).

Simply put, instructors may have lofty goals, share high-quality content, and even utilise advanced instructional designs, but most assessment strategies tend to focus on what is easy to measure rather than what is important. Figure 5.7 illustrates the eight critical factors that must be aligned within a learning design for it to be effective. Alignment within a learning design cannot be over-emphasised. If an undergraduate course is designed based upon a constructivist learning theory (Fosnot, 1996), the remaining factors must be in alignment with the pedagogical design. A description of these factors follows.

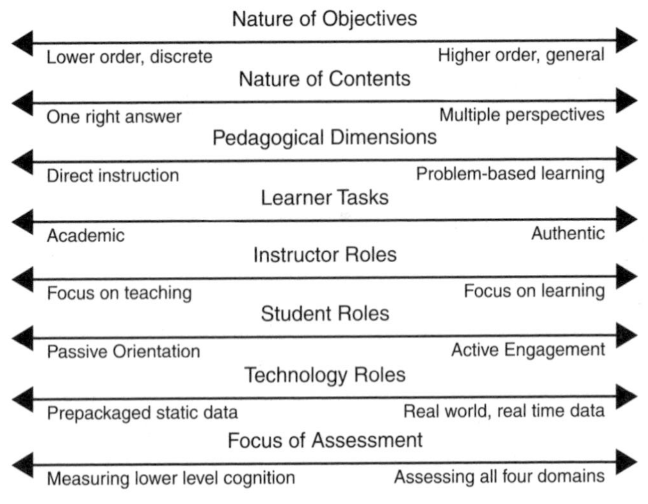

Figure 5.7 Critical factors in learning design alignment.

Nature of Objectives

The objectives of a learning course define the knowledge, skills, attitudes, and intentions that students should develop as a result of participating in that environment, such as a course in Ecology. Objectives are ideally stated as measurable outcomes ranging from discrete knowledge (e.g., students will be able to identify distinguishing properties of an ecosystem) to higher-order thinking (e.g., students will exhibit a robust mental model of how climate change threatens the Amazonian ecosystem).

Nature of Content

The information and data that encompass the subject matter to be taught, studied, and learned are defined by the content accessible within a learning setting. More often than not in undergraduate courses, content is presented in highly structured formats such as textbooks, but content can also be accessed in ill-structured, real-world formats such as original historical documents or scientific data from remote sensors. Indeed, the increasingly ubiquitous nature of the Web means that the content within an authentic e-learning course is for all practical purposes, limitless.

Instructional Design

The overall arrangement of activities, resources, structure, and activities that an e-learning course provides to promote learning is ideally organised by an appropriate instructional design. Traditional instructional designs found in higher education are focused on teacher talk (through lectures), static content (through textbooks), and fixed assessment (through tests seeking one right answer). Such designs are commonplace, but the evidence for the efficacy of these instructional methods is unacceptably weak. Alternative instructional designs include authentic tasks, problem-based learning (Hmelo & Evensen, 2000), project-based learning (Markham, Mergendoller, Larmer, & Ravitz, 2003), and service learning (Butin, 2005).

Learner Tasks

The strategies used to engage students in meaningful learning are ideally more authentic than academic. The NSSE studies (Kuh, 2003) point out that students are often inadequately engaged by traditional academic tasks such as writing term papers or cramming for multiple-choice tests of lower-level cognitive knowledge. By contrast, there is great potential for undergraduate learners to be engaged by authentic tasks such as conducting real-world inquiry (Fink, 2003).

Instructor Roles

Traditionally, the instructor provides most of the learning support (e.g., scaffolding) that students require when they are engaged in learning. Instructors accustomed to a didactic teaching approach, wherein they deliver pre-packaged information to students in the form of lectures and assigned readings, may struggle with the necessity of allowing their students to grapple with the inevitable complexities of authentic tasks or service learning. Bain (2004) describes how the best teachers surrender some of their power as experts and become co-learners with their student.

Student Roles

When students experience real-world tasks, dynamic content, collaboration, and the other components of an authentic e-learning course, their roles inevitably change as they become actively involved in the cognitive, psychomotor, affective, and conative learning domains. Students accustomed to more passive roles in the college lecture hall may initially resist the active requirements of authentic learning pedagogy. Effective learning designs often require collaboration and teamwork, and students who resist working in groups may balk at this. Resistance to changing roles may be especially strong among the students most often rewarded with high grades within the traditional teacher-text-test-centered pedagogy.

Technological Affordances

The cognitive tools, visualisations, simulations, role-playing games, and other interactive resources provided by today's Web 2.0 technologies are impressive (Ebner, Holzinger, & Maurer, 2007), but they must be viewed as secondary to instructional design. An affordance is the interaction possibilities posed by objects in the real or cyber worlds. Thinking of technology as a cognitive tool is an especially effective strategy in higher education (Kim & Reeves, 2007; Jonassen & Reeves, 1996).

Assessment Strategies

The methods used to estimate student accomplishment of the course objectives can range from formative to summative (Taras, 2005) and from traditional to alternative (Wiggins, 1998). Historically, this has been one of the weakest aspects of both traditional and innovative course design and implementation in higher education (Shipman, Aloi, & Jones, 2003). In most undergraduate courses, assessment and grading are usually based upon multiple-choice tests or academic essays. In an authentic learning design, assessment is based upon observations of student engagement and analysis of artefacts produced in the process of completing the tasks. Rather than using just one method, robust assessment requires the critical analysis of multiple forms of evidence that learning outcomes have been attained.

Putting it all Together

The failure to align these eight dimensions will undermine the successful design and implementation of any learning course, regardless of whether it is offered in a classroom, online, or via a blended model. The efficacy of any one or a few of these factors cannot be evaluated in isolation from the others.

Technology presents higher education with unparalleled opportunities for rapid and radical change, but decisions about making such changes should be made on the basis of painstaking instructional design. The next chapter describes the practical aspects of designing and producing authentic e-learning courses.

Chapter 6

Designing and Producing Authentic e-Learning Courses

Understanding and knowing the elements that are to be incorporated into an e-learning course still leaves a teacher some distance from being able to design the e-learning program itself. This chapter explores strategies by which teachers can select and plan the various elements that are needed to successfully create authentic e-learning courses.

Planning an e-learning course from scratch is usually the best way to create an authentic learning experience for students, and this method arguably has the best chance of success. However, it is possible to take an existing course and give it an authentic "makeover." This can often be done without the need to write and create new resources, or indeed to change much of the work that has gone into the original design. Sometimes, all that is required is the reconceptualisation of the tasks that students complete as they study the course, together with a revision of the means of assessment. In this way, the existing course resources and activities reside within a more purposeful task, and students can see meaning in the activities because they will contribute to the creation of a genuine product. As noted in Chapter 3, in any authentic learning design, there may be a role for a podcast lecture, there may be a role for self-assessed quizzes, and there may be a role for teacher-directed resources—but in themselves, they are inadequate. An overarching intent of authenticity is required.

Revising an Existing Course

Revising a course to include both authentic elements and existing resources can be done quite effectively. For example, in a multimedia project developed to teach statistics and research methods (described in Herrington & Standen, 2000), eight modules comprising 26 multimedia lessons had been developed in an extensive package for teaching statistics and research methods in a business degree. The resulting "electronic textbook" had some advantages over traditional lectures and tutorials, but formative evaluation showed it did not really solve a major problem of the course: that the technical material was boring when studied in isolation from its application, and students lacking work experience could not make connections. The trial revealed no improvement in students' motivation to work through the many steps needed to understand the material.

An authentic task and assessment were created for the course. Instead of systematically working through lessons, students were given a summer job with a fictitious company "Acumen Research" to undertake research for a client, a large bank. Resources, and a folder containing information on the project were provided in their office at "Acumen" (Figure 6.1). The folders on *research* and *statistics* on the filing cabinet are the original multimedia lessons. Students no longer need to laboriously make their way through them—but refer to them as they wish, to supplement learning from other sources to complete the project. In pairs, students design and conduct a research study for the client using data that have been "collected" by a group of telephone surveyors employed by the

Figure 6.1 The office interface for statistics and research methods.
Source: Peter Standen & Jan Herrington, Edith Cowan University

research agency. The data are downloaded, analysed in a standard statistics package, and written up. The report is assessed by the teacher authentically, in the same way that its real-world counterpart would be.

Rather than completely removing these multimedia lessons from the course, instead a real-life context and meaning were provided to the learning that the students were required to do as they worked with the program. Learning of theory was driven by the need to use it.

Revising with Existing Content

The content and resources of any course can be retained for use by students as they solve authentic problems. It is not necessary when revising a course to completely start from scratch, as many existing elements can be used as useful resources. The existing course can be reviewed against elements of authentic environments and tasks, as described in Chapters 1 and 2. Elements that are lacking can then be designed for the course as required.

The key to this approach is to ensure that the decision-making about how and when to use these resources is principally left to students themselves, rather than as directed by the teacher. The teacher's role becomes more supportive in suggesting appropriate resources at particular times, rather than setting the scope, sequence and timing of the course content in an inflexible manner.

Designing a New Course

The elements of authentic learning described in Chapter 1 can be used almost as a checklist to guide the design of a new e-learning course. Table 3.2 in Chapter 3, can also be used to gauge the authenticity of the environment.

How might a teacher designing an online course apply such principles? An example is given below.

Designing an Introductory Instructional Technology Course

Imagine you have been asked to design and teach an introductory online course on the use of the internet in education (Herrington, Oliver, & Herrington, 2007). The principal aim of the course is to introduce students to a wide range of online technologies and to promote understanding of how they might be used in educational contexts.

One way to approach this challenge would be to list 12–15 different web-based technologies (to correspond to the number of weeks in the semester), and create weekly online lectures, tasks and readings on each. Topics and tasks could become more complex as the course progressed, and three major assignments would be required at evenly spaced intervals throughout the semester. This represents a typical pattern of teacher-directed activities with little choice for students, an approach that is arguably the most commonly found learning design for online courses.

An alternative approach, based on the authentic learning principles described in this book, would be more student-centered, more engaging, and designed around authentic tasks.

Authentic Context

The first crucial consideration is to create an authentic context that reflects the way the knowledge would be used in real life. This might involve the development of a story or scenario that is capable of carrying or instantiating all the concepts and skills associated with the course curriculum. Suppose you decide to focus your course on the creation of a webpage; how could you incorporate a range of web technologies in a realistic and pedagogically appropriate way?

You decide to create a scenario around a family reunion, due to take place in the near future. Capturing the "scene" will enable you to introduce students to web technologies in a realistic and meaningful way. Suppose that the family is large, and a website is required to mark the occasion and to focus all family members on the upcoming celebrations.

Authentic Tasks

The most important decision for the design of your e-learning course is to create authentic tasks for students to complete as they study the course. Because you have established a meaningful and authentic context, design of authentic tasks is usually readily achieved. Because of real-life university constraints that require you to set three assignments, rather than the one complex task that you are planning, you need to divide the creation of the family website into three (assessable) stages, but you can incorporate this quite creatively into the scenario. The three tasks you set are:

Task 1: A distant cousin has written to you, telling you about a planned family reunion, and asking if you would be able to develop a family website. The first stage of the site is required for a family reunion, to be held in five weeks' time. At the reunion, you need to show a fully functioning website which includes an appropriate interface, 6–10 main menu items with pages, links to outside sites and several family photographs (Task due Week 5).

Task 2: The family reunion was a huge success and you and your cousin managed to acquire many useful resources to put onto the site. For example, people have sent old home movies on videotapes, audio recordings, recipes handed down from great-grandmothers, war histories, information about famous and infamous ancestors, newspaper clippings, family trees, old letters, telegrams, slide transparencies and many more relevant existing internet links. Your next task is to include some of these items into your webpage. As a further consideration, the copyright of many of the items you receive is owned by outside parties (professional photographs, newspaper articles, television interviews, etc.), you need to include a page on your website explaining copyright regulations and how you have satisfied them (Task due Week 10).

Task 3: The family is delighted at the progress of the website and you are receiving many emails, phone calls and letters almost on a daily basis. The reunion has put many people in touch with each other after many years and they are keen to keep contact. You decide to add some communication elements to the site. First, you decide to survey the family to find out how they would like to communicate (create an online feedback form), then based on that feedback, you establish a blog, a wiki on the site, social networking spaces, discussion forums, chats, podcasts and other participatory elements as required (Task due final week of semester).

While based on a scenario, students could create real, enduring sites to suit their own needs. In this way, they create a genuine and useful product rather than learn weekly set topics without reference to how the technologies might be used in the real world.

Expert Performances and the Modelling of Processes

To create a product such as the one that is required through fulfilment of these tasks, students need access to expert performances and the modelling of processes. Who are the experts in this situation? Because of the nature of the tasks, experts can be thought of as those people who have successfully completed this kind of task before. In creating the learning design, you could give students access to other websites and the methods that have been used to create such sites. As teacher, you can also model the process of developing a website yourself in an online tutorial. Students have the capacity to compare themselves to others in varying stages of expertise.

Multiple Roles and Perspectives

In any complex learning design, a single perspective such as that offered through a textbook or the teacher's online "lectures" is insufficient to reflect the authentic nature of the task. It is important to provide the kinds of *multiple roles and perspectives* that are available in real-life challenges. While a single textbook on creating webpages would be useful and informative, it is insufficient. The affordances of the internet enable alternative perspectives to be readily accessed through directed resources or search engines, and online readings or specific databases can be targeted for particular tasks.

Collaborative Construction of Knowledge

The authentic tasks in this e-learning course lend themselves to individual endeavour, where students could use their own family histories to resource the site. Nevertheless, this task allows *collaborative construction of knowledge* through construction of web tools that could be used jointly, or through collaboration on the entire course through the creation of a fictitious or an historical site using wikis.

Opportunities for Reflection

By allowing students to choose their own pathways through the tasks and resources, rather than providing a single step-by-step approach, the learning environment provides many *opportunities for reflection.* The social nature of learning could be supported by participatory web communications (e.g., on different aspects of the task, such as uploading, interface design, authoring tools, etc.). Students could also keep a reflective journal or blog to document their learning journey, enabling them to reflect *on* action as well as *in* action (Boud, 2006).

Opportunities for Articulation

Participatory functions of the Web (such as blogs, wikis, social networking and forums) not only allow active reflection, but also provide *opportunities for articulation* of students' growing understanding of their work. Formulating arguments or questions, and using the vocabulary of the discipline area, help to strengthen students' professional role in their learning.

Coaching and Scaffolding

The role of the instructor changes in authentic learning designs *to coaching and scaffolding*—less the "sage on the stage" and more "guide on the side" (Laurel, 1993), or as "expert learner" along with novice learners in a community of learners. Rather than simplifying topics for students, teachers should search for new ways to provide appropriate scaffolding and support. There is no longer a need to focus specifically on content and information, or on direct instruction about how to build a website, as these are available through rich resources and searching capacity within the learning setting. Instead, the teacher is able to focus on support for students at the metacognitive level.

Authentic Assessment

Instead of assessing solely by essays, quizzes or examinations, the tasks would be assessed using integrated and *authentic assessment.* The activities, and the website they produce, form the entire focus of the course, and it is on those products that students would be assessed. Students working in this example e-learning course would have a goal, and emerge with a real and tangible product. They would become effective performers with the knowledge they have acquired, and able to craft polished products.

Attending to Tasks, Resources and Supports

Consciously attending to the nine principles of authentic learning is one way to design an e-learning course. Another is to focus on the component groups of tasks, resources and supports (Oliver & Herrington,

2001). These three elements can provide a sound focus for the design of authentic e-learning courses, and they are now described in more depth.

Learning Tasks

Learning tasks (as described in detail in Chapter 2) reflect the kind of problem professionals would face in real life. The problem needs to be chosen carefully to ensure that students will learn and apply the knowledge and content required in the curriculum. The task needs to be the central organising device for the students' learning.

In authentic learning, there are particular forms which the tasks could take, and they are typically complex and ill-defined. They are intended to be substantial problems designed to engage the learners in ways that bring about the intended conceptual change. It is important to remember that the purpose of an authentic task is to provide a meaningful context for the planned learning in a discipline or subject. The task provides a means to enable learners to acquire a planned set of knowledge and skills. For this reason, the task is seen as a means to an end. The important outcomes from the learning problem are the skills and knowledge acquired and this knowledge development is ideally demonstrated through the successful completion of the task.

Learning Resources

Alongside the learning tasks, the course setting needs to provide learners with access to a variety of resources—the content—that can be used in the completion of the tasks. Resources need to be selected, planned and/or developed as appropriate to the task. These resources should not be limited and should include links to outside sources and databases to provide different perspectives and access to expert thinking. Textbooks, other books and library resources may be recommended for use in combination with web resources.

Learning Supports

Supports need to be put in place to scaffold learning. The teacher's role is more coach than source of knowledge. Collaboration between students is required or encouraged to enable them to support each other's learning. Technologies need to be put in place or suggested to help students explore solutions, including participation in listserves, wikis, blogs and microblogs to enable them to access and participate in worldwide discussion on relevant issues. Authentic e-learning courses take learners beyond their comfort zones and enable them to undertake activities that initially are unfamiliar and can be quite daunting. For this reason, supports for learners are crucial.

Framework of Constituent Elements of Tasks, Resources and Supports

Figure 6.2 shows the framework of the constituent elements, and through overlapping circles, it suggests that each is not a discrete component in its own right. It is interesting to note in Figure 6.2 the places where the circles overlap and the elements of an e-learning course that might share the features of two or more of the constituent elements. In any learning setting, there are items that arguably feature aspects of both learning *tasks* and learning *resources*, some that feature learning *tasks* and learning *supports*, and similarly, learning *supports* and learning *resources*. The usefulness of this distinction is illustrated below, when example designs are explored in more detail.

Designing Authentic Learning Tasks

The learning task is the starting point for the design and development of an authentic e-learning course. The authentic task creates the context for the planned learning experience and needs to be designed so that the scope and forms of engagement that are needed to bring about the planned conceptual change are derived from its successful completion.

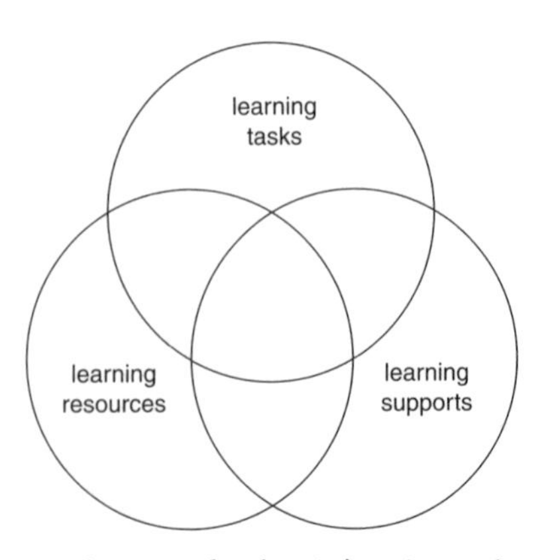

Figure 6.2 Constituent elements of authentic learning settings.

As has been described, the best forms of authentic learning tasks are those that are ill-defined, open-ended, quite complex and which lead to the development of a useful product.

There are a number of different forms by which learning tasks of this nature can be expressed. For example:

- As a problem, an open-ended task requiring an analysis, the development of a solution strategy, and a solution process
- A project, the development of a product/artefact through a planning and implementation process
- An inquiry, an investigation of a topic or event through a purposeful study based on a series of questions and the collection of data to enable a conclusion to be drawn.

The development of appropriate authentic learning tasks is not an easy exercise for many teachers. It usually takes considerable time to develop the expertise needed to be able to design strong learning tasks capable of supporting higher-order learning. Being able to incorporate all the elements into a single task is a challenging process and one which is aided considerably by previous experience in real-world application of the knowledge in question. Some of the difficulties associated with the design of a powerful and enabling authentic task include:

- Choosing a task where successful completion involves all the forms of learner engagement needed
- Choosing an appropriate degree of specificity. Providing enough information to enable the intention of the tasks to be understood whilst not constraining the learning process unnecessarily
- Designing a task where the outcome provides a product that will be useful in its own right—there are many degrees of utility and the best task leads to the product with the most valuable applications
- Presenting the task in a way so that the learner clearly recognises what needs to be known to successfully complete it but leaving space for the learner to have to make their own decisions.

Learning Outcomes

The starting point for planning the authentic learning task is a close examination of the intended learning outcomes for the course of study. It is important to align the desired outcomes of the course curriculum with the authentic learning task. In particular, it is important to have learning outcomes that are expressed in the form of learner capabilities rather than in terms of content to be covered. For example, in a computer science course, the objectives of a unit in computer programming might be described in a form that emphasises the content and knowledge to be gained. For example:

> At the end of this course, the student will have learned about:
>
> - Data types,
> - Programming control structures,
> - Data structures and sorting algorithms,
> - File-handling routines,
> - Recursion.

These stated intended learning outcomes do not reflect a capacity to use and apply this knowledge. It is likely that a closed book examination would be amongst the best ways to measure the more limited achievement of such learning outcomes rather than the authentic assessment required for an authentic task.

Authentic e-learning tasks are best used in the context of courses of study where the intended learning outcomes reflect students' capabilities to meaningfully apply what has been learned. Such courses are those where it is intended that the learners will not only develop a knowledge and understanding of the content but also the capacity to successfully apply it to meaningful settings.

To be suited to an authentic e-learning context, the computer programming course described above would need to have its intended outcomes revised and expressed in terms of capabilities rather than content covered. For example a better form would be:

> At the end of this course the student will be able to solve programming problems involving:
>
> - The choice and application of appropriate data types,
> - The application of programming control structures,
> - The use of appropriate data structures and sorting algorithms,
> - Successfully implementing file handling routines with data checking functionality,
> - Involving recursion where appropriate.

It is only when the course or unit is considered in terms of the meaningful application or use of what has been learned that a successful authentic task can be chosen as the basis for the learning activities.

Because an authentic task is normally large and complex, of necessity, it will need be broken down into a series of smaller tasks by the students. This decision-making is critical to the success of the task, and it is crucial that it is the students, rather than the teacher, who first attempt to perform this reflective role. However, learners can make choices that might limit the capacity of the task to support their learning. They might, for example, choose a very narrow focus, or choose a very simple solution and the learning experience might be limited. The teacher's scaffolding role is important here in ensuring that students do not feel completely overwhelmed by the task, nor limit it to narrow outcomes that do not support the intended learning.

There are three elements to the learning task represented in the framework. The first element is the task itself, as we have discussed above. The other two elements are represented in the framework in the intersection between task and resource (task-resource) and the intersection between the task and supports (task-support) (these are illustrated in the overlapping circles in Figure 6.2). Each of these elements needs deliberate planning and selection.

"Learning Task-Learning Resource" Elements

When designing an authentic task, a number of resources will be needed by the learners to successfully complete the task. These resources are very much task-dependent and need to be planned and developed as part of the creation of the learning task. Consider, for example, an authentic task that is set within a virtual company. The learning design will need to provide students with access to the forms of resources a real company might hold. This component of the framework describes these resources.

Teachers sometimes use fictitious companies and organisations as the context for authentic problems. It is usually impractical to use the resources of real organisations, because they will not be able to make the necessary information public, so the resources need to be created from scratch for the purpose of the learning task. Once developed, however, a website or set of documents for a fictitious company or organisation can be shared and reused. The generic nature of the information can make it quite reusable for other learning purposes.

Other forms of resources that are developed for authentic learning settings include case studies. In an authentic setting, if the teacher decides to change the task, these contextualised resources will also typically need to be changed.

"Learning Task-learning Support" Elements

As well as the task involving context-specific resources, there will usually be some learning supports that need to be designed into the task specification. In designing the task, it is important to consider strategies that might be able to support learners through the difficult phases of the project. Supports that can be developed as part of the task specification might include:

- Having learners work in collaborative teams,
- Providing suggestions for breaking the task down,
- Providing templates for the learner to complete aspects of the task,
- Providing guidelines and strategies for a possible solution process,
- Including feedback stages for the project.

All these supports need to be considered as part of the design of the learning task. They are included to enable all students to make progress with the task and can be varied depending on the needs of the students. The task-specific nature of these supports means that if the teacher wishes to change the task, many of these supports may also need to be changed.

The provision of appropriate supports for authentic learning is an important component of the design process. The scope and extent of the supports that are provided to assist students in the completion of the task need to be planned carefully. The support to be provided will depend on the nature of the learning outcomes being sought, the previous experience of the students in this form of learning setting, and the difficulty and complexity of the task that has been planned. Teachers also need to monitor learner progress in the e-learning course in order to ensure students are adequately supported.

Choosing Authentic e-Learning Resources

As mandated in curriculum, higher education courses involve the acquisition of particular forms of knowledge and the development of skills and understanding. In any authentic e-learning course, an important component of the design and development process is the provision of access to the content and information that represents the knowledge to be acquired. The learning task is intended to provide the context that will enable the students to meaningfully engage with this content and information.

The information and content provided to students in an authentic e-learning setting can take many forms. These forms include:

- reference materials in both printed and electronic forms,
- webpages and websites,
- primary sources of information, for example, government and agency online materials,
- online journals and publications,
- real-life/workplace examples associated with the task.

In an authentic e-learning course, these resources are usually provided for learners to reflect upon and use as they choose. Typically more information is provided than is usually needed to provide learners with valuable experience in selecting appropriate resources, and being able to view and assess materials developed from different perspectives. These resources are derived from the objectives of the course or unit, and are often prescribed when the outcomes and objectives are set as a starting point for the students' research for the task.

"Learning Resources-learning Supports" Elements

In designing an authentic learning task, the teacher needs to consider the knowledge and concepts that the learner will apply in the solution process. An authentic e-learning setting should always include a range of opportunities for the learners to develop the underlying knowledge and skills needed for the successful completion of the authentic task solution.

In classroom settings, teachers can assist in the appropriate development of learners' knowledge and development through specific activities. Similarly, in e-learning settings, learners can be directed to online resources that can be used to develop this knowledge, for example learning objects, tutorials and information sources with interactive elements. In strongly authentic e-learning settings, learners are able to discover and choose the information and knowledge they need to be able to complete the task. Different learners will take different paths according to their needs. These forms of flexibility greatly enhance learning experiences. Learners with previous experience can get on with the authentic task without having to spend unnecessary time covering content that they are already familiar with. Learners with gaps in their knowledge can address these areas as appropriate.

It is important that in completing the authentic task, the learners are making sound decisions based on informed judgments. The e-learning design needs to make obvious to the learners what underpinning skills and knowledge are needed in the task solution. However, teachers do not necessarily have to "reinvent the wheel" and develop these resources themselves. There are many useful resources available as sharable entities on the Web. A search of the web will likely provide many more resources that can possibly be used. The problem will inevitably be that there are too many resources to choose from, rather than too few.

Once again, these resources tend to be independent of the task. They represent the instructional elements associated with the content and would be the same irrespective of the task that is chosen and developed. The important thing to note is that it is the student who chooses the means required to complete the task, rather than the teacher who mandates the necessary resources.

Planning Learning Supports

The framework in Figure 6.3 identifies three related forms of support that need to be considered and planned when developing an authentic e-learning course. We have discussed the first form of scaffold in the description of the learning task (in the section *Learning Task-Learning Support Elements*).

Most learners are incapable of solving a problem or undertaking an investigation in a subject area which they know little about. Yet this is precisely what authentic learning proposes that they do. In order to enable learners to work beyond the realms of their existing capability, authentic e-learning courses need to provide a variety of learning supports in the form of scaffolds to facilitate the learning process.

In the description of the learning resources, we have discussed a second set of supports, resource-supports (in the section *Learning Resources-Learning Support Elements*), those associated with helping learners to acquire the underpinning knowledge and skills in the subject area being studied. These supports are not directly related to task completion. They relate to the need to ensure the learner is adequately informed and skilled in the subject matter that is needed for successful completion of the task.

For example, in a course seeking to develop students' knowledge of legal principles requiring students to "work" in a fictitious company, learners might need to know and understand some aspects of company law. The authentic setting might provide learners with online tutorials to enable them to develop specific knowledge and understanding. These tutorials represent this second set of scaffolds—scaffolds for the actual course content and information. In face-to-face classes, teachers will often provide some directed teaching to scaffold knowledge acquisition, and similarly in e-learning settings this expert knowledge can be provided.

Another set of scaffolds are needed to support learners generally, represented by the third form of supports. For example, learners need to be motivated and encouraged, and given feedback on progress in much the same way as a mentor might in the workplace. These forms of support can take a variety of forms and need to be planned when developing the environment. Typical forms of general support for learning include:

- Course schedules and timelines
- Teacher interventions
- Online discussion forums
- Teacher feedback and monitoring of learning
- Workplace mentors, buddies and peers
- Reflective journals.

Of course, many of these supports can be used in any type of learning setting. They are not unique to authentic e-learning courses and are typically provided in well-planned learning environments.

Knowing how much support to provide learners in authentic e-learning is a skill that teachers need to develop. In instances where the support is too plentiful and too specific, much of the value to be gained from the authentic learning setting can be lost. Learners need to work at times beyond their comfort zones and to take risks as they seek to develop their solutions as part of the learning process. Too much guidance can unwittingly limit the learning opportunities of the setting. The support systems need to ideally assist students at the point of need at the metacognitive level.

Framework for Elements

Figure 6.3 shows example forms of task, resource and support in the learning design framework described above, and demonstrates the different elements that could be considered and planned in the process of designing an authentic e-learning course.

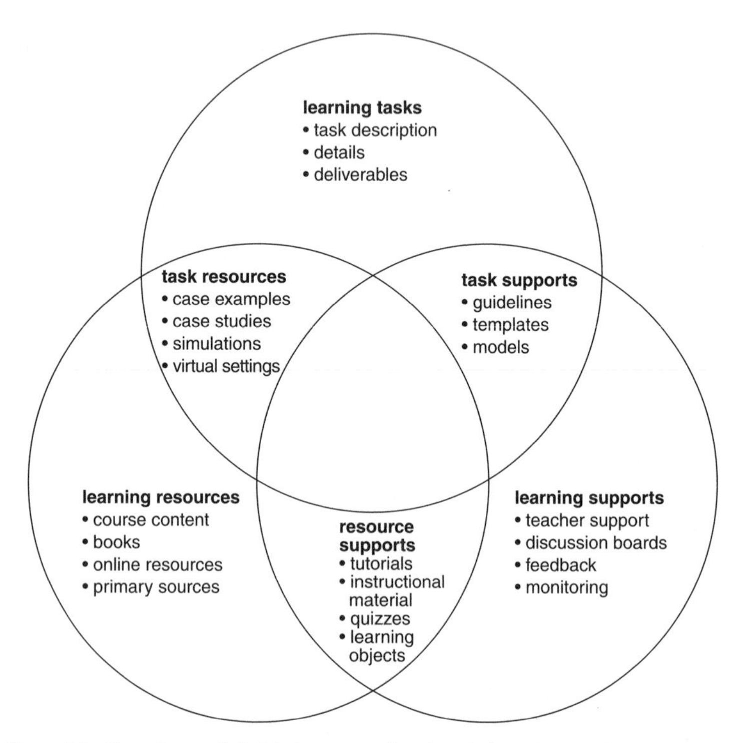

Figure 6.3 Constituent hybrid elements of authentic learning settings.

Case Study Example

It is useful to illustrate the related elements of task, resources and supports with references to a case study. This case is taken from the *Employment Consultant Skills Course* developed by the Australian Flexible Learning Framework. It showcases the various elements involved in the design of an authentic e-learning course.

The aim of the course is to train employment consultants who can assist people in the process of job seeking. The course has been designed for online delivery. Throughout the course, the learners are cast as employment consultants working within a simulated employment service called "JobFill."

The Authentic Task

In the module, *Develop and Monitor Employment Plans*, the authentic task on which the learning is contextualised involves the development of an employment plan for a client (Figure 6.4).

Task-Supports

The module has been designed with a number of task-supports to assist the learners in the design and development of the employment plan. When the development of an employment plan is undertaken for real-life clients, there are several stages in the process. In this course, the task has been divided into three stages that mirror those conducted in a real workplace, each of which is guided by online activities and directions.

Figure 6.5 shows the three stages represented by entries in the diary of the employment consultant. Through simple cues such as the workplace diary, the online task-supports maintain the authenticity of a workplace setting.

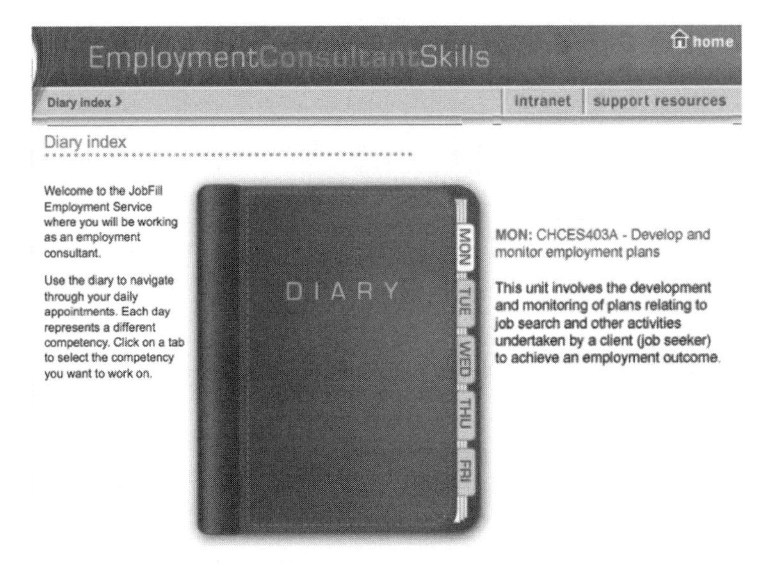

Figure 6.4 The authentic task for the module *Develop and Monitor Employment Plans.*
Source: Australian Flexible Learning Framework, © Commonwealth of Australia

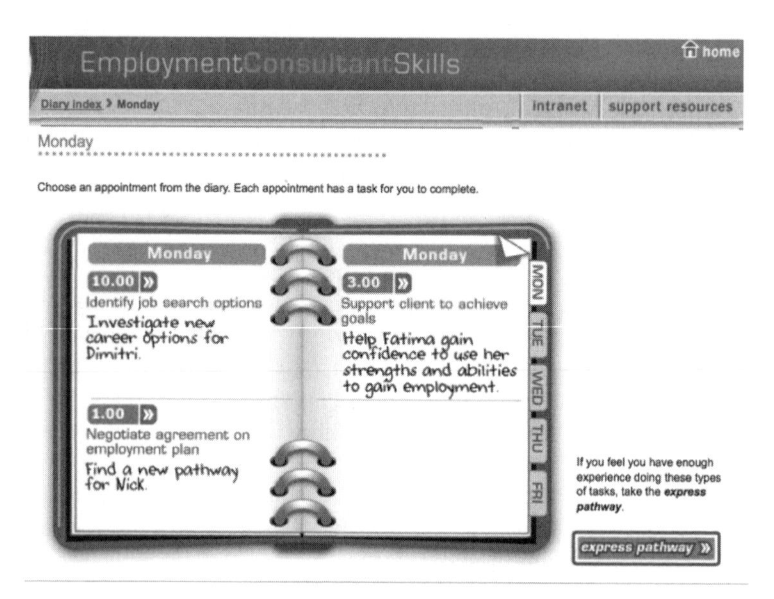

Figure 6.5 The phases of the authentic task represented in the student's work diary.
Source: Australian Flexible Learning Framework, © Commonwealth of Australia

Task-Resources

Because the learning is set in a simulated workplace setting, there is a need for task-related information and resources. The online setting provides the learner with the kind of resources that one would expect to find in the workplace. Figure 6.6 shows the online intranet for the fictitious company. Within this intranet, learners can view resources like the personal files of all the fictitious jobseekers who are registered, employer files, policies and procedures and company forms. For privacy and confidentiality reasons, it is not hard to see why these resources need to be fictitious rather than real files from a real company.

Content and Information Resources

In learning to be an employment consultant, there is clearly a range of general content and information about employment and people that the consultant needs to know. Students themselves can locate much of the general content and information that they will need to apply as they undertake their authentic tasks. However, key resources can also be

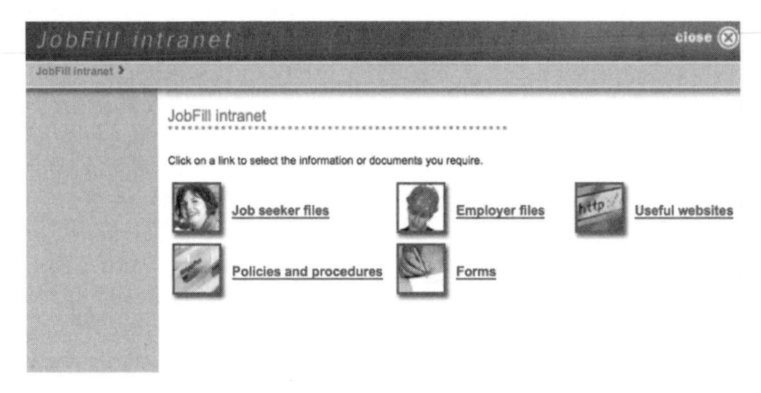

Figure 6.6 The task-related company intranet resource.
Source: Australian Flexible Learning Framework, © Commonwealth of Australia

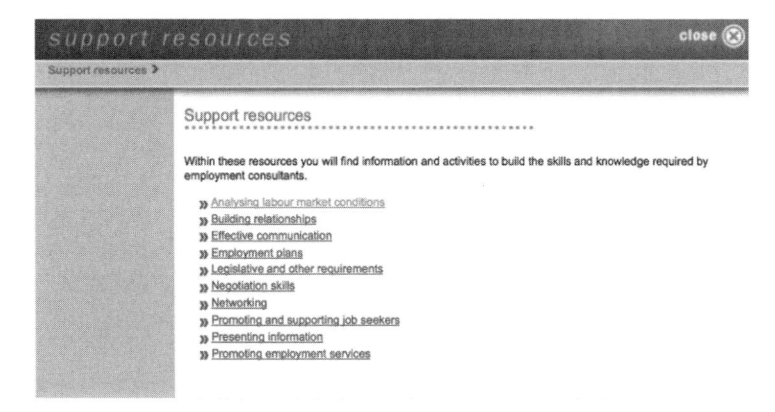

Figure 6.7 The general content resources to support the authentic task.
Source: Australian Flexible Learning Framework, © Commonwealth of Australia

provided in the online environment and included as part of the design process (Figure 6.7). This material is not specific to the task and could be sourced from many different locations.

Resource-Supports

Resource-supports are the resources that are provided to assist the learners to develop expertise with specific related skills, some of which may require practice. In any learning setting, there is generally a considerable amount of information and content that learners need to become familiar with. In online settings, these resources can be small files with instructional elements whose use promotes learners' understanding of the resources. They may take the form of tutorials, self-assessed quizzes, learning objects and similar discrete learning activities. Typically they present salient information and use prompts and interactions to help the student to reflect and review their learning.

In the resource-supports developed for the Employment course, an interactive module has been designed to help learners understand how to deal with people who speak very quickly on the telephone. The learners who choose to use this resource are able to practice listening and working with a very fast-speaking person to develop their skills in effective communications, and to better position them to plan employment options for the client (Figure 6.8). This resource provides generic information and includes a planned learning activity, hence its distinction from the other resources.

Learning Supports

The remaining section in the design framework is that describing the general learning supports. These are often difficult to plan and illustrate

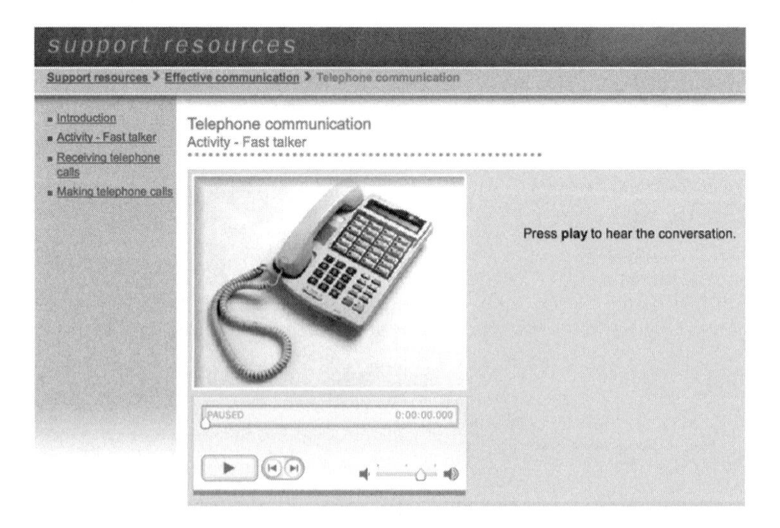

Figure 6.8 Resource-support activity to develop communication skills.
Source: Australian Flexible Learning Framework, © Commonwealth of Australia

because they tend to be teacher-dependent and relate mainly to the actions and activities of the teacher supporting the learners in the class. For example, the teacher can respond directly to student questions via email, or the course website. Bulletin boards and discussion forums are often used effectively as general supports for student learning through their heightened capacities to support interaction and communication.

A Final Comment on Design

Designing strong authentic learning tasks, resources and supports is very much an art and a science. The most important part of the design process is the development of the authentic task. The process gets easier with experience. The more authentic tasks one designs, the better one gets. Once the authentic task has been chosen, the other elements in the learning setting are relatively easy to design and develop. The task-resources and task-supports come from the task itself and the resources and resource-supports tend to be generic resources that can often be borrowed from repositories and existing sources.

The descriptions of the various authentic tasks in this book provide readers with principles, examples and ideas to start the creative processes needed to design and develop authentic e-learning tasks for their own subject areas.

Implementing Authentic e-Learning Courses

Once an authentic e-learning course is designed, it needs to be taught. As you would expect, teaching an authentic e-learning course can be quite unlike a conventional course, and the roles of both the teacher and the learner can be quite different.

Nevertheless, there are key activities associated with both the setting up and delivery of authentic e-learning that are similar to those required for any online course. In this section, we do not seek to repeat the excellent advice that exists for those wishing to learn more about effective online tutoring (e.g., Goodyear, Salmon, Spector, Steeples, & Tickner, 2001; Salmon, 2004), but simply to point out some of the key areas that are critical to authentic e-learning.

Setting up an Authentic e-Learning Site

As noted in Chapter 4, in the discussion about the degree of realism required in authentic e-learning courses, the learning setting or website can range from full simulation to simple text description of a problem area. A learning experience can be drawn as a fully realistic simulation, such as within a virtual world (e.g., *Second Life*), as a programmed website with professional graphics and animations, or as a set role-play where students enact different perspectives of a problem within a well-described learning setting. Such representations of a problem area can be very effective and immersive—and indeed authentic as we have described it here—but this level of verisimilitude is not essential for an e-learning course to have the cognitive realism required to engage with the task in an authentic way.

With all the readily accessible and (very often) free tools and programs available on the web, an authentic e-learning course could be offered in a truly simple form. A one-paragraph text description of a task could be emailed or published on a teacher's blog along with recommended resources and strategies; communication could be maintained throughout the semester through regular group email and/or web or mobile messages; and students could submit their assignments as URLs.

More typically, however, a course will be offered through a learning management system, such as Blackboard or Moodle. While LMSs can prompt teachers to revert to more conventional week-by-week content and resources, it does not have to be this way. The affordances of these programs can be used appropriately to support authentic learning if thought is given to the design of the site. Rather than a weekly schedule, the design can emphasise the tasks, resources and supports required. In particular, it is essential to set up the communication tools for students to use, such as discussion forums, chat facilities, wiki spaces, blogs or spaces for personal journals, and other participatory technologies that provide a means for students to share ideas and collaborate. Spaces for private group work are also useful for group members only.

In much the same way that a mentor might suggest useful resources as a starting point for a mentee to become more expert in an area of study, a list of seminal works or quintessential resources can be given on the course website. While such resources should not be seen as self-contained and sufficient, they are a useful starting point for students in the learning journey.

Try to ensure that there is a framework of elements that are in full working order prior to the start of the course. It is important, too, to adapt and add to the site as needed both in the provision of resources and links, and the scaffolding role provided by the teacher. The site should be dynamic, and used regularly as a central point of communication by both teacher and learners.

Supporting Learners in the First Weeks

The first two to three weeks of the semester are the most crucial for learners in coming to terms with the complexity of authentic tasks. It is important to support the learners fully at this time, and these early weeks could require the most intense and frequent communications with individual students by the teacher. If a student is not keeping in touch, it is often a sign that he or she is floundering and not able to cope with the demands of the course. A useful strategy in these early days is to provide online ice-breaking activities so that students have an easy way to start communicating with the group. It is important to follow up personally with students who drop out of these early communications to determine whether their non-participation is personal, or related to the difficulty of the task.

Ideally, with good communication tools and collaborative tasks, the early intense support provided by the teacher is eventually shared across the group. Nevertheless, there is always a need for the teacher to keep an eye out for the progress of each student. One strategy suggested by Reeves and Hedberg (2003) is to conduct a mid-semester interview to gauge how individual students are coping with the course.

Reviewing Implementation Problems

In Chapter 8, we describe methods of evaluating authentic e-learning courses. Formative and effectiveness evaluations can help a teacher to determine whether the implementation of the course is effective for the cohort of students and the subject matter. A common response to student difficulties, however, is to compromise elements of authenticity in revisions of the course. If students report difficulty in understanding how to tackle the complexity of the task, a teacher will sometimes respond by providing a more structured, content-based approach, thereby undermining the strength of the authentic e-learning design. A better approach is to work at the metacognitive level, providing greater support and scaffolding for students rather than capitulating to the implicit demand for more direct, instructivist pedagogy. Students who are slow to accept authentic learning are often the ones who gain the most from the approach, and immerse themselves fully in the creation of real products.

In the next chapter, we discuss assessment in authentic e-learning courses.

Chapter 7

Assessment of Authentic e-Learning

Alignment of authentic elements in any e-learning course is essential. If a teacher specifies higher-order outcomes for a course, every effort must be made to assess those outcomes in the most reliable, valid, and feasible manner possible. If the learner tasks are appropriately complex and challenging, the instructor must assemble the necessary real-world and technological resources to scaffold students as they strive to accomplish those tasks. For example, there is little point creating a well-considered and complex authentic e-learning task and then assessing it by testing factual knowledge in a multiple-choice test.

Although in general higher education practice, innovative approaches to teaching are more the exception than the rule, there are good examples in the higher education literature of undergraduate courses where an appropriate level of alignment has been reached (Bain, 2004). But the weakest component of most designs is assessment, perhaps because both instructors and students are so accustomed to thinking of assessments in traditional ways. Better assessment and enhanced alignment in university teaching and learning will require a larger investment in assessment and evaluation than most institutions are expending at this time.

Assessment versus Evaluation

Although the terms *assessment* and *evaluation* are commonly used interchangeably, they have two distinct meanings. Assessment is defined as the activity of measuring student learning and other human characteristics such as aptitude, whereas evaluation is focused on judging the effectiveness and worth of educational programmes, practices, and products. It may help to think that *people are assessed* and *things are evaluated* (Reeves & Hedberg, 2003). In this chapter, we focus on the assessment of students in authentic e-learning courses.

The Issue of Assessment

In the 1990s, the Cognition and Technology Group at Vanderbilt University, Nashville declared the exploration of alternative approaches to assessment "one of the major issues of the decade" (1993a). Innovative and appealing ideas about a range of alternative assessment methods have been espoused over the last decade and more, perhaps in response to the challenges and opportunities offered by new technologies, in particular, e-learning (Reeves, 2000).

When courses began to be offered online, they were no longer constrained by the requirement for fixed and regular timetabled classes, allowing teachers to use more complex and sustained product-based assessments. However, it could be argued that higher education teachers today are generally not well informed when it comes to the practical implementation and use of alternative, authentic assessment methods. As is often the case with technology-based learning (Mioduser, Nachmias, Oren, & Lahav, 1999), just as these assessment doors were opening, further developments were reducing opportunities, with the widespread adoption of learning management systems. Such systems, most noticeably in their early years, enticed teachers to design their courses in weekly segments with regular assessments that were often easily marked on a computer, such as multiple-choice tests.

The Value of Assessment

"We assess what we value and we value what we assess." This well-known maxim on assessment resonates with many who respond to the idea that, as teachers, we have the means to recognise and assess significant learning.

However, in reality, assessment is often undertaken with less noble intentions and with less useful outcomes. For example, in Clarke's research, one teacher gave the reason for assessment as little more than "a kind of official announcement that the topic is over and we will be moving on to the next one" (Clarke, 2003, p. 2). How often is assessment conducted not to improve educational outcomes, but simply because it is expected? Many universities require a mandatory number of assessment points within a semester unit or course, and the number and form of assessment items need to comply.

In discussing assessment there is an often-used analogy of a drunk person searching for lost keys under a lamp-post, not because that is where they might be found, but because the light is better there. It prompts the question: do we assess only what we can see (or measure)? And do we value what we assess? Within courseware management systems, teachers are often prompted to use assessment means and measures that are inbuilt into the program and readily customisable for the subject matter, such as multiple-choice tests and quizzes. Statistics of online presence and contributions are also readily obtainable, such as the number of minutes students are online and the number of posts to chats and forums. While such metrics can give useful supplementary information on the involvement of the students with the online course material, they should not be used as a principal measure for assessment purposes. If indeed we assess what we value, such assessment clearly values lower-order factual knowledge, time spent in the online course site, and quantity rather than quality of involvement. There can be, as noted by Siemens (2006), a tendency to measure usage statistics as a measure of success:

> Much like we used to measure "bums in seats" for program success, we now see statistics of "students enrolled in our LMS" and "number of page views by students" as an indication of success/progress. The underlying assumption is that if we just expose students to the content, learning will happen (p. 5).

Assessment and Student Learning

Many have argued that it is futile to apply standardised, norm-referenced tests to the assessment of learning in constructivist learning environments. For example, Entwhistle, Entwhistle and Tait (1993) contended that assessment procedures profoundly affect the way students learn, and that "providing a constructivist teaching environment will have little effect on the quality of learning while conventional assessment procedures remain in place" (p. 353). Further, Gardner (1992) maintained that norm-referenced, formal tests and assessment materials are not sensitive enough to account for cultural differences, and they are rarely useful in determining students' level of competence. As evidence, he cited the work of some of the researchers into learning in context (Lave et al., 1984; Lave & Wenger, 1991; Rogoff, 1984; Scribner, 1984), pointing out that these studies have revealed that often those who fail on formal measures of calculating or reasoning are able to exhibit excellent command of the same skills in their everyday context. The belief that written tests can assess understanding in mathematics has been undermined by research by Clements and Ellerton (1996). They have shown that students may give correct answers to pen-and-paper mathematics tests but often have little understanding of the mathematical concepts that the tests were designed to measure. Their data also indicated that conversely, students who had full or partial understanding of the tested mathematical concept sometimes gave incorrect answers.

The still widespread use of conventional methods of norm-referenced tests, essays and examinations is generally based on the assumption that there is an objective reality that can be judged right or wrong, or they are used to effectively deal with assessment of students in large classes. Thus, testing items must, of necessity, be confined to low-level assessment items that can be marked by a computer.

Institutional assessment policy requirements and restrictions often further compound the issue when it comes to the use of authentic assessment.

Restraints of Institutional Assessment Policies

Quality standards and greater accountability measures in universities have contributed to pressures on teachers to conform to set standards. Most universities have introduced assessment policies which in many instances run counter to constructivist philosophies and situated approaches to learning. For example, the requirement for courses to have a mandatory minimum number of assessments means complex course-based assessments are impractical. Similarly, restrictions on the amount of group work permissible for assessment often make collaborative, large-scale projects unworkable.

Concerns about restricted or ad hoc assessment policies and their implications on course design and teacher practices have been reported in the literature (e.g., Ecclestone & Swann, 1999). Perhaps the major assessment concerns in higher education currently are those that are largely at the institutional level, such as grade inflation, plagiarism, large classes and their impact on assessment (James & McInnis, 2001), and the potential for student litigation (Ecclestone & Swann, 1999). For the university teacher wishing to use effective and authentic assessment in his or her own courses, such issues can create genuine constraints, and further confusion can also arise from the different interpretations of the nature of authentic assessment (as described in detail by Cumming & Maxwell, 1999). The requirement to give a mandatory examination or online test, for example, can be antithetical to a teacher's fundamental pedagogical beliefs, and the teacher complies only in bad faith.

Other policy-driven assessment practices must also be questioned. Despite clear educational advantages to be derived from collaboration (e.g., Qin et al., 1995), assessment strategies that take advantage of the use of group work may be used only minimally because of assessment rules and policies. For example, a university might limit the assessable component of group work to 40% or less of course assessments. In such cases, the focus is on each student learning—and being assessed—independently of the social context in which that learning takes place, and as pointed out by Hooper (1992) there is little incentive for co-operation when students within a group compete for grades. Young (1995) too, has argued that it is misleading to judge students individually when one of the most important skills they develop is "the ability to distribute wisely problem-solving tasks among members of a group" (p. 91).

As alternatives to norm-referenced, standardised tests, McLellan (1993) suggested that assessment can take the form of a number of evaluation measures which do not include formal tests, such as portfolios, summary statistics of learners' paths through multimedia programs, diagnosis, and reflection and self-assessment. Maclellan (2004) has argued that students' perception of an assessment task has a profound effect on the level of their engagement and depth of learning, creating a clear imperative for the need to examine the nature of assessment, and to measure what is truly important.

Characteristics of Authentic Assessment

Many authors have provided criteria with which to design and evaluate authentic assessment. For example, Newmann and Wehlage (1993) listed five discrete standards of authentic assessment. Similarly, Wiggins (1990; 1993; 1989), Reeves (2000), Reeves and Okey (1996) and others have provided guidelines or elements that help to explain the nature of authentic assessment. More practice-based guidelines include the characteristics of "rich assessment tasks" developed by Clarke (2003). Rich assessment tasks:

- connect naturally with what has been taught,
- address a range of outcomes in the one task,
- engage the learner,
- can be successfully undertaken using a range of methods or approaches,
- provide a measure of choice or "openness",

- encourage students to disclose their own understanding of what they have learned,
- allow students to show connections they are able to make between the concepts they have learned,
- are themselves worthwhile activities for students' learning,
- help teachers to decide what specific help students may require in the relevant content areas,
- authentically represent the ways in which the knowledge and skills will be used in the future (pp. 5–6).

Morgan and O'Reilly (2006) developed 10 key qualities specifically for online assessment, which they argue need special attention. Online assessment needs to comprise:

- A clear rational and consistent pedagogical approach,
- Explicit values, aims, criteria and standards,
- Relevant authentic and holistic tasks,
- Awareness of students' learning contexts and perceptions,
- Sufficient and timely formative feedback,
- A facilitative degree of structure,
- Appropriate volume of assessment,
- Valid and reliable,
- Certifiable as students' own work,
- Subject to continuous improvement via evaluation and quality enhancement (pp. 86–87).

A Framework for Authentic and Integrated Assessment

Building on Herrington and Herrington's (1998; 2006) summary of the essential characteristics of authentic assessment, the list below attempts to provide a synthesis of the recent literature and research while considering four key factors of assessment *context, student factors, task factors* and *indicators.* Using these guidelines, assessment is most likely to be authentic if it satisfies the following criteria.

Context

- Requires fidelity of the task to the conditions under which the performance would normally occur (Reeves & Okey, 1996; Meyer, 1992; Wiggins, 1993);
- Requires connectedness and transfer to the world beyond the classroom (Newmann & Wehlage, 1993; Newmann & Archbald, 1992).

Student Factors

- Requires problem-solving skills and higher order thinking (Reeves, 2000; Newmann & Wehlage, 1993);
- Requires production of knowledge rather than reproduction (Newmann & Archbald, 1992);
- Requires significant student time and effort in collaboration with others (Linn, Baker, & Dunbar, 1991; Kroll, Masingila, & Mau, 1992) (Reeves, 2000);
- Is characterised by substantive conversation (Newmann & Wehlage, 1993);
- Requires students to be effective performers with acquired knowledge, and to craft polished performances or products (Wiggins, 1990; 1993; 1989);
- Promotes depth of knowledge (Newmann & Wehlage, 1993).

Task Factors

- Stimulates a wide range of active responses (Reeves, 2000);
- Involves complex, ill-structured challenges that require judgment, multiple steps, and a full array of tasks (Wiggins, 1990; 1993; 1989; Linn, Baker, & Dunbar, 1991; Torrance, 1995) (Reeves, 2000);
- Requires the assessment to be seamlessly integrated with the activity (Reeves & Okey, 1996; Young, 1995).

Indicators

- Provides multiple indicators of learning (Lajoie, 1991; Linn, Baker, & Dunbar, 1991);
- Achieves validity and reliability with appropriate criteria for scoring varied products (Wiggins, 1990; Lajoie, 1991; Resnick & Resnick, 1992).

Such guidelines enable teachers to create e-learning designs using authentic contexts and scenarios that ensure assessment measures whether students can use their knowledge effectively and realistically, as opposed to the reproduction of surface knowledge that is quickly forgotten after an examination or test.

However, as noted by Reeves (2000), higher education teachers rarely receive adequate training in the use of assessment strategies, and the use of authentic assessment provides further challenges for many because of the sometimes limiting assessment policies adopted by universities.

Teachers are often unsure about the process of marking authentic assessment, and the principles that must be brought into effect if an authentic task is not to be undermined by teachers inadvertently applying standardised or norm-referenced criteria in their marking of the varied products presented by students. The importance of alignment between a task and its assessment is at the heart of this problem, and is discussed in more detail in the next section.

Alignment of Task and Assessment

In order to explore the alignment of an authentic task and its assessment, consider the situation where a teacher of an introductory research methods course develops an authentic task.

The task requires students to produce a research report for publication in a magazine (such as a consumer awareness magazine like *Consumer Reports*, *Choice*, *Ethical Consumer* and *Consumer Magazine*). The task is presented in the form of a scenario to capture the authentic nature of the task, where the students are asked by the editors of the magazine to produce a report comparing five products, such as five different types of detergent powder or yoghurt or car insurance. The students are able to choose a product of their own choice, and design the research to test the product.

If the assessment is to be aligned with the task, the teacher must take care to use the principles of the authentic scenario to assist with the assessment of the task. It would not be aligned if, for example, the teacher marked the work according to the guidelines for writing a research report, and took marks off because the students did not have a literature review or a section describing the "Significance of the research" or "Limitations and delimitations of the research," as might be required in a formal research report. It would be important for the assessment to use the purpose of the work to guide its assessment, and thereby assess the work on its research, design and execution as appropriate for publication in a consumer magazine.

A most useful distinction between the content and context of assessment has been described by Cumming and Maxwell (1999), who distinguish between the *first-order expectations* of a task, and the *second-order expectations*. They draw on the work of Wiggins (1993) to explain the construct. Wiggins gave an example of students required to learn historical analysis through the examination of author perspective in a text. The scenario within which this task was set was a trial in a courtroom, where the student was required to take the role of a prosecutor or defence lawyer in a trial brought to court by a parent group seeking to forbid the use of a particular novel as a textbook in a high school. In this example, Cumming and Maxwell described the historical analysis of author perspective as the *first-order expectation*, and the skills required to present the workings of a courtroom as the *second-order expectation.* They questioned the usefulness of the second-order scenario in this example on the grounds of its lack of "personal and practical usefulness," the emphasis on "courtroom behaviour rather than historical analysis," and the uncertainty about whether or not the issue needed to encompass "the notion of censorship" (p. 186).

This example illustrates how important it is to ensure that the second-order expectations of a task (usually providing the purpose for an activity in an authentic context) are realistic and fully in keeping with the expectations of the academic requirements of the task. However, if care is taken to ensure that this is done, such an authentic context is a powerful tool in giving meaning and justification to the assessment of any student product.

We use this principle in our own assessment tasks. For example, in a course on leaders in educational technology (taught by Reeves), students select an esteemed person in the field to research in depth. Students prepare an article for submission to *Educational Technology* magazine and are assessed on their suitability as a scholarly biographical article on the leader's achievement in the field. These articles are regularly published in the magazine.

In an introductory course on digital technologies (taught by Oliver), students in a communications degree in their first year of university develop the fundamentals of design while learning to apply a range of electronic tools. The course seeks to develop learners' capabilities to create attractive and effective documents, interfaces and graphics across a wide range of computer-based applications including a word processor, a spreadsheet, presentation software, drawing software and web-page development software. The assessment for the unit involves students developing a personal website to showcase the work from their university studies in the form of a personal portfolio. The development of the portfolio website involves them in planning and creating an interface that reflects the personal impressions that they want their site to convey to users. At the same time the site needs to include the forms of functionality required to enable users to navigate and browse easily and for the site to be easily maintained and grown. This product forms the basis of the assessment in the course. It has personal relevance and provides a strong context for the application and development of both the design skills and technical skills sought by the course.

Similarly, in a course on design research (taught by Herrington), students learn about this research approach by actually conducting it, albeit in condensed form focusing on a single iteration. Students choose a significant educational problem, conduct a literature review and consult with practitioners, plan an intervention, obtain ethical approval if required, and implement and evaluate it. The students write the research up as a brief paper for a conference, using the specifications and guidelines of the conference of their choice. The work is assessed as a scholarly paper submitted for review, and it is assessed as such. Many of these papers have been accepted for conferences (if the student later submitted the paper).

Further published illustrative examples of this principle in higher education practice are given below.

Project Management

In a course on project management, McLoughlin and Luca (2006) described the authentic task students perform as they form teams to create a multimedia website for a fictional client. Students are required to draw up contracts, create management models, plan roles and responsibilities for each team member, document progress, and produce an effective website to meet client needs. The websites are assessed by the teacher, and peer-assessed by the other teams, in accordance with the needs of the client, the proposed purpose of the website and its quality.

Evaluation of Technology-Based Learning

In a course designed to teach evaluation of technology-based learning environments, Agostinho (2006) described how students are invited to participate in a scenario where they are new recruits to an evaluation company. It is within this context that they learn evaluation skills and strategies, and each task is given within the context of a realistic evaluation. In the major task, students are asked to prepare a proposal for an evaluation of a post-graduate course. They do this as representatives of the company, and in an accomplished and professional manner, with reference to a real online course. The teacher's role in assessing each assignment readily reflects the realistic role of an assessor of an evaluation proposal (rather than a teacher marking an assignment), and realistic criteria can be brought to bear on the final marks.

Fiction and Film

Fitzsimmons' (2006) description of a literature course showed a similar alignment between an authentic task and its assessment. In a course on North American fiction and film, one task is to write a critical review of a book for publication in an electronic journal. This is a real journal established for the course and it is published each time the course runs. The students not only submit their book reviews for consideration but also act as members of the editorial review board for the journal. Thus, students and teacher jointly and authentically assess journal papers and select the best for publication, in direct contrast to a teacher simply marking an essay.

Learning Italian

In an undergraduate Italian language course (Pais Marden, Herrington, & Herrington, 2007), students in teams plan and organise a trip to Australia for a group of Italian university students, and develop an itinerary and comprehensive travel guide in Italian. Learners in Australia and Italy collaborate and interact with each other and with a group of Italian native speaker facilitators, using the communication tools provided in the course website and relevant resources. Students also draw on knowledge from other subject areas in order to create their final product, which is shared among community members. The students extend their understanding of the conventions of language use by engaging in the kinds of authentic activities likely to be found in real-world contexts, and the itineraries and travel guides are assessed as genuine products for Italian tourists travelling in Australia.

Authentic Assessment for Authentic Learning

The alignment between an authentic task and its assessment is frequently neglected in e-learning courses where the persuasive appeal of computer-based, easily marked tests is paramount. Failure to effect this alignment can lead to the negation of the impact of any authentic task used by teachers no matter how good the intention. Alignment between task and assessment effectively frees the teacher from a judgmental, teacher-driven perspective to one where realistic criteria are used to assess real products. In so doing, it is crucial to the effective use of authentic assessment in higher education.

Neil Postman (1992), in his social comment on the role of computers in modern society, has spoken of the "loss of confidence in human judgement and subjectivity." He goes on to say "We have devalued the singular human capacity to see things whole in all their psychic, emotional and moral dimensions, and we have replaced this with faith in the powers of technical calculation" (p. 118). This comment reflects the faith many educators have in standardised assessment procedures as true indicators of learning, and provides a cogent argument for the further development and refinement of the role of authentic assessment within e-learning.

This chapter has focused on the assessment of student learning in authentic e-learning courses. In the next chapter, we describe strategies for evaluation of e-learning courses.

Chapter 8

Evaluating Authentic e-Learning Courses

Evaluation in an authentic e-learning course may be required at various points throughout the life cycle of a course, from the planning stages, through to formative and effectiveness evaluation, and after a course has been running for some time, impact and maintenance evaluation.

In this chapter, we give guidance on planning a formal evaluation of an e-learning course and how to plan such an evaluation (cf. Reeves & Hedberg, 2003 for a full description of functions of evaluation appropriate to interactive learning systems). Evaluation is not "rocket science," but it is a complex enough activity to require careful planning and managing strategies. Preparing a detailed evaluation plan is essential before undertaking an evaluation.

An evaluation plan is a written document that spells out the "who, what, when, where, why, and how" of an evaluation. The plan will likely go through several stages of revision before it is optimised, and even then it is likely to be modified during its implementation. Negotiating an evaluation plan with all the relevant stakeholders represents a major part of the effort required to evaluate authentic e-learning. However, trying to evaluate without a sound plan will almost always be disastrous.

Evaluation Planning

Beyond the obvious benefits, an evaluation plan has at least two other distinct advantages. First, the process of preparing a plan helps to understand the size and scope of an evaluation. That understanding is needed to establish a meaningful timeline and a reasonable budget for the evaluation. Second, the planning process provides an opportunity to establish rapport with clients (the people paying for the evaluation) and other stakeholders (anyone who may use the information from the evaluation for decision making). The major components of an evaluation plan are:

- The *Introduction* section lists the major sections of the plan as well as the primary people involved in writing the plan.
- The *Background* section describes all the information needed to provide the reader with an understanding of the background of the authentic e-learning course to be evaluated.
- The *Purposes* section clarifies the purposes of the evaluation. A single plan can address a variety of purposes. Clients must clearly understand and sign off on the purposes for the evaluation to be successful.
- The *Stakeholders* section specifies the clients and all the primary and secondary stakeholders in the evaluation. It is recommended to open up the evaluation to as many stakeholders as the client will allow.
- The *Decisions* section specifies the anticipated decisions to be informed or guided by the evaluation. This section is often difficult to prepare, but it should be included if the evaluation is to have impact on decision making. After all, evaluation is not an end in itself. Most clients do not wish to anticipate negative outcomes, but these too must be considered.
- The *Questions* section delineates the questions addressed by the evaluation design and data collection methods. The clearer the questions, the more likely the evaluation will provide useful answers. Each decision will have one or more evaluation questions associated with it.
- The *Methods* section describes the evaluation design and procedures. There are numerous distinctive designs and procedures that can be used. You should strive to match these options to the purposes and questions of your clients while keeping within the budget and timeline of the study.
- The *Participants* section specifies which learners, teachers, and other personnel will participate in the evaluation. If a sample is used, a rationale for the sample size used should be included.
- The *Instruments* section specifies all the evaluation instruments and tools to be used. Actual instruments should be included in appendices for review and approval.
- The *Limitations* section spells out any limitations to the interpretation and generalisability of the evaluation. This section also describes potential threats to the reliability and validity of the evaluation.

- The *Logistics* section specifies who will be responsible for the various implementation, analysis, and reporting aspects of the evaluation.
- The *Timeline* section presents the schedule for implementation, analysis, and reporting of the evaluation.
- The *Budget* section clarifies the finances for the evaluation. Personnel time is usually the major cost factor. Other significant costs may be instrument development, analysis, and report preparation.

As noted above, a difficult, but exceedingly important, aspect of this approach to evaluating authentic e-learning is that it encourages close collaboration with clients and other stakeholders to identify in advance decisions that must be made about the authentic e-learning program being evaluated. Frankly, unless an evaluation is designed to guide or influence specific decisions, it should not be conducted in the first place. Identifying decisions upfront is often quite challenging because when people are involved in something as innovative as authentic e-learning, there is a natural inclination to assume it is going to be effective. But even the best designs can go awry. As many decisions as possible that might be made about the e-learning being developed or implemented should be anticipated. For each decision, questions must be answered to help clients or others make better decisions. Only then should a decision be made on an evaluation design or the selection of specific data collection methods for the evaluation.

Evaluation planning requires political savvy and astute negotiation skills. Just as politicians must engage in persuasion and negotiation to get things accomplished within legislative bodies, evaluators of e-learning often find themselves in the position of having to persuade their clients of the value of asking hard questions or addressing difficult issues in an evaluation. Unwilling or unable to confront the complexities that may be involved in an e-learning evaluation, clients and other stakeholders may desire direct and simple answers to complex questions. Experienced evaluators know that direct and simple answers are extremely rare, and that "it depends" and other conditional statements are the most likely finding of even the best evaluations. A sound evaluation plan will expose as many of these conditionals as possible upfront while at the same time keeping the clients committed to the evaluation process.

Preparing an Evaluation Proposal: An Example

In the following sub-sections of this chapter, each component of an evaluation plan is explained in more detail. Examples of each component are provided within the context of evaluating a hypothetical authentic e-learning program used in an undergraduate ecology course. Students in this course are challenged to serve on the management team for a large public botanical garden that is threatened by several local environment problems, such as polluted runoff from a nearby swine farm.

Introduction Overview

This section introduces the major sections of the plan as well as the primary people involved in writing it. An example of a typical Introduction section appears below. It is a good idea to introduce the reader to the type and amount of information upon which the planning is based, both in terms of human input and review of other materials.

Introduction (Example)

> This plan describes the background, purposes, limitations, stakeholders, decisions, questions, methods, sample, instruments, procedures, logistics, and timeline for the evaluation of the *Botanical Gardens Management Simulation* to be used in *ECOL 2000: Ecological Applications* course at The University of Georgia. This online simulation program is being developed with funding by the National Science Foundation (NSF) to engage undergraduate students in the management of an ecological environment under threat. The methodology, procedures, and instrumentation included in this plan are based on several meetings between members of the development team (Gwen Glass, Bobbi Burgess, and Lou Landers) and the evaluation team (Rod Ross and Sally Simpson), as well as a review of several draft design documents and the original NSF funding proposal.

Background Overview

This section describes any information that is needed to provide the reader with an understanding of the background of the authentic e-learning program being evaluated. The reader should be given enough information to understand the unique nature of the program being evaluated, but not so much detail as to become overwhelmed. Explain any jargon used in describing the e-learning program if the plan will be read by stakeholders unfamiliar with technical terms, or the latest buzzwords used by e-learning developers.

Although evaluation plans may make for dry reading, it does not have to be that way. An evaluation plan can tell a story that is interesting, and it can be illustrated with screen images from the e-learning program. If lengthy background materials are needed, you should put them in an appendix.

Background (Example)

> The e-learning program under development is called "Botanical Gardens Management Simulation" (BGMS). This simulation will be used over a 10-week period within an undergraduate course called *ECOL 2000: Ecological Applications* at The University of Georgia. The catalogue description of the course is: "This course presents current ecological approaches used to quantify and reduce the impacts of natural and human disturbances on ecosystem structure and function. Case studies and an online simulation illustrate impacts and management strategies related to issues such as environmental toxicology, conservation ecology, and restoration ecology."
>
> The course is unique in its use of pedagogy based on authentic tasks. In traditional undergraduate science courses, information is presented in encapsulated formats, often via abstract presentations and texts, and it largely is left up to the student to generate any possible connections between conditions (such as a problem) and actions (such as the use of knowledge as a tool to solve the problem). There is ample evidence that students who are quite adept at "regurgitating" memorised information on tests rarely retrieve that same information when confronted with novel conditions that warrant its application. Most knowledge acquired through traditional instruction is "inert" except within the confined structure of traditional tests, and even then it is easily forgotten.
>
> The BGMS authentic e-learning program is being developed with funding from NSF to present a real-world problem situation that will serve as a focus for collaborative learning among students in the course. The BGMS is intended to be intrinsically interesting, problem-oriented, and challenging. In response to the BGMS, students are expected to be highly motivated as they are confronted with realistic problems (e.g., a runoff from a local swine farm is threatening the water quality of the

streams that run through a large botanical garden). Within the BGMS, they must solve the problems that impact the local fauna and flora in the garden.

The ECOL 2000 course is traditionally taught in a face-to-face course that combines classroom lectures with actual field experiences in the Georgia State Botanical Gardens, which is located near and managed by The University of Georgia. The BGMS is being developed for use in an online version of ECOL 2000 that will be offered to students enrolled in the Georgia eCore, a program that allows University System of Georgia (USG) students the opportunity to complete their first two years of their collegiate careers in an online environment.

Purposes Overview

This section thoroughly describes the purposes of the evaluation. An evaluation can address a variety of purposes, but all must be stated clearly. Evaluation resembles a political process. As such, all clients and most stakeholders must agree upon its purposes if the evaluation is to succeed.

Sometimes the purposes relate to a mix of formative and summative goals or functions. A formative evaluation provides information to guide decisions about creating, debugging, and enhancing an authentic e-learning course at various stages of its development. Some of the primary activities carried out during formative evaluation include expert review, user observations, and usability testing. A summative evaluation drives decisions about the marketing and implementation of an e-learning program. The overall purpose of effectiveness evaluation is to determine whether the authentic e-learning program accomplishes its objectives within the immediate context of its implementation (Did students learn?) and longer-term context (Was student learning retained and transferred to a broader context of application?). Some of the primary summative evaluation activities include alpha, beta, and field tests, observations, interviews, and performance assessment.

Given that the nature of the e-learning product or program being evaluated is almost sure to change over time, trying to anticipate all the evaluation functions or roles in advance is difficult, and flexibility is required throughout the evaluation planning and implementation process. Despite the inherent complexity, the more effort that is put into clarifying the purposes of the evaluation, the more likely stakeholders are to sign off on them.

Purpose (Example)

> The overall purpose of this evaluation is to provide the course teacher and the instructional designers at the Center for Teaching and Learning at the University of Georgia (CTL, UGA) with the timely, accurate information required to support decisions regarding the enhancement, extension, and/or marketing of the BGMS e-learning program. A list of anticipated decisions is presented in a separate section below. This evaluation is primarily formative in the sense that the information collected will be used as the basis for improvements in the BGMS e-learning program during its development. As a result of this evaluation and the decisions and actions stemming from it, the BGMS e-learning program should be ready for beta testing within the eCore during the Fall Semester of 2011. Specific sub-purposes of this evaluation are:
>
> - to collect information for improving the BGMS e-learning program from selected content and instructional experts;
> - to collect information for improving the BGMS e-learning program from members of the target audience (undergraduate eCore students and their teachers);
> - to establish procedures for a beta test of the BGMS e-learning program; and,
> - to establish procedures for the ongoing collection of information for improving the BGMS e-learning program after statewide deployment.

Stakeholders Overview

This section specifies the clients as well as the primary and secondary stakeholders or consumers of the evaluation. The *clients* are the people who are usually paying for an evaluation and who accordingly often have the highest stake or interest in the results. In general, it is recommended to share information about an evaluation with as many other stakeholders as the clients will allow. In some situations, for example e-learning development projects funded by government agencies such as the National Science Foundation, the plans and findings of evaluations may be "public domain" information and thus can be shared with anyone. By contrast, commercial clients may wish to restrict the sharing of evaluation plans and findings to only specific parties.

Primary stakeholders include the people most directly involved in or affected by the evaluation, such as the students intended to use an authentic e-learning program. *Secondary audiences* are any people judged to have a stake in the evaluation and thus a right to know about its methods and results (e.g., members of an accreditation agency who review educational degree programs for certification purposes).

As Patton (1997) wrote, "... stakeholders typically have diverse and often competing interests" (p. 42). Which stakeholders will receive evaluation reports may be a major focus for negotiation between you and your clients.

Stakeholders (Example)

> The clients for this evaluation are the members of the Center for Teaching and Learning (CTL) design and development team at The University of Georgia (UGA) and the primary teacher of ECOL 2000. Important secondary stakeholders include the managers of the Georgia Board of Regents eCore program and the students who will eventually use the BGMS. Dissemination of the evaluation plans and results will be controlled by the clients. The designers and implementers of this evaluation are Rod Ross and Sally Simpson, evaluation specialists from the Department of Educational Psychology at UGA who have been designated as the evaluators for this e-learning development project.

Decisions Overview

As noted earlier in this chapter, this section is often the most difficult part of a plan to prepare, but it should be included if the evaluation is to have meaningful impact on decision making. Trying to anticipate the decisions that can be influenced by an evaluation takes foresight and trust. Many clients do not wish to anticipate negative outcomes for their efforts, but these too must be considered.

Obviously, you cannot create an exhaustive list of all the decisions that will be made about an e-learning program. Although there will almost always be unanticipated decisions that must be confronted, you should work with your clients to identify all major decisions in advance. If you don't, your evaluation efforts are unlikely to be as influential as they could be.

Decisions (Example)

To empower this evaluation to provide timely and accurate information to support decision making, we have identified a set of anticipated decisions that will be made about the BGMS e-learning program during its development. Most of these decisions must be made regardless of the quantity and quality of information available to the decision makers, but the evaluation will ensure that the decisions are informed by the best possible information. The following decisions are anticipated:

- Delivery options for the BGMS e-learning program will be established
- Modifications will be made in the BGMS e-learning program to improve its effectiveness and appeal
- Marketing decisions will be made about the BGMS e-learning program by the managers of the Georgia eCore.

Questions Overview

A key element of a sound evaluation plan is careful specification of the questions to be addressed by the evaluation design and data collection methods. The clearer and more detailed these questions are, the more likely that you will be able to provide reliable and valid answers to them. Whenever decisions are made, questions are asked and alternatives are considered, formally and/or informally.

In order to influence the decisions identified during the evaluation planning process as well as other unanticipated decisions, your evaluation must provide answers to a variety of questions that enable "informed" decision making. Another challenge in evaluation planning is limiting the questions to those most relevant to the decisions that must be made without exceeding the amount of time, money, and other resources allocated for evaluation. In most cases, there will be far more questions that could be asked than your resources will allow, and therefore some difficult choices must be made about which questions will actually be addressed. You should make these choices in collaboration with your clients well in advance of any data collection for the evaluation.

Questions (Example)

The following questions will be addressed during this evaluation:

- What are the technical requirements for using the BGMS e-learning program?

- What are learner reactions to the BGMS e-learning program?
  - appeal
  - motivation
  - usability
- What are teacher reactions to the BGMS e-learning program?
  - appeal
  - utility
- What are expert reactions to the BGMS e-learning program?
  - content
  - instructional design
  - human-computer interface
- What corrections must be made to the BGMS e-learning program?
- What enhancements can be made to the BGMS e-learning program?

Methods Overview

The Methods section of the plan describes the overall evaluation design and data collection strategies to be employed in your evaluation. There are numerous designs and many data collection strategies that can be used. The keys to successful evaluation are matching these options to the purposes and questions of your client while keeping within the budget and timeline of the study.

Most evaluation textbooks do not provide sufficient practical guidance regarding methodology because the examples they include are usually based upon the assumption that one design will suffice (e.g., a quasi-experimental design comparing an instructional innovation such as authentic e-learning with a "traditional" one such as classroom instruction). Experienced evaluators can attest that most evaluations demand mixed-methods designs (Creswell & Plano-Clark, 2006) and multiple data collection strategies.

One of the reasons that you will probably include multiple methods in your evaluation is the need to "triangulate" your findings. You can triangulate findings by using more than one method to collect data about an issue in the evaluation. For example, suppose you are interested in student attitudes toward the use of a new learning management system (LMS) in an online course. A general questionnaire designed to elicit their opinions of the LMS would be one way of collecting that data, but students are often turned off by questionnaires, and they may provide you with little detailed information about their real reactions to the LMS. A better strategy would be:

1 Begin your data collection by interviewing a few selected students about their reactions to the LMS
2 Design a questionnaire based upon the interview data and distribute it to a larger group of students, and
3 Follow up the questionnaire with a focus group of students to elaborate or clarify the results of the questionnaire.

A good way to succinctly present how your evaluation methods align with your questions is to use a matrix. On one axis of the matrix the questions that are to be addressed by the evaluation are listed. On the other axis of the matrix, all the data collection strategies that are reliable, valid, and feasible for this particular evaluation are listed.

One advantage of using a matrix is that you and your clients can review the alignment among the evaluation questions and proposed methods of collecting data to address these questions. The matrix not only provides an overview of the evaluation methods. It also allows you to ensure that each question is addressed by one or more data collection strategies.

Although it is not always possible in every evaluation, it is desirable to triangulate most questions with more than one evaluation data collection strategy. Examples of the instruments used with each method are usually placed in appendices to the plan.

Methods (Example)

No single evaluation design can encompass the six major questions specified for the evaluation of the BGMS e-learning program. Therefore, a mixed methods evaluation design and multiple data collection strategies will be utilised to collect the information required to address these questions. The data collection strategies include:

a teacher interviews
b learner questionnaires
c learner focus groups
d usability testing
e online data collection
f expert review.

The example table below is a matrix that illustrates the relationship between specific questions and the data collection strategies used in this evaluation.

Questions / Methods	Teacher interviews	Learner questionnaires	Learner focus	Usability testing	Online data	Expert review
What are the technical requirements for using the BGMS e-learning program?	✗			✗	✗	
What are learner reactions to the BGMS e-learning program?	✗	✗	✗			
What are teacher reactions to the BGMS e-learning program?	✗					
What are expert reactions to the BGMS e-learning program?						✗
What corrections must be made to the BGMS e-learning program?	✗	✗		✗	✗	
What enhancements can be made to the BGMS e-learning program?	✗	✗	✗	✗		✗

Participants Overview

This section specifies exactly which learners, teachers, experts, and other personnel will participate in the evaluation. If sampling is used in the data collection process, a rationale for sample sizes should be included as well. Sampling is used when the population of potential participants in the evaluation is larger than you can afford to collect data from given the limits of your evaluation budget and timeline.

Involving people as participants in an evaluation should not be done carelessly because you are asking for their valuable time and energy. The nature of any sampling strategies you may use will vary considerably depending upon the purpose of your evaluation and the completion status of the program or product being evaluated. For example, early in the stages of development of a new authentic e-learning program, you will usually use fewer participants for longer and more intensive evaluation sessions. On the other hand, an authentic e-learning program that is ready for field testing can be shared with large numbers of reviewers around the world who might try it out and complete a brief survey about it after the trial period.

Participants (Example)

The participants in this formative evaluation will be:

- The primary teacher for ECOL 2000
- 30 students enrolled in the classroom version of ECOL 2000
- 3 e-learning design experts.

Instruments Overview

This section describes the instruments to be used in the e-learning evaluation. Copies of instruments should be included in appendices for review by your clients or other designated reviewers. The descriptions in this section should provide enough information to permit readers to judge the various purposes and uses of different instruments. Some e-learning evaluations will require the development of new instruments, in which case the plan may include only an outline of how the instruments will be developed. Whatever types of instruments you use, you'll need to be concerned with reliability and validity.

The reliability and validity of instruments must be considered in light of the purposes of the evaluation (Patton, 1997). Reliability deals with the consistency of measurement. For example, a bathroom scale that provides the same weight if you step on it ten times in a row is probably reliable. Validity is about the degree to which an instrument achieves its aims. For example, if you want an accurate report of your weight, your reliable bathroom scale will need to be calibrated with another scale of recognised accuracy. It could be giving you the same weight ten times in a row, but be off by 2 kilograms!

Although any evaluator should know the fundamentals of establishing the reliability and validity of evaluation instruments, it may be necessary to hire measurement specialists to provide expert consultation in this area, especially when new instruments are being developed.

Instruments (Example)

Appendix A includes a protocol for the teacher interview. Appendix B includes the Learner Questionnaire that the students participating in this evaluation will complete after they use the prototype BGMS e-learning program for three weeks. Appendix C includes the protocol

> for a Learner Focus Group that will be conducted with selected students and teachers who have used the prototype BGMS e-learning program for 10 weeks. Appendix D includes a description of the protocols to be followed when using the portable usability lab to record student interactions with the prototype BGMS e-learning program. Appendix E includes a list of all the data to be collected by the computer while users are trying the prototype BGMS e-learning program. These data include both navigation paths and response choices. Appendix F includes brief resumes of five e-learning experts from whom a panel of three will be selected to review the prototype BGMS.

Limitations Overview

This section spells out the inevitable limitations to the interpretation and generalisability of the evaluation. People sometimes put too much faith in the findings of evaluations, perhaps assuming that if they read a report in print, it must be true. Every evaluation has limitations and/or room for alternative explanations.

The limitations section of your plan should describe potential threats to the reliability and validity of the evaluation design and instrumentation.

Limitations (Example)

> Two constraints on this evaluation should be clarified. First, all contents of the BGMS e-learning program must be regarded as changeable during the formative evaluation phase, and indeed they are expected to be modified in response to findings. The "moving target" nature of the BGMS e-learning program should be viewed as an advantage in that its flexibility increases the likelihood that the information yielded by the formative evaluation will be used to make substantive improvements in the structure and operation of the program. The second constraint has to do with the motivation of the learners participating in this evaluation. These students are not accustomed to taking online courses whereas the eventual learners for the BGMS are students enrolled in the online eCore program. The on-campus learners may have different expectations for the BGMS than the eventual target students.

Logistics Overview

This section spells out who will be responsible for the various data collection, analysis, and reporting aspects of the evaluation. Much of the data you collect in an evaluation is time-sensitive. For example, the responses that you get from a student immediately after trying a new e-learning program will be different from the responses you get after a delay of only a few hours. Sometimes, you will want to delay data collection, but most often you will want to collect evaluation data while someone actually uses a new program, or as soon as possible thereafter. It is all too easy for various data collection and data management activities to be forgotten in the midst of an evaluation project and therefore assigning clear authority and responsibility for these tasks is essential.

Logistics (Example)

Rod Ross and Sally Simpson will coordinate the implementation of this evaluation plan, including scheduling, data collection, and data transmission, with the CTL design and development staff, primarily Gwen Glass, who is the course manager for this project. All data will be processed, analysed, interpreted, and reported by Rod Ross and Sally Simpson. All reports will be provided to managers and members of the development team at the UGA CTL. Further dissemination of the evaluation findings will be determined by Gwen Glass. Additional details about the logistics are found in the timeline section of this plan. The due dates for various deliverables are also specified in the timeline.

Timeline Overview

This section clarifies the schedule for implementing and reporting the evaluation. Project management software is helpful in preparing a timeline for evaluations, although these programs can be somewhat complex to use. However, if you conduct many evaluations, developing expertise with project management software is a good investment of your money and time.

Timeline (Example)

This evaluation plan has been revised based on an earlier draft prepared in July. The final evaluation plan will be reviewed, revised, and approved by August 14. The initial data collection phase of the evaluation itself will commence August 21 in the ECOL 2000 course taught at UGA during the fall semester. The first interim report will be delivered by September 15, and subsequent interim reports will be provided on the 15th day of October and November. The final report will be delivered by December 10. Additional interim reports will be produced as requested.

Budget Overview

This section clarifies the costs of the evaluation. Evaluation is very much a people-intensive process. In fact, most of the money spent on evaluation usually will be for personnel and consultant costs. If specialised equipment and facilities such as a software usability laboratory are used, additional costs will be incurred.

Budgeting for evaluation is always a challenge because many e-learning developers are somewhat reluctant to spend money for evaluation in the first place. When things get tight during a development project, they often look at cutting the evaluation budget first. Your clients may ask you to recommend a percentage of an e-learning program development budget to be devoted to evaluation. This is difficult to do without the details of any given project, but a general estimate of 10% of the development budget should be devoted to formative evaluation activities. Summative evaluations will usually require additional allocations.

Budget (Example)

Item	*Rate*	*Cost*
Evaluators: Rod Ross and Sally Simpson	100 hours at $100/hour Planning: 20 hours Implementing: 30 hours Analysis: 30 hours Reporting: 20 hours	$10 000
Expert consultants	5 hours at $300/hour for 3 experts	$4500
Student incentives	30 × $50 gift certificates	$1500
Usability testing costs	10 hours at $100/hour	$1000
	TOTAL COST	$17 000

Evaluation Project Management

Managing evaluations is just as important as planning them. There are several time-tested strategies that can help to meet the management challenge. These include evaluation diaries, status reports, and sign-off forms.

Evaluation Diary

An evaluation diary is an online collection of documents that can be used to keep track of the planning, implementing, analysing, and reporting aspects of an evaluation. You can use various forms of free or commercial online programs to maintain your diary, such as Google docs, a blog, or a wiki. A diary is an excellent management tool, especially for large-scale evaluations. Some of the typical items kept in an evaluation diary follow.

Evaluation Plan: A copy of the most current plan plus various revisions that it went through during negotiations with clients.

Status Reports: Copies of the periodic evaluation status reports (weekly are recommended) provided to clients.

Correspondence: Copies of memos, letters, sign-off forms, and copies of emails if relevant.

Financial Records: Detailed financial records, including printouts of budgeting spreadsheets, receipts, invoices, and so on.

Instrumentation: Copies of evaluation instruments that were obtained, developed, and/or revised for the evaluation.

Data: Backup copies of all the data (raw and processed) collected during the evaluation.

Analyses: Printouts of the analyses of the data, both quantitative and qualitative.

Reports: Copies of all the interim and final reports generated during the evaluation.

Timeline: Timeline and documentation for any changes that may have been made in the schedule.

Notes: Copies of your personal notes and anecdotal records from evaluation meetings, observations, and other aspects of the evaluation.

You will need to take special security measures such as login and password protection with data collected and stored in an evaluation diary, especially in situations when confidentiality is a major issue.

Generally, the evaluation diary is not made available to your clients or other members of a development or implementation team, especially when you are an external, as opposed to an internal, evaluator. An external evaluator is someone hired from the outside to provide a more objective evaluation. An internal evaluator is a member of the development and/or implementation team, and his/her perspective is more likely to be biased in favor of the project than the perspective of the external evaluator.

Regardless of your role, the evaluation diary is a management tool for you and others who are involved directly in the evaluation effort rather than a type of evaluation report. There are certainly other types of documentation that can be maintained in an evaluation diary or log. The important thing is to begin maintaining detailed records from the very beginning of the evaluation. It is extremely difficult and in some cases impossible to document your evaluation efforts later in the process. In the age of the "paper-less office," all the documentation for an evaluation can be maintained online. However, in light of computer thefts, crashes, and other mischief, we recommend keeping several backups of all your evaluation documents.

Status Reports

Evaluation status reports are brief reports distributed to evaluation team members, your clients, and sometimes to selected primary or secondary audiences for the evaluation. Status reports serve two essential purposes: first, updating everyone about the current status of the evaluation, and second, documenting controversial decisions and other important events.

How often status reports are issued depends upon the schedule and intensity of an evaluation effort. In larger-scale e-learning evaluations, they are often prepared on a weekly basis, whereas on longer-term or smaller-scale evaluations, less frequent reports may suffice. Generally, it is better to err on the side of keeping your clients and other stakeholders over-informed about the status of the evaluation effort than to leave them under-informed.

Status Report (Example)

Status Report: Botanical Gardens Management Simulation (BGMS)E-learning Evaluation
Date: September 15

From: Sally Simpson
Accomplishments (Since August 21):

- Began the BGMS e-learning evaluation with ECOL 2000 class on schedule;
- 24 students have completed the online questionnaires;
- Focus group is scheduled for Friday, October 22, in the Ecology Department classroom.

Pending items:

1 Schedule interview with teacher.
2 Select experts for review.
3 Analyse questionnaire data.
4 Begin to prepare draft final report.

Concerns and recommended actions:

1 It is proving more difficult to get experts to review the e-learning program than expected. We may not have all three as hoped.
2 There are major problems in the BGMS e-learning program with respect to data tracking. These bugs must be fixed as soon as possible.

Remarks:
The programmers from the CTL development team are working hard to fix the bugs in the program, but they are also having trouble with the learning management system. The problems may be beyond their control. What contingency plans do we have if the LMS does not function as hoped?

Sign-off Forms

A sign-off form is a valuable tool for managing an e-learning evaluation project. The sign-off form documents client approval of an evaluation plan, interim report, final report, or any other document considered important within the context of the evaluative effort. For example, most evaluators prepare draft reports at regular intervals. Draft reports should be reviewed carefully by your clients, and their review process should be documented. The sign-off form indicates the client's approval to proceed with the next step of the evaluation and to pay for work completed, if applicable. A sign-off form will help you keep your evaluation effort making desirable progress and prevent the client from constantly changing the evaluation plans.

Of course, sometimes the client will have good reasons for wanting to change the questions addressed or methods used in an evaluation. If you have carefully documented previous negotiations, you will be in a stronger position to request the additional finances, time, or personnel that may be required to fulfill requests for significant changes in an evaluation plan. Here is what a sign-off form might look like:

Status Report (Example)

Sign-off form

Project: BGMS e-Learning Evaluation

I have reviewed and approved the Interim Report of the evaluation of the BGMS program being conducted for the CTL at UGA by Rod Ross and Sally Simpson, the consultants from Educational Psychology Department. I hereby give approval to proceed with preparing the final report of this evaluation. I also give my approval for evaluators to invoice the CTL for satisfactory completion of this phase of the evaluation plan.

I understand that further changes to the evaluation (aside from those specified in the plan dated August 14) will likely result in a delay in the final report date and could result in additional charges to the CTL.

[signature] .... [date] ....
Gwen Glass, Project Manager

Evaluation Reporting

E-learning evaluations yield information intended to influence important decisions about the design and implementation of e-learning programs, but this will happen only if the information is provided to decision makers and others in formats that are timely and efficient. In presenting e-learning evaluation results, remember that most decision makers and other stakeholders want more than "just the facts" in an evaluation report. They expect you to explain how you have collected the data and how you arrived at the interpretations and recommendations in your report. They want the whole story. The full story of an e-learning evaluation involves the following:

- Describe both the e-learning program itself and the context in which the program was evaluated;
- Clarify the decisions and questions that drove the evaluation;
- Explain the methods used in reference to specific evaluation questions;
- Report the information collected in reference to specific decisions and questions;
- Summarise the findings and make recommendations.

Although other reporting formats such as video and interactive web-pages should definitely be considered, most evaluations are still reported as written documents. A final written report should contain all the elements that will make it useful to the decision makers and other stake-holders. Most reports include an executive summary, which summarises the findings and presents the recommendations along with a brief rationale for each recommendation. In addition, most evaluation reports include appendices that provide greater detail about various aspects of the evaluation such as instruments and transcripts of data.

A good presentation of the results from an evaluation will not over-whelm the readers with technical details. After all, the intent of an evaluation report is to inform people, not to impress them with your technical expertise. If your recommendations are to have strength, the links among recommendations and sources of data must be clearly delineated. Present the data you have collected clearly, and employ summary formats (such as graphs and tables) to make comparisons possible.

The links between the decisions and questions that have driven the evaluation and the recommendations that stem from the answers to the questions should be clear. This might sound too obvious to state again, but providing useful recommendations based upon appropriate evidence requires you to have deep insight into the effective workings of the e-learning program that has been evaluated. This is a skill that takes experience to build. Make sure that you address each issue and provide practical information so that the decision makers (e.g., developers, potential adopters, and/or users of the e-learning program) can utilise the findings to inform the decisions they must make.

In preparing recommendations, don't forget that sometimes there are unintended outcomes that might have been overlooked in the set of initial questions. Useful evaluation reports describe unexpected, as well as expected, issues that were revealed by the evaluation that the clients and other stakeholders should consider carefully in their decision making. For example, an authentic e-learning program might be used to engage students in the simulated management of an ecological threat. This program may also have the unintended, but beneficial, impact of encouraging students to become more environmentally active.

Your recommendations should be pragmatic. Creating a list of unrealistic recommendations that will fail when implemented because they lack relevance to the context is just as useless as not providing any recommendations at all. Try to show how each recommendation is a practical solution to any problems that may be involved in making decisions about the e-learning program. Your awareness of what types of changes and actions are acceptable within a given context will ensure that your evaluation report will influence decision makers to the fullest extent possible. For example, if you know that your clients have invested heavily in a specific interactive delivery option and that they are not in a position to change delivery systems, recommending that they move from one delivery system to another would be unwise in most situations.

No aspect of an evaluation report should be given more attention than the recommendations. The following guidelines for making practical and useful recommendations from Patton (1997) should be followed:

1. The format and nature of the final report should be negotiated with the evaluation clients and other stakeholders as far in advance as possible.
2. Recommendations should clearly be supported by the evaluation results.
3. Some decision makers prefer receiving several options rather than recommendations advocating only one course of action.
4. Insofar as it is possible, when making recommendations, particularly major ones involving substantial changes in program operations or policies, evaluators should study, specify, and include in their reports some consideration of the benefits and costs of making the suggested changes, including the costs and risks of not making them.
5. Focus on actions within the control of the clients and other stakeholders.
6. Exercise political sensitivity in writing recommendations.
7. Allow yourself sufficient time to do a good job of writing the recommendations. Recommendations should rarely, if ever, surprise your clients or stakeholders.

8 Develop strategies for getting recommendations taken seriously, e.g., help clients assign responsibility to people for follow-up actions in response to recommendations.

Video is a potentially powerful format for e-learning evaluation reports. Video reports usually consist of recordings of actual learners interacting with an e-learning program, such as learners explaining their interactions via a think-aloud protocol. Videos of learner interactions may be interspersed with interviews with learners, expert statements, or video displays of the program with a voice-over explanation of the results. Some decision makers may not have the time or patience to read a printed report, but they may be willing to watch a brief video report that illustrates the findings of an evaluation. Generally, video reports should not be longer than 15 to 20 minutes. The widespread availability of digital video editing software and screen capture hardware enables the production of sophisticated video reports highlighting problems with interface design and other usability issues related to e-learning programs. Video reports can be distributed via videotapes, DVDs, or as downloadable videos on the Web, depending on the video delivery system preferred by the clients and other stakeholders.

The Web is another powerful medium for the preparation and dissemination of e-learning evaluation reports. Websites are especially useful when the e-learning program being evaluated is online, given that there can be links from the report to the program itself. As long as the clients agree, web-based reports can be easily reviewed by all members of the relevant stakeholder community. Logins and passwords can also protect reports from distribution beyond the intended stakeholders. The Web allows evaluation reports to be interactive in the sense that stakeholders can move quickly from data displays to interpretations, or vice versa. Alternatively, print-based reports can be made available through the Web by converting them to Adobe Acrobat pdf files for easy downloading.

Regardless of the medium, effectively communicating the recommendations to your clients is critical to the success and utility of the whole evaluation enterprise. You should ask several people (including, if possible, representatives of the stakeholders for the evaluation) to review your draft reports to ensure that you have told the story as clearly and compellingly as possible and have supported each recommendation with valid evidence.

You may also need to develop different forms of reporting for different groups of stakeholders. For example, whereas the clients of an e-learning evaluation may expect or require a formal printed report, other audiences may be more receptive to alternative formats, such as the aforementioned two-page format or an interactive website format. Videos are especially useful when you want to have a focus group reflect upon the evaluation findings. Websites are useful when the findings of an evaluation must be frequently updated or widely disseminated.

Summary

This chapter has introduced the process of planning, managing, and reporting evaluations of authentic e-learning programs. Obviously, you can't be expected to become expert in these processes instantly. Substantial experience is required to refine knowledge and skills in these areas. Much of the expertise required for planning, managing, and reporting evaluations involves negotiation skills. It is beyond the scope of this book to provide an introduction to the art of negotiation, but most libraries and bookstores contain useful volumes on the process of negotiating. It might be worthwhile reading one or two of these books or perhaps even attending a workshop on negotiating skills. Evaluation often involves clashes of values and goals (Patton, 1997). Negotiation skills are essential for successful evaluators.

Evaluation is an important and powerful tool within the overall initiative to develop and implement authentic e-learning. But research is needed as well. The final chapter describes a unique "design research" approach to conduct inquiry in this context.

Chapter 9

Researching Authentic e-Learning

There is much anecdotal evidence to suggest that authentic e-learning courses and tasks are an effective approach to facilitate students' higher-order learning. However, while authentic learning designs as described here, are theoretically sound, more research is required to assist teachers in design and implementation strategies to fully realise the potential of the approach.

Complex tasks by their very nature create considerable diversity of outcomes, and it is often difficult to foresee the design, implementation, and maintenance challenges that will inevitably arise. In our research, we have noticed that the teachers using these approaches have a deep commitment to the educational philosophy of authenticity, and a capacity for hard work above and beyond the usual level required (or recognised) for the development of an e-learning course. The problems they encounter are complex and not easily solved, ranging from institutional factors (such as restrictive university policy, the costs of development, and the unreliability of technology infrastructure), to personal teaching factors (such as the necessity to learn a new teaching role), and to learning issues (such as the level of support and guidance needed by students and how to help them deal with their inevitable anxieties).

Because this is new territory, teachers are left without appropriate guidelines in often difficult circumstances. There is a huge gap between the theoretical ideal and the practical realisation of these innovative approaches, and effective models, principles and guidelines are needed by faculty members, educational designers, and academic administrators who are prepared to challenge the dominant teaching practices in higher education today.

There is a need for ongoing research in authentic e-learning to provide the guidelines needed across a range of discipline areas and problem contexts in education in higher education.

The Need for a Different Kind of Research

The February 9, 2004 issue of the *New Yorker* magazine included a short piece entitled "Chew On" by Ben McGrath. The story described an educational computing research study undertaken in dentistry at New York University by Dr Kenneth L. Allen and colleagues. The aims of the research, as also reported at the annual conference of the International Association of Dental Research (Allen, Galvis, & Katz, 2004), were:

1. To compare two methods of teaching dental anatomy: "CD + lab" versus "standard lecture + lab," and
2. To determine whether actively chewing gum during lecture, lab and studying would have an effect on learning.

According to the *New Yorker* article, Allen and his colleagues originally intended only to compare the effectiveness of an interactive CD-ROM about dental anatomy and a standard dental anatomy lecture, but lacking funding, they incorporated chewing gum into the study at the behest of the Wrigley's company which was interested in the effects on learning of chewing its products.

No one familiar with the frustrating history of instructional technology's impact on learning (Clark, 2001; Cuban, 2001) will be surprised that there were no statistically significant differences found between the test scores of the students using the dental anatomy CD-ROM versus those who attended a dental anatomy lecture. Although the chewing gum results also failed to reach statistical significance, the authors concluded that the finding that "the chewing gum group ($n = 29$) had an average of 83.6 [on a 25-question objective exam] vs. 78.8 for the no chewing gum group ($n = 27$)" appeared to be "educationally significant."

The *New Yorker* writer poked fun at Dr Allen, suggesting that he might want to extend his research to investigations of the impact on learning of chewing tobacco or biting fingernails, but there is little doubt that Dr Allen, like numerous other faculty members from virtually every academic discipline, sincerely hoped to find that the interactive multimedia CD-ROM was a more effective instructional treatment than a traditional lecture.

What motivates this widespread belief in the potential of virtually any form of interactive technology itself among so many higher educators despite the considerable evidence (Dillon & Gabbard, 1998; Russell, 1999) that such faith is misplaced? And why are such comparative studies so frequently conducted in educational research?

Comparative Studies

Research is needed to meet the types of challenges facing e-learning educators, but not the type of research that has dominated education technology for the past fifty years. The most common type of study found in the research literature compares changes in delivery medium (e.g., online versus lecture) instead of comparing differences in pedagogical design (e.g., engaging in authentic tasks versus attending lectures). Clearly, there is an urgent need for *design research* (also known as *design-based research, development research* and *design experiments*) (van den Akker, 1999; van den Akker, et al., 2006a) to provide design guidelines for enhancing e-teaching and e-learning.

Design research is distinctly different from the experimental research methods that have long been applied in our field (Ross, Morrison, & Lowther, 2005). Most instructional technology and e-learning research reported in the higher education literature has studied the effects of relatively small changes to specific courses. The chewing gum study by Allen et al. (2004) is a case in point in that the researchers compared one 50-minute lecture within a dental anatomy course with the use of an interactive multimedia CD-ROM. Decades of similar small-scale, isolated studies have failed to provide academics with a robust set of design principles that can guide them in the integration of computers and other technologies into teaching and learning at the postsecondary level. Although there is renewed enthusiasm for experimental research designs among some educational researchers (cf. Feuer, 2002), we do not believe that this is the most fruitful path for a design field such as e-learning.

Changing the mental models of researchers from those that are primarily experimental to those that are developmental is not an easy task, especially given the prevalence of media comparison studies using experimental methods in the field of educational technology for nearly a century.

Saettler (1990) found evidence of experimental comparisons of educational films with classroom instruction in the US as far back as the 1920s, and comparative research designs have been applied to every new educational technology since then, including programmed instruction, instructional television and computer-based instruction. However, for decades the results of such media comparison research studies have usually reported "no significant differences" (Russell, 1999). Not surprisingly, much of the existing research related to e-learning continues in the same vein, that is, comparing online courses with so-called "traditional" classroom courses (e.g., Cheng, Lehman, & Armstrong, 1991; Koory, 2003; MacDonald & Bartlett, 2000).

Recently, Bernard, Lou, Abrami, Wozney, Borokhovski, Wallet, Wade, and Fiset (2003) reported a comprehensive meta-analysis of 157 empirical comparisons of distance education courses with face-to-face instruction courses between 1985 and 2003. Although not all the distance education courses in the studies analysed were online, many were. Altogether they found over 1000 comparison studies in the research literature, but the majority of the studies did not meet their criteria for inclusion in the meta-analysis.

Earlier reviews have found that comparison studies are often flawed by problems such as specification error, lack of linkage to theoretical foundations, inadequate literature reviews, poor treatment implementation, major measurement flaws, inconsequential learning outcomes for research participants, inadequate sample sizes, inaccurate statistical analyses, and meaningless discussions of results (Reeves, 1993c). Bernard et al. (2003) reported a very small, but statistically "significant, positive mean effect size for interactive distance education over traditional classroom instruction on student achievement" as well as small, but statistically significant, "negative effect for retention rate" (p. 2). Further analysis indicated that synchronous communication and two-way audio and video were among the conditions that contributed to effective distance education. While this meta-analysis is excellent in its design and reporting, its findings, as well as those derived from other related meta-analyses (Cavanaugh, 2001; Machtmes & Asher, 2000), fall far short with respect to specifying design guidelines for e-learning.

Design Research

To provide design guidelines for developing and implementing effective e-learning designs, there is an urgent need for design research (Bannan-Ritland, 2003; Design-Based Research Collective, 2003; Kelly, 2003; van den Akker, et al., 2006b). Van den Akker (1999) provided a succinct description of design research:

> More than most other research approaches, [design] research aims at making both practical and scientific contributions. In the search for innovative "solutions" for educational problems, interaction with practitioners . . . is essential. The ultimate aim is not to test whether theory, when applied to practice, is a good predictor of events. The interrelation between theory and practice is more

> complex and dynamic: is it possible to create a practical and effective intervention for an existing problem or intended change in the real world? The innovative challenge is usually quite substantial, otherwise the research would not be initiated at all. Interaction with practitioners is needed to gradually clarify both the problem at stake and the characteristics of its potential solution. An iterative process of "successive approximation" or "evolutionary prototyping" of the "ideal" intervention is desirable. Direct application of theory is not sufficient to solve those complicated problems (pp. 8–9).

Design research has its origins in educators' pragmatic desire to improve learning, not in a purely functional sense, but from an informed theoretical perspective. It is grounded in the practical reality of the teacher, from the identification of significant educational problems to the iterative nature of the proposed solutions. However, theoretical foundations and claims are crucial to the design of solutions—as noted by Cobb, Confrey, diSessa, Lehrer, and Schauble (2003), "the theory must do real work" (p. 10). Theory informing practice is at the heart of the approach, and the creation of design principles and guidelines enables research outcomes to be transformed into educational practice. Design research:

- focuses on broad-based, complex problems critical to education,
- involves intensive collaboration among researchers and practitioners,
- integrates known and hypothetical design principles with technological affordances to render plausible solutions to these complex problems,
- conducts rigorous and reflective inquiry to test and refine innovative learning designs as well as to reveal new design principles,
- requires long-term engagement that allows for continual refinement of protocols and questions, and
- maintains a commitment to theory construction and explanation while solving real-world problems.

At this stage in the development of e-learning, there is a clear need to further the understanding of the more effective and successful approaches and their relationships with underpinning theoretical principles and technological affordances (Anderson, 2003). There is a huge gap between the theoretical ideal and the practical realisation of these innovative approaches, and effective models, principles and guidelines are needed by teachers, instructional designers, and academic administrators who are prepared to challenge the dominant teaching practices in higher education today. Design research is an effective way to address this need.

Phases of Educational Design Research

Design research is an iterative and lengthy process, but Reeves (2006) proposed that it can be viewed as four connected phases (Figure 9.1). Each of these four phases is described below, together with a description of the practical considerations in each phase and guiding questions for educators planning the research.

PHASE 1: Analysis of Practical Problems by Researchers and Practitioners

There are three key processes and products that form the first phase of design research.

The Problem

In design research in education, the identification and exploration of a significant educational problem is a crucial first step. It is this problem that creates a purpose for the research, and it is the creation and evaluation of a potential solution to this problem that forms the focus of the entire study. Many researchers, particularly those using educational technologies, start by thinking of a solution—such as a technology-based intervention, an educational game, an e-learning site, or a tech-

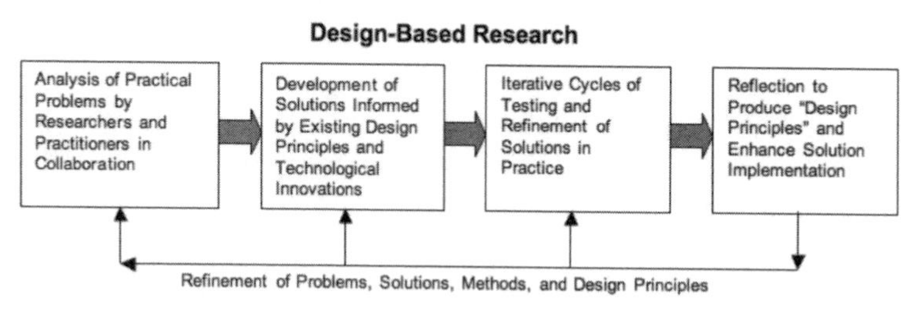

Figure 9.1 Four phases of design research (Reeves, 2006, p. 59).

nology tool—before they even begin to consider the educational problem it could solve. Problems then arise when the solution is revealed to be a stand-alone, pre-conceived product rather than a genuine attempt to solve an educational problem.

Edelson (2006) commented on the basic assumptions of design research, pointing out that:

> It begins with the basic assumption that existing practices are inadequate or can, at least, be improved upon, so that new practices are necessary. The underlying questions behind design research are the same as those that drive innovative design: What alternatives are there to current educational practices? How can these alternatives be established and sustained? (p. 103).

The first step in design research is to identify and explore a significant educational problem. A practical question to consider is: What is the educational problem that the research will address?

The Practitioners

In the first phase, practitioners (such as teachers) and researchers together explore the nature of the educational issue or problem facing students. It is important for practitioners to be involved in this phase so that the full extent of the problem is known, rather than being interpreted solely by researchers. Questions such as the following help to focus this aspect of the inquiry:

- Who are the teachers/students/practitioners that are knowledgable about or "own" the problem?

  For example, colleagues who teach in a relevant course, teachers from other universities, or academics from professional associations might be consulted.

- What data will be collected from these practitioners?

  For example, practitioners might be interviewed individually (with the researcher audio-recording or taking notes), or focus group discussions could be conducted with all practitioners together.

- What questions will be asked?

For example, the practitioners might be asked their views on the problem, and their suggestions for how to solve it. Relevant issues that have been discussed in the literature might also be addressed.

- How will these data be analysed?

  For example, practitioners' comments might be organised to create a list of recurring themes, together with a list of suggestions and advice on how to improve the situation.

The Literature Review

A literature review is also conducted in this phase to refer to the work that has already been done in the area or in related areas, and how similar problems might have been addressed in another field. A question such as the following is relevant for this stage of the research:

- What are the key references in the area of interest?

  For example, conduct a keyword or database search, or a Google Scholar search to find key people working in the area, or use known papers to follow references. Include both seminal works and recent publications.

The Research Questions

After this initial investigation of the problem, related literature and practitioners' ideas, it should be possible to create research questions to guide the research.

By the end of this phase, there is a clear description of the problem and its educational context, a literature review, a summary analysis of practitioners' views, and preliminary research questions.

PHASE 2: Development of Solutions Informed by Existing Design Principles and Technological Innovations

In the second phase of design research, a solution to the problem (or intervention) is proposed that can be implemented in the educational setting. In order to create the solution, again the literature is consulted to find relevant theory that can guide thinking, as well as locate existing design principles that may have addressed a similar problem.

Draft principles in the literature

A literature review in design research does not only perform the usual functions associated with a review—such as, the identification, location and analysis of documents relating to the research problem (Gay, 1992), or the building of a logical framework for the research, and identification of gaps in research (Marshall & Rossman, 1999). The second literature review process is a critical stage in design research because it facilitates the creation of draft design guidelines to inform the design and development of the intervention that will seek to address the identified problem.

Once again the literature should be consulted for design principles that others have suggested. They may not be called design principles, but could appear to be advice on how to create particular learning tasks or address particular problems. For example, our own guidelines for authentic learning environments and authentic tasks in Chapters 1 and 2 are design principles.

The following example lists are also forms of design principles because they give advice on designing for particular circumstances or outcomes:

Example 1: Jonassen: Constructivist Learning Environments

Jonassen (1994) proposed that knowledge construction may best be facilitated by constructivist learning environments which:

- provide multiple representations of reality, which avoid oversimplification
- focus on knowledge construction, not reproduction
- present authentic tasks (contextualising rather than abstract instruction)
- provide real-world, case-based learning environments rather than pre-determined instructional sequences
- foster reflective practice
- enable context- and content-dependent knowledge construction
- support collaborative construction of knowledge through social negotiation, not competition (p. 35).

Example 2: Boud and Knights: reflection in learning

Boud and Knights (1996) proposed that the following are important in introducing and establishing a productive climate for reflection:

- articulating an educational rationale for the process
- introducing a simple exercise to illustrate reflection
- providing an opportunity for students to clarify their understanding of the idea
- introducing a framework or model to aid thinking about elements of reflection
- modelling a reflective approach in one's own presentation of the idea
- identifying areas of the process that students can make their own
- providing time
- treating reflection as a normal activity.

Other researchers in your field may have addressed a similar problem and determined design principles of relevance. A more focused literature search should help to locate these specific principles.

The next step is to create a list of draft principles to guide the design of the intervention or solution to the problem that was explored in Phase 1. This step can take some analysis, as it will need to combine theory of learning with existing principles, as well as the ideas collected from the practitioners. Some questions to consider at this stage include:

- What are the most relevant research papers that provide design principles or design advice?

  Choose several papers that seem closest to the problem area and extract their design principles where possible. These principles are not always conveniently listed as bullet points, but may be described in the papers in paragraphs or under headings.

- What learning theory or approaches are most helpful in addressing the problem?

  For example, does the proposed solution involve theory such as situated learning, distributed learning, communities of practice, or problem-based learning?

- What are the draft principles to guide the design of the solution?

  Using the theory and principles from the literature review, and the interviews conducted with the practitioners, principles can be drafted to guide the design of the intervention. This can be done in a table such as Table 9.1 above. Adapting and using the stem provided in the table will help to keep the principles quite specific and naturally prompt each to start with a verb (e.g., allow, provide

Table 9.1 Organising Matrix for Draft Design Principles

Draft principles	Source/Reference
[Condition x] may best be facilitated by learning designs which:	
Draft Principle 1:	
Draft Principle 2:	
Draft Principle 3: Etc.	

opportunities for, promote, enable, support, etc.). In the second column, reference can be given to the publication that was the source of the principle (e.g., Jonassen, 1994) or the consultation with practitioners.

Technological Affordances

Once the draft principles have been created, it is important to consider the best way to deliver or operationalise the intervention within the e-learning environment. Often the intervention is technology-based, so innovative technologies can be part of the solution. A guiding question could be:

- What technologies appear most useful for operationalising or implementing the intervention?

  Think about technologies that might be useful for the students to use as cognitive tools as well as for delivery of content, for example, computer programs, websites, mobile technologies, and collaborative tools such as wikis.

Once the draft principles have been created, the proposed solution is designed and developed (according to the draft principles) ready for implementation.

The Design of the Learning Environment

When the design principles that will guide the creation of the learning environment are clear, it is important to consider how each will be instantiated in the learning setting. Again, a table can be useful to describe how each of the draft principles will be reflected in practice in the learning environment. Table 9.2 provides a matrix to illustrate how each design principle can be explicitly stated (in Column 1), and how each principle will be implemented or operationalised (in Column 2).

By the end of this phase, draft design principles will have been produced, appropriate delivery technologies will have been selected, and a solution to the problem will have been planned and created ready for implementation in the e-learning course.

PHASE 3: Iterative Cycles of Testing and Refinement of Solutions in Practice

Once a learning solution or intervention has been designed and developed (in Phase 2), the next phase of design research is the implementation and evaluation of the proposed solution in practice.

Design research is not a methodology, but a research approach. While both qualitative and quantitative methods may be used, it is worth noting that: "Design researchers do *not* emphasize isolated variables.

Table 9.2 Implementation of Draft Design Principles

Draft principles	*Principle will be implemented in the learning environment by:*
Draft Principle 1:	
Draft Principle 2:	
Draft Principle 3:	
Etc.	

While design researchers do focus on specific objects and processes in specific contexts, they try to study those as integral and meaningful phenomena" (van den Akker, Gravemeijer, McKenney, & Nieveen, 2006b, p. 5).

The First Implementation/cycle

The solution designed in Phase 2 is implemented and evaluated in iterative cycles in Phase 3. The iterative nature of design research means that a single implementation is rarely sufficient to gather enough evidence about the success of the intervention and its effect on the problem situation. A typical design research study would have two or more cycles, where after the first implementation and evaluation changes are made to the learning design to further improve its ability to address the problem. This is in keeping with the focus suggested by Reeves (1999), who maintained that "our research and evaluation efforts should be primarily developmental in nature . . . the purpose of such inquiry should be to improve, not to prove" (p. 18).

The first implementation evaluation is planned in much the same way as any research study, where choice of participants, and data collection and analysis strategies are selected in relation to the research questions. Relevant questions here include:

- Who are the participants in the study?

  Consider the class, the students, any additional researchers or helpers, and so on. Because of the highly situated nature of this research, participants in a design research study in education are central to the investigation. As Reeves (2006) noted, "Design research is not an activity that an individual researcher can conduct in isolation from practice" (p. 59). Most often, participants are students in the researcher's (or cooperating practitioner's) own practice, or teachers, parents, support personnel or other people involved in the educational community that is the focus of the study.

- What procedure will be used to implement the solution with the students in the e-learning course?

  Practical steps need to be planned to implement and evaluate the intervention.

- What data will be collected to answer the research questions?

The method of data collection in design research can involve the collection of qualitative and/or quantitative data, and it may be collected in cycles of several weeks, or even semesters or years. "In view of the wide variation of possible interventions and contexts, a broad range of (direct/indirect; intermediate/ultimate) indicators for 'success' should be considered" (van den Akker, 1999, p. 8). Plan the multiple data sources (triangulation) to ensure that evidence on the success of the solution is collected from different sources. For example, data sources such as:

- Interviews
- Surveys
- Focus groups
- Anecdotal records
- Artefacts (or student work)
- Participant journals
- Published evaluation instruments
- Questionnaires
- Observation
- Activity logs
- Usability tests
- Content analysis
- Statistical tests

- How will data be analysed?

Specify how data from each source will be analysed. This will depend upon the data types and research design.

Further Iterative Cycles

After the first implementation of the solution and the analysis of the data, evidence on the success or otherwise of the approach will be collected. A review of this evidence will enable changes to be made to the intervention to improve it. It is important to see this process as an opportunity to continually improve the e-learning strategy rather than to see it as a one-off test of its effectiveness. With the strong foundation of the intervention in theory and practice it is unlikely that the first attempt will be completely ineffective so that it requires the teacher to abandon the approach completely. Instead, the e-learning design is refined and then implemented again. Often the refined second implementation is quite similar to the first but with a different group of students (such as the next time the unit or course runs). The data collected may be the same, or could be modified because of the analysis and findings.

PHASE 4: Reflection to Produce Design Principles and Enhance Solution Implementation

Once a learning design or intervention has been implemented, evaluated and refined in cycles, the last phase is to reflect on the entire process to produce design principles that can inform future development and implementation decisions. There are potentially at least three useful outcomes of design research:

- The design principles
- Designed products or artefacts: the physical representations of the learning environment (e.g., website, CD-ROM)
- Societal outputs, such as professional development and learning.

Design Principles

A distinctive element of design research, and one that sets it apart from other research approaches (such as action research), is the production of design principles to advance both practical and theoretical understanding of the problem area. After the implementation and evaluation of the proposed solution, the draft principles that have guided the design of the solution need to be revisited. As a result of the findings from Phase 3, principles may need to be refined, revised, reorganised, combined, reduced, and possibly new principles will need to be added.

Practical Output of Design Research

The intervention that is designed and implemented in design research is often a computer-based or technology-based product that could be published or shared widely. The product of the design is viewed as a major output. However, a less tangible product may be the approach or method used (such as a particular pedagogical approach) rather than a physical one.

Societal Output of Design Research

The collaboration that is so integral to the process of designing and accomplishing a design research project has an additional benefit in that it enhances the professional development of all people involved, not only the students. For example, the project may have involved computer programmers, graphic designers, professional developers and so on, as well as the practitioners, academic colleagues and students involved directly in the study.

Reporting Design Research

Many teachers and faculty members, especially those working in institutions classified as research universities, recognise but rarely admit publicly, that the primary reason that they conduct research is that they are bound by the publish-or-perish rule, that is, they must publish in refereed research journals or fail to achieve tenure or be promoted. In this regard, publishing design research papers has particular limitations and problems.

Design research is such a new approach to educational inquiry that many journal editors and reviewers are unfamiliar with it. Many reviewers confuse the method with simple evaluations of software, or unfairly emphasise the *development* at the expense of the *research.* In addition, the narrative nature of design research reports means that they often easily exceed the word number limitations of traditional print journals.

Therefore, design researchers must be creative in their efforts to disseminate the findings of their research endeavours. First, we recommend that they regularly present in-progress reports of their design research initiatives at general international conferences as well as at discipline-specific conferences. There are several places within the phases of the approach where findings can usefully be shared in conferences. For example, by the end of Phase 2, a significant educational problem has been identified, the literature has been examined, practitioners have been consulted and importantly, a theory-based solution has been designed—all worthy of dissemination to colleagues at scientific gatherings. There is also the added benefit that peers can give advice and feedback on the proposed solution. Such a paper may not be acceptable at conferences where data analysis is a requirement for acceptance, but many conferences do take brief or in-progress papers where such dissemination would be most appropriate.

Second, researchers could create a project website with regular updates and a series of numbered interim reports of their findings. Additional related resources and links could also be featured on such a website.

Third, from time to time, researchers should submit syntheses of their conference papers and interim reports to both print and online journals. Online journals are particularly appropriate to design research on authentic e-learning as links can be made to the research website or possibly the learning site itself.

Fourth, at the conclusion of a major design research cycle, researchers should seek to publish a book and associated web resource that summarises the methods, results, and design principles emerging from the project. This may sound easy, but it requires a sharply focused attention to dissemination. Such a process is important as it helps to encapsulate the findings of each iterative cycle or stage into a whole and substantial contribution to the educational community, in the form of frameworks or guidelines for others to apply.

A Research Agenda for Authentic e-Learning

What questions should be pursued over the next decade to advance the state of the art of authentic e-learning?

There are many practical and theoretical impediments to the widespread use of the approach that have been discussed in earlier chapters that require solutions, such as:

- The difficulty of designing convincing tasks to carry complex and sustained learning;
- The role of participatory, social technologies in facilitating the creation and publication of genuine products;
- The impact of restrictive administrative and assessment policies in higher education;
- The means to reduce the high workload associated with e-learning student support;
- The impact of reduced funding and resources for e-learning course development in universities;
- The most appropriate means to share authentic e-learning designs;
- Restrictions of mandatory use of learning management systems and virtual learning environments;
- Potential lack of student engagement (at least initially by some students);
- The means to provide authentic assessment within learning management systems;
- The role of motivation in student accomplishment in authentic e-learning.

These areas of research in particular provide opportunities to advance understanding about authentic e-learning and to respond to the widespread use of technologies and web-based tools in society generally.

Design research offers a way forward towards more significant and socially responsible research. It requires that researchers in education:

- Explore significant educational problems, rather than conduct research for its own sake;
- Define a pedagogical outcome and create learning settings that address it;
- Emphasise content and pedagogy rather than technology;
- Give special attention to supporting human interactions and nurturing learning communities;
- Modify the learning design until the pedagogical outcome is reached;
- Reflect on the process to reveal design principles that can inform other teachers and researchers, and future development projects.

Nonetheless, the dominant mental models of educational technology research must evolve.

Certainly, the need for a more socially responsible research agenda in e-learning has never been greater. Instead of continuing to tinker around the edges of teaching and learning challenges by conducting quasi-experimental studies focused on small changes in learning environments, or even conducting one-off qualitative studies of esoteric cases, instructional technology researchers and their colleagues in other academic disciplines must begin to tackle the huge problems we face in the first quarter of the 21st Century. Design research offers a positive step in that incredibly important quest.

Conclusion

In reflecting on her role as a university teacher, Hogan (1996) made this observation:

> I was struck by the irony that I did an enormous amount of reading and thinking about education in order to prepare my lectures, plan effective workshops and select readings and texts for my students, while the students did relatively little. I was the most active learner in my classes—because I had total responsibility for what was learned and how it was presented (p. 79).

Hogan's observation resonates with many teachers and academics who spend hours preparing lectures, classes and online teaching sites for students. Many teachers express the view that they have never truly understood a concept or issue until they were required to teach it. Perhaps it is so with e-learning sites—the teachers or creators have a wonderful time ordering and simplifying concepts, presenting ideas and gathering resources, and the students just "do" the work. Using an authentic learning approach, the principal responsibility for what to learn and when to learn is no longer the teacher's. Instead, responsibility for learning rests with the learner.

The use of authentic e-learning in higher education has the capacity to reinvigorate online courses through the use of new participatory learning technologies, not only for delivery, but also as powerful cognitive tools and publication platforms. It has the potential to renew individual teachers' enthusiasm for their online teaching by challenging them to create innovative and complex tasks which are so carefully crafted that they have the ability to facilitate student learning across a whole semester unit or a large part of it.

Academic staff members are under increasing pressure to design e-learning courses in ways that help students to achieve higher-order outcomes such as thinking like experts, being able to accomplish work-related professional roles, and developing robust mental models of complex processes. But most of them are unable to accomplish this without design guidelines and substantial support. This book has been written to provide exactly this type of support.

References

Agostinho, S. (2006). Using characters in online simulated environments to guide authentic tasks. In A. Herrington & J. Herrington (Eds.), *Authentic learning environments in higher education* (pp. 88–95). Hershey, PA: Information Science Publishing.

Alessi, S. (1988). Fidelity in the design of instructional simulations. *Journal of Computer-Based Instruction, 15*(2), 40–47.

Alessi, S.M. (1996). Seeking common ground: Our conflicting viewpoints about learning and technology [Electronic Version]. *ITForum*, available online at http://itech1.coe.uga.edu/itforum/paper11/paper11.html.

Allen, D. (1999). *When twins marry twins* [Electronic Version]. Retrieved 17 February, 2006, from http://www.udel.edu/pbl/curric/biology-prob.html

Allen, I.E., & Seaman, J. (2003). *Sizing the opportunity: The quality and extent of online education in the United States, 2002 and 2003.* Needham, MA: The Sloan Consortium.

Allen, K.L., Galvis, D.L., and Katz, R.V. (2004). Evaluation of CDs and chewing gum in teaching dental anatomy. Paper presented at the *International Association for Dental Research 82nd General Session [Electronic Version].* Retrieved June 17, 2004, from http://iadr.confex.com/iadr/2004Hawaii/techprogram/abstract_40091.htm

Ambat, W.L. (2008). Localization and digitization: An approach to appreciating Shakespeare's plays. In *The 3rd National ICTs in Basic Education Conference.* Cebu City, Philippines: FitEd. http://www.fit-ed.org/congress2008/.

Ambrose, D.W. (1991). The effects of hypermedia on learning: A literature review. *Educational Technology, 31*(10), 51–55.

Anderson, L.W., & Krathwohl, D.R. (Eds.). (2001). *A taxonomy for learning, teaching and assessing: A revision of Bloom's Taxonomy of educational objectives.* New York: Longman.

Anderson, T. (2003). Modes of interaction in distance education: Recent developments and research questions. In M. G. Moore & W.G. Anderson (Eds.), *Handbook of distance education* (pp. 129–144). Mahwah, NJ: Lawrence Erlbaum Associates.

Angus, M., & Gray, J. (2002). *Description of a situated learning approach in a research Methods postgraduate subject.* Retrieved 17 February, 2004, from http://www.learningdesigns.uow.edu.au/exemplars/info/LD13/

Atwell, P., Lavin, D., Domina, T., & Levey, T. (2006). New evidence on college remediation. *Journal of Higher Education Policy and Management, 77*(5), 886–924.

Bain, J.D. (2003). Slowing the pendulum: Should we preserve some aspects of instructivism? In P. Kommers & G. Richards (Eds.), *World Conference on Educational Multimedia, Hypermedia and Telecommunications 2003* (pp. 1382–1388). Honolulu: AACE.

Bain, K. (2004). *What the best college teachers do.* Cambridge, MA: Harvard University Press.

Bannan-Ritland, B. (2003). The role of design in research: The integrative learning design framework. *Educational Researcher, 32*(1), 21–24.

Barab, S.A., & Landa, A. (1997). Designing effective interdisciplinary anchors. *Educational Leadership, 54*, 52–55.

Barab, S.A., Squire, K.D., & Dueber, W. (2000). A co-evolutionary model for supporting the emergence of authenticity. *Educational Technology Research & Development, 48*(2), 37–62.

Beetham, H., & Sharpe, R. (Eds.). (2007). *Rethinking pedagogy for a digital age.* London: Routledge.

Bereiter, C. (1984). How to keep thinking skills from going the way of all frills. *Educational Leadership, 42*, 75–77.

Bernard, R.M., Lou, Y., Abrami, P.C., Wozney, L., Borokhovski, E., Wallet, P. A., Wade, A., & Fiset, M. (2003). *How does distance education compare to classroom instruction? A meta-analysis of the empirical literature.* Paper presented at the Annual Meeting of the American Educational Research Association, April 2003, Chicago, IL. Available at: http://doe.concordia.ca/cslp/.

Bloom, B.S. (1956). *Taxonomy of educational objectives: The classification of education goals. Handbook 1: Cognitive domains.* New York: Longman.

Bloom, B.S. (1971). *Mastery learning.* New York: Holt, Rinehart, & Winston.

Bloom, B.S. (1977). Favorable learning conditions for all. *Teacher, 95*(3).

Bok, D. (2007). *Our underachieving colleges: A candid look at how much students learn and why they should be learning more.* Princeton, NJ: Princeton University Press.

Bottge, B.A., & Hasselbring, T.S. (1993). Taking word problems off the page. *Educational Leadership, 50*(7), 36–38.

Boud, D. (2006). Creating a space for reflection. In D. Boud, P. Cressey, & P. Docherty (Eds.), *Productive reflection at work* (pp. 158–169). London: Routledge.

Boud, D., Keogh, R., & Walker, D. (1985). Promoting reflection in learning: A model. In D. Boud, R. Keogh, & D. Walker (Eds.), *Reflection: Turning experience into learning* (pp. 18–40). London: Kogan Page.

Boud, D., & Knights, S. (1996). Reflective learning for social work: Research, theory and practice. In N. Gould & I. Taylor (Eds.), *Reflective learning for social work: Research, theory and practice* (pp. 23–34). Aldershot: Ashgate Publishing.

Brabazon, T. (2007). *The University of Google: Education in the [post] information age.* Hampshire: Ashgate.

Bransford, J.D., Sherwood, R.D., Hasselbring, T.S., Kinzer, C.K., & Williams, S.M. (1990). Anchored instruction: Why we need it and how technology can help. In D. Nix & R. Spiro (Eds.), *Cognition, education and multimedia: Exploring ideas in high technology* (pp. 115–141). Hillsdale, NJ: Lawrence Erlbaum.

Bransford, J.D., Vye, N., Kinzer, C., & Risko, V. (1990). Teaching thinking and content knowledge: Toward an integrated approach. In B.F. Jones & L. Idol (Eds.), *Dimensions of thinking and cognitive instruction* (pp. 381–413). Hillsdale, NJ: Lawrence Erlbaum.

Britto, M. (2002). *An exploratory study of the development of a survey instrument to measure the pedagogical dimensions of web-based instruction.* Unpublished Doctoral Thesis. The University of Georgia.

Brophy, J., & Alleman, J. (1991). Activities as instructional tools: A framework for analysis and evaluation. *Educational Researcher, 20*(4), 9–23.

Brown, A.L. (1997). Transforming schools into communities of thinking and learning about serious matters. *American Psychologist, 52*(4), 399–413.

Brown, A.L., & Campione, J.C. (1994). Guided discovery in a community of learners. In K. McGilly (Ed.), *Classroom lessons: Integrating cognitive theory and classroom practice* (pp. 229–270). Cambridge, MA: MIT Press.

Brown, J.S., Collins, A., & Duguid, P. (1989a). Debating the situation: A rejoinder to Palincsar and Wineburg. *Educational Researcher, 18*(5), 10–12.

Brown, J.S., Collins, A., & Duguid, P. (1989b). Situated cognition and the culture of learning. *Educational Researcher, 18*(1), 32–42.

Brown, J.S., & Duguid, P. (1993). Stolen knowledge. *Educational Technology, 33*(3), 10–15.

Brown, J.S., & Duguid, P. (1994). Practice at the periphery: A reply to Steven Tripp. *Educational Technology, 34*(10), 9–11.

Burton, L. (1992). Who assesses whom and to what purpose? In M. Stephens & J. Izard (Eds.), *Reshaping assessment practices: Assessment in the mathematical sciences under challenge* (pp. 1–18). Hawthorn, Vic: ACER.

Burton, R.R., Brown, J.S., & Fischer, G. (1984). Skiing as a model of instruction. In B. Rogoff & J. Lave (Eds.), *Everyday cognition: Its development in social context* (pp. 139–150). Cambridge, MA: Harvard University Press.

Butin, D.W. (Ed.). (2005). *Service-learning in higher education: Critical issues and directions.* New York: Palgrave.

Candy, P., Harri-Augstein, S., & Thomas, L. (1985). Reflection and the self-organized learner: A model for learning conversations. In D. Boud,

R. Keogh, & D. Walker (Eds.), *Reflection: Turning experience into learning* (pp. 100–116). London: Kogan Page.

Carroll, J.B. (1963). A model of school learning. *Teachers College Record, 64*, 723–733.

Carroll, J.B. (1989). The Carroll model: A 25-year retrospective and prospective view. *Educational Researcher, 18*(1), 26–31.

Cavanaugh, C.S. (2001). The effectiveness of interactive distance education technologies in K-12 learning: A meta-analysis. *International Journal of Educational Telecommunications, 7*(1), 73–88.

CEO Forum on Education and Technology. (2001). *Student achievement in the 21st Century: Assessment, alignment, accountability, access, analysis.* Retrieved February 12, 2009, from http://www.ceoforum.org/

Chee, Y.S. (1995). Cognitive apprenticeship and its application to the teaching of Smalltalk in a multimedia interactive learning environment. *Instructional Science, 23*, 133–161.

Cheng, H.-C., Lehman, J., & Armstrong, P. (1991). Comparison of performance and attitude in traditional and computer conference classes. *The American Journal of Distance Education, 5*(3), 51–64.

Choi, J., & Hannafin, M. (1995). Situated cognition and learning environments: Roles, structures and implications for design. *Educational Technology Research & Development, 43*(2), 53–69.

Clark, R.E. (Ed.). (2001). *Learning from media: Arguments, analysis, and evidence.* Greenwich, CT: Information Age Publishing.

Clarke, D.M. (2003). Changing assessment for changing times. In S. Jaffer & L. Burgess (Eds.), *Proceedings of the 9th National Congress of the Association for Mathematics Education of South Africa* (Vol. 1, pp. 1–10). Cape Town, South Africa: AMESA.

Clayden, E., Desforges, C., Mills, C., & Rawson, W. (1994). Authentic activity and learning. *British Journal of Educational Studies, 42*(2), 163–173.

Clements, M.A., & Ellerton, N.F. (1996). *Mathematics education research: Past, present and future.* Bangkok, Thailand: UNESCO.

Cobb, P., Confrey, J., diSessa, A., Lehrer, R., & Schauble, L. (2003). Design experiments in educational research. *Educational Researcher, 32*(1), 9–13.

Cognition and Technology Group at Vanderbilt. (1990a). Anchored instruction and its relationship to situated cognition. *Educational Researcher, 19*(6), 2–10.

Cognition and Technology Group at Vanderbilt. (1990b). Technology and the design of generative learning environments. *Educational Technology, 31*(5), 34–40.

Cognition and Technology Group at Vanderbilt. (1993a). Anchored instruction and situated cognition revisited. *Educational Technology, 33*(3), 52–70.

Cognition and Technology Group at Vanderbilt. (1993b). Toward integrated curricula: Possibilities from anchored instruction. In M. Rabinowitz (Ed.),

Cognitive science foundations of instruction (pp. 33–55). Hillsdale, NJ: Lawrence Erlbaum Associates.

Cole, N. (1990). Conceptions of educational achievement. *Educational Researcher, 19*(3), 2–7.

Collen, A. (1996). Reflection and metaphor in conversation. *Educational Technology, 36*(1), 54–55.

Collins, A. (1988). *Cognitive apprenticeship and instructional technology.* Cambridge, MA: BBN Labs Inc.

Collins, A. (1991). The role of computer technology in restructuring schools. *Phi Delta Kappan, 73*(1), 28–36.

Collins, A., & Brown, J.S. (1988). The computer as a tool for learning through reflection. In H. Mandl & A. Lesgold (Eds.), *Learning issues for intelligent tutoring systems* (pp. 1–18). New York: Springer-Verlag.

Collins, A., Brown, J.S., & Holum, A. (1991). Cognitive apprenticeship: Making thinking visible. *American Educator, 15*(3), 6–11, 38–46.

Collins, A., Brown, J.S., & Newman, S.E. (1989). Cognitive apprenticeship: Teaching the crafts of reading, writing, and mathematics. In L.B. Resnick (Ed.), *Knowing, learning and instruction: Essays in honour of Robert Glaser* (pp. 453–494). Hillsdale, NJ: LEA.

Commonwealth of Australia. (2001). *Universities in crisis.* Retrieved July 13, 2008, from http://www.aph.gov.au/senate/Committee/eet_ctte/completed_inquiries/1999-02/public_uni/report/contents.htm

Conole, G., & Fill, K. (2005). A learning design toolkit to create pedagogically effective learning activities. *Journal of Interactive Media in Education, 8*(08), 1–16.

Coomes, M.D., & DeBard, R. (Eds.). (2004). *Serving the millennial generation: New directions for student services.* San Francisco: Jossey-Bass.

Creswell, J.W., & Plano-Clark, V.L. (2006). *Designing and conducting mixed methods of research.* Thousand Oaks, CA: Sage.

Cronin, J.C. (1993). Four misconceptions about authentic learning. *Educational Leadership, 50*(7), 78–80.

Csikszentmihalyi, M. (1992). *Flow: The psychology of happiness.* London: Rider.

Cuban, L. (2001). *Oversold and underused: Computers in the classroom.* Cambridge, MA: Harvard University Press.

Cumming, J.J., & Maxwell, G.S. (1999). Contextualising authentic assessment. *Assessment in Education, 6*(2), 177–194.

Davydov, V.V. (1995). The influence of L.S. Vygotsky on education theory, research and practice. *Educational Researcher, 24*(3), 12–21.

Del Marie Rysavy, S., & Sales, G.C. (1991). Cooperative learning in computer-based instruction. *Educational Technology Research & Development, 39*(2), 70–79.

Design-Based Research Collective. (2003). Design-based research: An emerging paradigm for educational inquiry. *Educational Researcher, 32*(1), 5–8.

Dick, W., & Carey, L. (1990). *The systematic design of instruction* (3rd ed.). Glenview, IL: Scott Foresman.

Dillon, A., & Gabbard, R. (1998). Hypermedia as an educational technology: A review of the quantitative research literature on learning comprehension, control and style. *Review of Educational Research, 68*(3), 322–349.

Dreyfus, H., & Dreyfus, S. (1989). Why computers may never think like people. In T. Forester (Ed.), *Computers in the human context: Information technology, productivity and people.* Oxford: Basil Blackwell.

Duchastel, P.C. (1997). A Web-based model for university instruction. *Journal of Educational Technology Systems, 25*(3), 221–228.

Dunlap, J.C., & Grabinger, R.C. (1996). Rich environments for active learning in the higher education classroom. In B.G. Wilson (Ed.), *Constructivist learning environments: Case studies in instructional design* (pp. 65–82). Englewood Cliffs, NJ: Educational Technology.

Dwyer, D. (1995). Finding the future in the past: Readying schools for the 21st century. In R. Oliver & M. Wild (Eds.), *Proceedings of the Australian Computers in Education Conference* (Vol. 1, pp. 19–30). Perth: ECAWA.

Ebner, M., Holzinger, A., & Maurer, H. (2007). Web 2.0 technology: Future interfaces for technology enhanced learning? *Lecture Notes in Computer Science, 4556*(559–568).

Ecclestone, K., & Swann, J. (1999). Litigation and learning: Tensions in improving university lecturers' assessment practice. *Assessment in Education, 6*(3), 377–389.

Edelson, D.C. (2006). Balancing innovation and risk: Assessing design research proposals. In J. van den Akker, K. Gravemeijer, S. McKenney, & N. Nieveen (Eds.), *Educational design research* (pp. 100–106). London: Routledge.

Edelson, D.C., Pea, R.D., & Gomez, L. (1996). Constructivism in the collaboratory. In B.G. Wilson (Ed.), *Constructivist learning environments: Case studies in instructional design* (pp. 151–164). Englewood Cliffs, NJ: Educational Technology Publications.

Ehrenberg, R.G. (2005). Method or madness? Inside the USNWR college rankings. *Journal of College Admission, 189*, 29–35.

Entwhistle, N., Entwhistle, A., & Tait, H. (1993). Academic understanding and contexts to enhance it. In T.M. Duffy, J. Lowyck, & D.H. Jonassen (Eds.), *Designing environments for constructive learning* (pp. 331–357). Heidelberg: Springer-Verlag.

Feuer, M.J., Towne, L., & Shavelson, R.J. (2002). Scientific culture and educational research. *Educational Researcher, 31*(8), 4–14.

Fink, L.D. (2003). *Creating significant learning experiences: An integrated approach to designing college courses.* San Francisco: Jossey-Bass.

Fitzsimmons, J. (2006). Speaking snake: Authentic learning and the study of literature. In A. Herrington & J. Herrington (Eds.), *Authentic learning environments in higher education* (pp. 162–171). Hershey, PA: Information Science Publishing.

Flavell, J.H. (1979). Metacognition and cognitive monitoring: A new area of psychological inquiry. *American Psychologist, 34,* 906–911.

Forman, E.A., & Cazden, C.B. (1985). Exploring Vygotskyan perspectives in education: The cognitive value of peer interaction. In J.V. Wertsch (Ed.), *Culture, communication and cognition: Vygotskian perspectives* (pp. 323–347). Cambridge: Cambridge University Press.

Fosnot, C. (1996). *Constructivism: Theory, perspectives, and practice.* New York: Teachers College.

Friedman, T.L. (2005). *The world is flat: A brief history of the twenty-first century.* New York: Farrar, Straus and Giroux.

Gagné, R.M., Briggs, L.J., & Wager, W.W. (1992). *Principles of instructional design* (4th ed.). Orlando FL: Harcourt, Brace, Jovanovich.

Gardner, H. (1992). Assessment in context: The alternative to standardized testing. In B.R. Gifford & M.C. O'Connor (Eds.), *Changing assessment: Alternative views of aptitude, achievement and instruction* (pp. 77–119). Boston: Kluwer.

Gawande, A. (2007). *Better: A surgeon's notes on performance.* New York: Picador.

Gay, L.R. (1992). *Educational research: Competencies for analysis and application* (4th ed.). New York: Merrill.

Gick, M.L., & Holyoak, K.J. (1980). Analogical problem solving. *Cognitive Psychology, 12,* 306–355.

Goodman, F.L. (1995). Practice in theory. *Simulation and gaming, 26,* 178–190.

Goodyear, P., Salmon, G., Spector, J.M., Steeples, C., & Tickner, S. (2001). Competencies for online teaching. *Educational Technology Research & Development, 49*(1), 65–72.

Gordon, R. (1998). Balancing real-world problems with real-world results. *Phi Delta Kappan, 79,* 390–393.

Gott, S.P., Lesgold, A., & Kane, R.S. (1996). Tutoring for transfer of technical competence. In B.G. Wilson (Ed.), *Constructivist learning environments: Case studies in instructional design* (pp. 33–48). Englewood Cliffs, NJ: Educational Technology.

Green, M.E., & Sulbaran, T. (2006). Preview of using distributed virtual reality in construction scheduling education. In T.C. Reeves & S.F. Yamashita (Eds.), *Proceedings of ELearn Conference 2006* (pp. 51–56). Chesapeake, VA: AACE.

Greenfield, P.M. (1984). A theory of the teacher in the learning activities of everyday life. In B. Rogoff & J. Lave (Eds.), *Everyday cognition: Its development in social context* (pp. 117–138). Cambridge, MA: Harvard University Press.

Greenhalgh, M. (2002). Learning art history in context: A model of Borobudur and the limits of reality. *The Journal of Education, Community and Values: Interface on the Internet, 2*(6), 1–14.

Griffin, M.M. (1995). You can't get there from here: Situated learning, transfer and map skills. *Contemporary Educational Psychology, 20*, 65–87.

Harley, S. (1993). Situated learning and classroom instruction. *Educational Technology, 33*(3), 46–51.

Harrow, A.J. (1972). *A taxonomy of the psychomotor domain: A guide for developing behavioral objectives.* New York: David McKay.

Herrington, J., & Herrington, A. (1998). Authentic assessment and multimedia: How university students respond to a model of authentic assessment. *Higher Education Research & Development, 17*(3), 305–322.

Herrington, J., & Herrington, A. (2006). Authentic conditions for authentic assessment: Aligning task and assessment. In A. Bunker & I. Vardi (Eds.), *Research and Development in Higher Education Volume 29, Critical visions: Thinking, learning and researching in higher education* (pp. 146–151). Milperra, NSW: HERDSA.

Herrington, J., Mantei, J., Herrington, A., Olney, I., & Ferry, B. (2008). New technologies, new pedagogies: Mobile technologies and new ways of teaching and learning. In *Proceedings ascilite Melbourne 2008* (pp. 419–427). Melbourne: ASCILITE. Available http://www.ascilite.org.au/conferences/melbourne08/procs/herrington-j.pdf.

Herrington, J., & Oliver, R. (2000). An instructional design framework for authentic learning environments. *Educational Technology Research and Development, 48*(3), 23–48.

Herrington, J., & Oliver, R. (2006). Professional development for the online teacher: An authentic approach. In A. Herrington & J. Herrington (Eds.), *Authentic learning environments in higher education* (pp. 283–295). Hershey, PA: ISP

Herrington, J., Oliver, R., & Herrington, A. (2007). Authentic learning on the web: Guidelines for course design. In B. Khan (Ed.), *Flexible learning in an information society* (pp. 26–35). Hershey, PA: ISP.

Herrington, J., Oliver, R., & Reeves, T.C. (2003). Patterns of engagement in authentic online learning environments. *Australian Journal of Educational Technology, 19*(1), 59–71 http://www.ascilite.org.au/ajet/ajet19/res/herrington.html.

Herrington, J., Reeves, T.C., & Oliver, R. (2007). Immersive learning technologies: Realism and online authentic learning. *Journal of Computing in Higher Education, 19*(1), 65–84.

Herrington, J., Reeves, T.C., Oliver, R., & Woo, Y. (2004). Designing authentic activities in web-based courses. *Journal of Computing in Higher Education, 16*(1), 3–29.

Herrington, J., & Standen, P. (2000). Moving from an instructivist to a constructivist multimedia learning environment. *Journal of Educational Multimedia and Hypermedia, 9*(3), 195–205.

Hersh, R.H., & Merrow, J. (Eds.). (2005). *Declining by degrees: Higher education at risk.* New York: Palgrave Macmillan.

Hmelo, C., & Evensen, D.H. (2000). Problem-based learning: gaining insights on learning interactions through multiple methods of enquiry. In C. Hmelo & D.H. Evensen (Eds.), *Problem-based learning* (pp. 1–16). Mahwah, NJ: LEA.

Hoffman, B., & Ritchie, D. (1997). Using multimedia to overcome the problems with problem based learning. *Instructional Science, 25*, 97–115.

Hogan, C. (1996). Getting students to do their reading, think about it and share their ideas and responses. In J. Abbott & L. Willcoxson (Eds.), *Teaching and learning within and across disciplines* (pp. 79–82). Perth, WA: Murdoch University.

Honebein, P.C., Duffy, T.M., & Fishman, B.J. (1993). Constructivism and the design of learning environments: Context and authentic activities for learning. In T.M. Duffy, J. Lowyck, & D.H. Jonassen (Eds.), *Designing environments for constructive learning* (pp. 87–108). Heidelberg: Springer-Verlag.

Hooper, S. (1992). Cooperative learning and computer-based design. *Educational Technology Research & Development, 40*(3), 21–38.

Howe, N., & Strauss, W. (2000). *Millennials rising: The next great generation.* New York: Vintage Books.

Hummel, H.G.K. (1993). Distance education and situated learning: Paradox or partnership? *Educational Technology, 33*(12), 11–22.

Iiyoshi, T., & Kumar, M.S.V. (2008). *Opening up education: The collective advancement of education through open technology, open content, and open knowledge.* Cambridge, MA: MIT Press.

Jacob, S.M., & Issac, B. (2008). Mobile technologies and its impact: An analysis in higher education context. *International Journal of Interactive Mobile Technologies, 2*(1), 10–18.

James, R., & McInnis, C. (2001). Strategically re-positioning student assessment: A discussion paper on the assessment of student learning in universities. Retrieved December 2006, from http://www.cshe.unimelb.edu.au/downloads/Assess.pdf

Jenkins, H. (2007). Confronting the challenges of participatory culture. Retrieved October 2008, from http://digitallearning.macfound.org/

Jonassen, D. (1991a). Context is everything. *Educational Technology, 31*(5), 35–37.

Jonassen, D. (1991b). Evaluating constructivistic learning. *Educational Technology, 31*(9), 28–33.

Jonassen, D. (1993). The trouble with learning environments. *Educational Technology, 33*(1), 35–37.

Jonassen, D. (1994). Towards a constructivist design model. *Educational Technology, 34*(4), 34–37.

Jonassen, D. (1995). Supporting communities of learners with technology: A vision for integrating technology with learning in schools. *Educational Technology, 35*(5), 60–63.

Jonassen, D., Mayes, T., & McAleese, R. (1993). A manifesto for a constructivist approach to uses of technology in higher education. In T.M. Duffy,

J. Lowyck, & D.H. Jonassen (Eds.), *Designing environments for constructive learning* (pp. 231–247). Heidelberg: Springer-Verlag.

Jonassen, D., & Reeves, T.C. (1996). Learning with technology: Using computers as cognitive tools. In D.H. Jonassen (Ed.), *Handbook of research on educational communications and technology* (pp. 693–719). New York: Macmillan.

Jonassen, D.H., & Grabowski, B.L. (1983). *Handbook of individual differences, learning, and instruction.* Hillsdale, NJ: Lawrence Erlbaum Associates.

Jones, S. (2006). Using IT to augment authentic learning environments. In A. Herrington & J. Herrington (Eds.), *Authentic learning environments in higher education* (pp. 172–181). Hershey, PA: Information Science Publishing.

Kantor, R.J., Waddington, T., & Osgood, R.E. (2000). Fostering the suspension of disbelief: The role of authenticity in goal-based scenarios. *Interactive Learning Environments, 8*(3), 211–227.

Katz, S., & Lesgold, A. (1993). The role of the tutor in computer-based collaborative learning situations. In S.P. Lajoie & S.J. Derry (Eds.), *Computers as cognitive tools* (pp. 289–317). Hillsdale, NJ: Lawrence Erlbaum.

Keen, A. (2007). *The cult of the amateur: How today's internet is killing our culture and assaulting the economy.* London: Nicholas Brealey Publishing.

Kelly, A.E. (2003). Research as design. *Educational Researcher, 32*(1), 3–4.

Kemmis, S. (1985). Action research and the politics of reflection. In D. Boud, R. Keogh, & D. Walker (Eds.), *Reflection: Turning experience into learning* (pp. 139–163). London: Kogan Page.

Kim, B., & Reeves, T.C. (2007). Reframing research on learning with technology: In search of the meaning of cognitive tools. *Instructional Science, 35,* 207–256.

Klein, G.A., & Hoffman, R.R. (1993). Seeing the invisible: Perceptual-cognitive aspects of expertise. In M. Rabinowitz (Ed.), *Cognitive science foundations of instruction* (pp. 203–226). Hillsdale, NJ: Lawrence Erlbaum Associates.

Knights, S. (1985). Reflection and learning: The importance of a listener. In D. Boud, R. Keogh, & D. Walker (Eds.), *Reflection: Turning experience into learning* (pp. 85–90). London: Kogan Page.

Koenders, A. (2002). Creating opportunities from challenges in on-line introductory biology. In A. Goody, J. Herrington, & M. Northcote (Eds.), *Quality conversations: Research and Development in Higher Education, Volume 25* (pp. 393–400). Jamison, ACT: HERDSA.

Kolbe, K. (1990). *The conative connection: Acting on instinct.* Reading, MA: Addison-Wesley.

Kolbitsch, J., & Maurer, H. (2006). The transformation of the web: How emerging communities shape the information we consume. *Journal of Universal Computer Science, 12*(2), 187–213.

Koory, M.A. (2003). Differences in learning outcomes for the online and F2F versions of An Introduction to Shakespeare. *Journal of Asynchronous*

Learning Networks, 7. Retrieved January 2007, from http://www.aln.org/publications/jaln/v7n2/index.asp

Krathwohl, D.R., Bloom, B.S., & Masia, B.B. (1964). *Taxonomy of educational objectives: The classification of educational goals. Handbook II: The affective domain*. New York: David McKay.

Kroll, D.L., Masingila, J.O., & Mau, S.T. (1992). Grading cooperative problem solving. *Mathematics Teacher, 85*(8), 619–627.

Kuh, G.D. (2001). Assessing what really matters to student learning: Inside the National Survey of Student Engagement (NSSE). *Change, 33*(3), 10–17, 66.

Kuh, G.D. (2003). What we're learning about student engagement from NSSE. *Change, 35*(2), 24–32.

Kuh, G.D., Kinzie, J., Schuh, J.H., & Whitt, E.J. (2005). *Student success in college: Creating conditions that matter*. San Francisco: Jossey-Bass.

Kuh, G.D., Laird, T.N., & Umbach, P. (2004). Aligning faculty activities and student behavior: Realizing the promise of greater expectations. *Liberal Education, 90*(4), 24–31.

Lajoie, S. (1991). A framework for authentic assessment in mathematics. *NCRMSE Research Review: The Teaching and Learning of Mathematics, 1*(1), 6–12.

Lajoie, S.P. (Ed.). (2000). *Computers as cognitive tools: No more walls*. Mahwah, NJ: LEA.

Laurel, B. (1993). *Computers as theatre*. Reading, MA: Addison-Wesley.

Lave, J., Murtagh, M., & de la Rocha, O. (1984). The dialectic of arithmetic in grocery shopping. In B. Rogoff & J. Lave (Eds.), *Everyday cognition: Its development in social context* (pp. 67–94). Cambridge, MA: Harvard University Press.

Lave, J., & Wenger, E. (1991). *Situated learning: Legitimate peripheral participation*. Cambridge: Cambridge University Press.

Lebow, D. (1993). Constructivist values for instructional systems design: Five principles toward a new mindset. *Educational Technology Research & Development, 41*(3), 4–16.

Lebow, D., & Wager, W.W. (1994). Authentic activity as a model for appropriate learning activity: Implications for emerging instructional technologies. *Canadian Journal of Educational Communication, 23*(3), 231–244.

Lee, B. (1985). Intellectual origins of Vygotsky's semiotic analysis. In J.V. Wertsch (Ed.), *Culture, communication and cognition: Vygotskian perspectives* (pp. 66–93). Cambridge: Cambridge University Press.

Lehrer, J. (2009). *How we decide*. Boston, MA: Houghton Mifflin Harcourt.

Leppisaari, I., Vainio, L., & Herrington, J. (2009). *Developing authentic e-learning through virtual benchmarking*. Paper presented at the *Ed-Media 2009 Conference*, Honolulu, Hawaii.

Linn, R.L., Baker, E.L., & Dunbar, S.B. (1991). Complex, performance-based assessment: Expectations and validation criteria. *Educational Researcher, 20*(8), 15–21.

Littlejohn, A., & Pegler, C. (2007). *Preparing for blended e-learning.* London: Routledge.

Liu, Y., Oh, E., & Reeves, T.C. (2009, April). *Self-regulated learning in an authentic, collaborative online learning environment.* Paper presented at the Annual Meeting of the American Educational Research Association, San Diego, CA.

Lockwood, F. (1992). *Activities in self-instructional texts.* London: Kogan Page.

Lombardi, M.M. (2007). *Approaches that work: How authentic learning is transforming higher education. ELI Report No 5.* Boulder, CO: EDUCAUSE.

MacDonald, M., & Bartlett, J.E. (2000). Comparison of Web-based and traditional delivery methods in a business communications unit. *Delta Pi Epsilon, 42*(2), 90–100.

Macedonia, M.R., & Rosenbloom, P.S. (2001). Entertainment technology and virtual environments for training and education. In M. Devlin, R. Larson, & J. Meyerson (Eds.), *The internet and the university: 2000 forum* (pp. 79–95). Boulder, CO: EDUCAUSE.

Machtmes, K., & Asher, J.W. (2000). A meta-analysis of the effectiveness of telecourses in distance education. *The American Journal of Distance Education, 14*(1), 27–46.

Maclellan, E. (2004). Authenticity in assessment tasks: A heuristic exploration of academics' perceptions. *Higher Education Research and Development, 23*(1), 19–33.

Maor, D., & Phillips, R. (1996). Developing a multimedia package for teaching thinking skills. In C. McBeath & R. Atkinson (Eds.), *The learning superhighway: New world? New worries?* (pp. 242–248). Perth, WA: Promaco Conventions.

Maor, D., & Taylor, P.C. (1995). Teacher epistemology and scientific inquiry in computerized classroom environments. *Journal of Research in Science Teaching, 32*(8), 839–854.

Marginson, S., & van der Wende, M.C. (2007). *Globalisation and higher education.* Paris: OECD/CERI.

Markham, T., Mergendoller, J., Larmer, J., & Ravitz, J. (2003). *Project based learning handbook* (2nd ed.). Novato, CA: Buck Institute for Education.

Marshall, C., & Rossman, G. (1999). *Designing qualitative research* (3rd ed.). Thousand Oaks, CA: Sage.

McKee, A. (2008). Reality versus authenticity: Mapping the scaffolding requirements for teaching intellectual skills for working in television. *Journal of Learning Design, 2*(2), 1–13.

McLellan, H. (1991). Virtual environments and situated learning. *Multimedia Review, 2*(3), 30–37.

McLellan, H. (1993). Evaluation in a situated learning environment. *Educational Technology, 33*(3), 39–45.

McLellan, H. (1994). Situated learning: Continuing the conversation. *Educational Technology, 34*(10), 7–8.

McLoughlin, C., & Luca, J. (2006). Applying situated learning theory to the creation of learning environments to enhance socialisation and self-regulation. In A. Herrington & J. Herrington (Eds.), *Authentic learning environments in higher education* (pp. 194–213). Hershey, PA: ISP.

McMahon, H., & O'Neill, W. (1993). Computer-mediated zones of engagement in learning. In T.M. Duffy, J. Lowyck, & D.H. Jonassen (Eds.), *Designing environments for constructive learning* (pp. 37–57). Heidelberg: Springer-Verlag.

Mercer, N. (1996). The quality of talk in children's collaborative activity in the classroom. *Learning and instruction, 6*(4), 359–377.

Meyer, C.A. (1992). What's the difference between authentic and performance assessment? *Educational Leadership, 49*(8), 39–40.

Milburn, D. (n.d.). Magellan's log: The willed suspension of disbelief. Retrieved July 2002, from www.texaschapbookpress.com/magellanslog8/disbelief.htm

Miller, G.A., & Gildea, P.M. (1987). How children learn words. *Scientific American, 257*(3), 86–91.

Miller, R. (2005). Integrative learning and assessment. *Peer Review, 7*(4), 11–14.

Ministerial Council for Education, E-Training and Youth Affairs (MCEETYA) (2005). *Learning in an online world: Contemporary learning.* Retrieved October 2008, from http://www.mceetya.edu.au/verve/_resources/

Mioduser, D., Nachmias, R., Oren, A., & Lahav, O. (1999). Web-based learning environments: Current states and emerging trends. In B. Collis & R. Oliver (Eds.), *Ed-Media 1999 World Conference on Educational Multimedia, Hypermedia and Telecommunications* (pp. 753–758). Seattle, WA: AACE.

Morgan, C., & O'Reilly, M. (2006). Ten key qualities of assessment online. In M. Hricko & S. Howell (Eds.), *Online assessment and measurement.* Hershey, PA: Information Science Publishing.

Morris, N.M., & Rouse, W.B. (1985). Review and evaluation of empirical research in troubleshooting. *Human Factors, 27*(5), 503–530.

Morrissey, P. (2006). *Not just a name on a wall.* Retrieved December, 2008, from http://www.notjustanameonawall.com/

Murray, C., & Cox, C. (1989). *Apollo: The race to the moon.* New York: Simon and Schuster.

Myers, S. (1993). A trial for Dmitri Karamazov. *Educational Leadership, 50*(7), 71–72.

Naidu, S. (2003). Designing instruction for e-learning environments. In M.G. Moore & W.G. Anderson (Eds.), *Handbook of distance education* (pp. 349–365). Mahwah, NJ: LEA.

New Media Consortium. (2008). *Horizon Report 2008: Australia-New Zealand.* Austin, TX: NMC.

Newfield, C. (2008). *Unmaking the public university: The forty year assault on the middle class.* Cambridge, MA: Harvard University Press.

Newmann, F.M., & Archbald, D.A. (1992). The nature of authentic academic achievement. In H. Berlak, F.M. Newmann, E. Adams, D.A. Archbald, T. Burgess, J. Raven, & T.A. Romberg (Eds.), *Toward a new science of educational testing and assessment* (pp. 71–84). Albany, NY: State University of New York Press.

Newmann, F.M., & Wehlage, G. (1993). Five standards of authentic instruction. *Educational Leadership, 50*(7), 8–12.

Norman, D.A. (1983). Some observations on mental models. In D. Gentner & A.L. Stevens (Eds.), *Mental models* (pp. 7–14). Hillsdale, NJ: LEA.

Norman, D. (1988). *The psychology of everyday things.* New York: Basic Books.

Norman, D. (1993). *Things that make us smart: Defending human attributes in the age of the machine.* Reading, MA: Addison-Wesley.

NSF Task Force on Cyberlearning. (2008). Fostering learning in the networked world: The Cyberlearning opportunity and challenge [Electronic Version]. Retrieved August 2008, from http://www.nsf.gov/pubs/2008/nsf08204/nsf08204.pdf

O'Reilly, M. (2000). Reinvigorating educational design for an online world. In R. Sims, M. O'Reilly, & S. Sawkins (Eds.), *Proceedings of the 17th Annual ASCILITE Conference* (pp. 255–264). Lismore, NSW: ASCILITE.

Oblinger, D., & Oblinger, J. (Eds.). (2005). *Educating the Net Gen.* Washington, DC: EDUCAUSE.

Oliver, R., & Herrington, J. (2001). *Teaching and learning online: A beginner's guide to e-learning and e-teaching in higher education.* Perth, WA: CRITC.

Oliver, R., & Omari, A. (1999). Using online technologies to support problem based learning: Learners responses and perceptions. *Australian Journal of Educational Technology, 15*(158–79).

Olney, I., Herrington, J., & Verenikina, I. (2009). Digital story telling using iPods. In J. Herrington, A. Herrington, M. Mantei, I. Olney, & B. Ferry (Eds.), *New technologies, new pedagogies: Mobile learning in higher education* (pp. 36–44). Wollongong: UOW.

Oosterhof, A., Conrad, R., & Ely, D. (Eds.). (2008). *Assessing learners online.* New York: Prentice Hall.

Oren, T. (1990). Cognitive load in hypermedia: Designing for the exploratory learner. In S. Ambron & K. Hooper (Eds.), *Learning with interactive multimedia* (pp. 126–136). Washington, DC: Microsoft Press.

Pais Marden, M., Herrington, J., & Herrington, A. (2007). Design-based research: Learning Italian at university in a community of learners. In C. Montgomerie & J. Seale (Eds.), *Proceedings of EdMedia 2007* (pp. 2966–2972). Chesapeake, VA: AACE.

Partnership for 21st Century Skills. (2007). *Beyond the three Rs: Voter attitudes toward 21st Century skills.* Retrieved March 2009, from http://www.21stcenturyskills.org/

Patton, M.Q. (1997). *Utilization-focused evaluation: The new century text* (3rd ed.). Thousand Oaks, CA: Sage.

Pea, R.D. (1991). Learning through multimedia. *IEEE Computer Graphics & Applications, 11*(4), 58–66.

Pearson, M., & Smith, D. (1985). Debriefing in experience-based learning. In D. Boud, R. Keogh, & D. Walker (Eds.), *Reflection: Turning experience into learning* (pp. 69–83). London: Kogan Page.

Pellegrino, J.W., Chudowsky, N., & Glaser, R. (Eds.). (2001). *Knowing what students know: The science and design of educational assessment.* Washington, DC: National Academy Press.

Pennell, R., Durham, M., Ozog, M., & Spark, A. (1997). Writing in context: Situated learning on the web. In R. Kevill, R. Oliver, & R. Phillips (Eds.), *Proceedings of the 14th Annual Conference of the Australian Society for Computers in Learning in Tertiary Education* (pp. 463–469). Perth, WA: Curtin University.

Perkins, D.N. (1991). What constructivism demands of the learner. *Educational Technology, 31*(8), 19–21.

Perreault, H.R. (1999). Authentic activities for business education. *Delta Pi Epsilon, 41*(1), 35–41.

Petraglia, J. (1998a). *Reality by design: The rhetoric and technology of authenticity in education.* Mahwah, NJ: LEA.

Petraglia, J. (1998b). The real world on a short leash: The (mis)application of constructivism to the design of educational technology. *Educational Technology Research & Development, 46*(3), 53–65.

Postman, N. (1992). *Technopoly: The surrender of culture to technology.* New York: Alfred A. Knopf, Inc.

Qin, Z., Johnson, D.W., & Johnson, R.T. (1995). Cooperative versus competitive efforts and problem solving. *Review of Educational Research, 65*(2), 129–143.

Rabkin, M.T. (2002). Patient simulators: Is it real or is it ultrasim? [Electronic Version]. *Prospective, 1.* Retrieved December 2008, from http://www.bidmc.harvard.edu/

Raschke, C. (2002). *The digital revolution and the coming of the postmodern university.* New York: RoutledgeFalmer.

Reeves, T.C. (1993a). Evaluating interactive multimedia. In D.M. Gayeski (Ed.), *Multimedia for learning: Development, application, evaluation* (pp. 97–112). Englewood Cliffs, NJ: Educational Technology Publications.

Reeves, T.C. (1993b). Interactive learning systems as mindtools. In P. Newhouse (Ed.), *Viewpoints 2* (pp. 2–11, 29). Perth: ECAWA.

Reeves, T.C. (1993c). Pseudoscience in computer-based instruction: The case of learner control research. *Journal of Computer-based Instruction, 20*(2), 39–46.

Reeves, T.C. (1999). A research agenda for interactive learning in the new millennium. In P. Kommers & G. Richards (Eds.), *Proceedings of EdMedia 1999* (pp. 15–20). Norfolk, VA: AACE.

Reeves, T.C. (2000). Alternative assessment approaches for online learning environments in higher education. *Journal of Educational Computing Research, 23*(1), 101–111.

Reeves, T.C. (2006). Design research from a technology perspective. In J. van den Akker, K. Gravemeijer, S. McKenney, & N. Nieveen (Eds.), *Educational design research* (pp. 52–66). London: Routledge.

Reeves, T.C., & Hedberg, J.G. (2003). *Interactive learning systems evaluation.* Englewood Cliffs, NJ: Educational Technology Publications.

Reeves, T.C., Herrington, J., & Oliver, R. (2005). Design research: A socially responsible approach to instructional technology research in higher education. *Journal of Computing in Higher Education, 16*(2), 97–116.

Reeves, T.C., & Laffey, J.M. (1999). Design, assessment, and evaluation of a problem-based learning environment in undergraduate engineering. *Higher Education Research and Development Journal, 18*(2), 219–232.

Reeves, T.C., & Okey, J.R. (1996). Alternative assessment for constructivist learning environments. In B.G. Wilson (Ed.), *Constructivist learning environments: Case studies in instructional design* (pp. 191–202). Englewood Cliffs, NJ: Educational Technology.

Reeves, T.C., & Reeves, P.M. (1997). Effective dimensions of interactive learning on the World Wide Web. In B.H. Khan (Ed.), *Web-based instruction* (pp. 59–66). Englewood Cliffs, NJ: Educational Technology.

Repman, J., Weller, H.G., & Lan, W. (1993). The impact of social context on learning in hypermedia-based instruction. *Journal of Educational Multimedia & Hypermedia, 2*(3), 283–298.

Resnick, L. (1987). Learning in school and out. *Educational Researcher, 16*(9), 13–20.

Resnick, L.B., & Resnick, D.P. (1992). Assessing the thinking curriculum: New tools for educational reform. In B.R. Gifford & M.C. O'Connor (Eds.), *Changing assessment: Alternative views of aptitude, achievement and instruction* (pp. 37–75). Boston, MA: Kluwer.

Ridley, D.S. (1992). Reflective self-awareness: A basic motivational process. *Journal of Experimental Education, 60*(1), 31–48.

Riesbeck, C.K. (1996). Case-based teaching and constructivism: Carpenters and tools. In B.G. Wilson (Ed.), *Constructivist learning environments: Case studies in instructional design* (pp. 49–61). Englewood Cliffs, NJ: Educational Technology.

Rist, R. (1973). *The urban school: A factory for failure.* Cambridge, MA: MIT Press.

Rogoff, B. (1984). Introduction: Thinking and learning in social context. In B. Rogoff & J. Lave (Eds.), *Everyday cognition: Its development in social context* (pp. 1–8). Cambridge, MA: Harvard University Press.

Rosenberg, M. J. (2006). *Beyond e-learning.* San Francisco: Pfeiffer.

Ross, S.M., Morrison, G.R., & Lowther, D.L. (2005). Using experimental methods in higher education research. *Journal of Computing in Higher Education, 16*(2), 39–64.

Russell, T.L. (1999). *The no significant difference phenomenon* Montgomery, AL: International Distance Education Certification Center.

Saettler, P. (1990). *The evolution of American educational technology.* Englewood, CO: Libraries Unlimited.

Salmon, G. (2004). *E-moderating: The key to teaching and learning online.* London: Routledge.

Sandberg, J., & Wielinga, B. (1992). Situated cognition: A paradigm shift? *Journal of Artificial Intelligence in Education, 3,* 129–138.

Savery, J.R., & Duffy, T.M. (1996). Problem based learning: An instructional model and its constructivist framework. In B.G. Wilson (Ed.), *Constructivist learning environments: Case studies in instructional design* (pp. 135–148). Englewood Cliffs, NJ: Educational Technology.

Schneider, C.G. (2005). Liberal education: Slip-sliding away. In R.H. Hersh & J. Merrow (Eds.), *Declining by degrees: Higher education at risk* (pp. 61–76). New York: Palgrave Macmillan.

Schoenfeld, A.H. (1991). On mathematics as sense making: An informal attack on the unfortunate divorce of formal and informal mathematics. In D.N. Perkins, J. Segal, & J. Voss (Eds.), *Informal reasoning and education* (pp. 311–343). Hillsdale, NJ: LEA.

Schooley, C. (2005). *Get ready: The millennials are coming! Changing workforce.* Cambridge, MA: Forrester Research.

Scribner, S. (1984). Studying working intelligence. In B. Rogoff & J. Lave (Eds.), *Everyday cognition: Its development in social context* (pp. 9–40). Cambridge, MA: Harvard University Press.

Sharples, M., Taylor, J., & Vavoula, G. (2005). Towards a theory of mobile learning. In H. van der Merwe & T. Brown (Eds.), *mLearn 2005. 4th World Conference on mLearning. Mobile Technologies.* Cape Town, South Africa: mLearn 2005

Shipman, D., Aloi, S.L., & Jones, E.A. (2003). Addressing key challenges in higher education assessment. *Journal of General Education, 52*(4), 335–346.

Siemens, G. (2006). *Learning or management system? A review of learning management system reviews.* Retrieved 20 April 2009, from http://ltc.umanitoba.ca/wordpress/wp-content/uploads/2006/

Slavin, R.E. (1996). Research on cooperative learning and achievement: What we know, what we need to know. *Contemporary Educational Psychology, 21,* 43–69.

Smith, P.E. (1986). *Instructional simulation: Research, theory and a case study.* Eric Document 267 793.

Smith, P.E. (1987). Simulating the classroom with media and computers. *Simulation and Games, 18*(3), 395–413.

Snow, R.E., Corno, L., & Jackson, D. (1996). Individual differences in affective and conative functions. In D.C. Berliner & R.C. Calfee (Eds.), *Handbook of Educational Psychology* (pp. 243–310). New York: Macmillan.

Sperber, M. (2005). How undergraduate education became college lite—and a personal apology. In R.H. Hersh & J. Merrow (Eds.), *Declining by degrees: Higher education at risk* (pp. 131–143). New York: Palgrave Macmillan.

Spiro, R.J., Feltovich, P.J., Jacobson, M.J., & Coulson, R.L. (1991a). Cognitive flexibility, constructivism, and hypertext: Random access instruction for advanced knowledge acquisition in ill-structured domains. *Educational Technology, 31*(5), 24–33.

Spiro, R.J., Feltovich, P.J., Jacobson, M.J., & Coulson, R.L. (1991b). Knowledge representation, content specification, and the development of skill in situation-specific knowledge assembly: Some constructivist issues as they relate to cognitive flexibility theory and hypertext. *Educational Technology, 31*(9), 22–25.

Spiro, R.J., Vispoel, W.P., Schmitz, J.G., Samarapungavan, A., & Boeger, A.E. (1987). Knowledge acquisition for application: Cognitive flexibility and transfer in complex content domains. In B.K. Britton & S.M. Glynn (Eds.), *Executive control processes in reading* (Vol. 31, pp. 177–199). Hillsdale, NJ: Lawrence Erlbaum Associates.

Standen, P., & Herrington, J. (1996). Multimedia simulations: A new use for technology in tertiary education. In *Proceedings of the Higher Education Research and Development Society of Australasia Conference* (pp. 832–836). Perth: HERDSA.

Sternberg, R.J., Wagner, R.K., & Okagaki, L. (1993). Practical intelligence: The nature and role of tacit knowledge in work and at school. In J.M. Puckett & H.W. Reese (Eds.), *Mechanisms of everyday cognition* (pp. 205–227). Hillsdale, NJ: LEA.

Surowiecki, J. (2004). *The wisdom of crowds: Why the many are smarter than the few and how collective wisdom shapes business, economies, societies, and nation.* New York: Doubleday.

Taplin, M. (2000). Problem-based learning in distance education: Practitioners' beliefs about an action learning project. *Distance Education, 21*(2), 284–307.

Tapscott, D. (1998). *Growing up digital: The rise of the net generation.* New York: McGraw-Hill.

Tapscott, D., & Williams, A.D. (2006). *Wikinomics: How mass collaboration changes everything.* New York: Penguin.

Taras, M. (2005). Assessment—summative and formative—some theoretical reflections. *British Journal of Educational Studies, 53*(4), 466–478.

Thatcher, D.C. (1990). Promoting learning through games and simulations. *Simulation and gaming, 21*(3), 262–273.

Torrance, H. (1995). Introduction. In H. Torrance (Ed.), *Evaluating authentic assessment: Problems and possibilities in new approaches to assessment* (pp. 1–8). Buckingham: Open University Press.

Traxler, J. (2007). Defining, discussing, and evaluating mobile learning: The moving finger writes and having writ . . . *International Review of Research in Open & Distance Learning, 8*(2), 1–12.

Tripp, S.D. (1993). Theories, traditions and situated learning. *Educational Technology, 33*(3), 71–77.

Twenge, J.M. (2006). *Generation me: Why today's young Americans are more confident, assertive, entitled—and more miserable than ever before.* New York: Free Press.

Twigg, C.A. (2003). Quality, cost and access: The case for redesign. In M.S. Pittinsky (Ed.), *The wired tower: Perspectives on the impact of the internet on higher education* (pp. 111–143). Upper Saddle River, NJ: Prentice Hall.

van den Akker, J. (1999). Principles and methods of development research. In J. van den Akker, N. Nieveen, R.M. Branch, K.L. Gustafson, & T. Plomp (Eds.), *Design methodology and developmental research in education and training* (pp. 1–14). The Netherlands: Kluwer.

van den Akker, J., Gravemeijer, K., McKenney, S., & Nieveen, N. (2006a). Introducing educational design research. In J. van den Akker, K. Gravemeijer, S. McKenney, & N. Nieveen (Eds.), *Educational design research* (pp. 3–7). London: Routledge.

van den Akker, J., Gravemeijer, K., McKenney, S., & Nieveen, N. (Eds.). (2006b). *Educational design research.* London: Routledge.

von Wright, J. (1992). Reflections on reflection. *Learning and Instruction, 2,* 59–68.

Vonderwell, S. (2003). An examination of asynchronous communication experiences and perspectives of students in an online course. *Internet and Higher Education, 6*(77–90).

Vygotsky, L.S. (1978). *Mind in society: The development of higher psychological processes.* Cambridge, MA: Harvard University Press.

Wertsch, J.V. (1985a). Introduction. In J.V. Wertsch (Ed.), *Culture, communication and cognition: Vygotskian perspectives* (pp. 1–18). Cambridge: Cambridge University Press.

Wertsch, J.V. (1985b). *Vygotsky and the social formation of the mind.* Cambridge, MA: Harvard University Press.

Whitehead, A.N. (1932). *The aims of education and other essays.* London: Ernest Benn Limited.

Wiggins, G. (1989). A true test: Toward more authentic and equitable assessment. *Phi Delta Kappan, 70*(9), 703–713.

Wiggins, G. (1990). *The case for authentic assessment.* Washington, DC: ERIC Clearinghouse on Tests, Measurement, and Evaluation.

Wiggins, G. (1993). *Assessing student performance: Exploring the purpose and limits of testing.* San Francisco: Jossey-Bass.

Wiggins, G.P. (1998). *Educative assessment: Designing assessments to inform and improve student performance.* San Francisco: Jossey-Bass.

Wilson, B.G. (Ed.). (1996). *Constructivist learning environments: Case studies in instructional design.* Englewood Cliffs, NJ: Educational Technology Publications.

Wineburg, S.S. (1989). Remembrance of theories past. *Educational Researcher, 18*(5), 7–10.

Winn, W. (1993). Instructional design and situated learning: Paradox or partnership. *Educational Technology, 33*(3), 16–21.

Winn, W., & Snyder, D. (1996). Cognitive perspectives in psychology. In D. Jonassen (Ed.), *Handbook of research for educational communications and technology* (pp. 112–142). New York: Macmillan.

Woo, Y., Herrington, J., Agostinho, S., & Reeves, T.C. (2007). Implementing authentic tasks in web-based learning environments. *Educause Quarterly, 2007*(3), 36–43.

Young, M.F. (1993). Instructional design for situated learning. *Educational Technology Research and Development, 41*(1), 43–58.

Young, M.F. (1995). Assessment of situated learning using computer environments. *Journal of Science Education and Technology, 4*(1), 89–96.

Young, M.F., & McNeese, M. (1993). A situated cognition approach to problem solving with implications for computer-based learning and assessment. In G. Salvendy & M.J. Smith (Eds.), *Human-computer interaction: Software and hardware interfaces* (pp. 825–830). New York: Elsevier Science Publishers.

Zemsky, R., Wegner, G.R., & Massy, W.P. (2005). *Remaking the American university: Market-smart and mission-centered.* Piscataway, NJ: Rutgers University Press.

Index